ANTI-SOCIAL BEHAVIOUR ORDER

SPECIAL BULLETIN

SECOND EDITION

ANTI-SOCIAL BEHAVIOUR ORDERS

SPECIAL BULLETIN

SECOND EDITION

Anesh Pema and Sharon Heels

JORDANS

2004

Published by
Jordan Publishing Limited
21 St Thomas Street
Bristol BS1 6JS

© Jordan Publishing Ltd 2004

All rights reserved. No part of this publication may be reproduced, stored in a retrieval system, or transmitted in any way or by any means, including photocopying or recording, without the written permission of the copyright holder, application for which should be addressed to the publisher.

Crown Copyright material is reproduced with the permission of the Controller of Her Majesty's Stationery Office

British Library Cataloguing-in-Publication Data
A catalogue record for this book is available from the British Library.

ISBN 0 85308 934 5

Typeset by Jordan Publishing Limited
Printed and bound in Great Britain by The Cromwell Press

ABOUT THE AUTHORS

Anesh Pema is a barrister at Zenith Chambers, Leeds, with extensive experience of representing and advising in anti-social behaviour applications. He has appeared in a number of the important decisions in the field and has conducted the largest multiple ASBO application in the country on behalf of Leeds City Council. He can be contacted at Zenith Chambers, 10 Park Square, Leeds LS1 2LH, DX Leeds 26412, telephone 0113 245 5438, fax 0113 245 1986 or by email (apema@zenithchambers.co.uk).

Sharon Heels is a senior solicitor with Kirklees Metropolitan Council. Specialising in nuisance, anti-social behaviour and housing law, she has considerable expertise in these matters and runs training and workshops in these areas. She can be contacted at Kirklees Metropolitan Council, telephone 01484 221527 or by email (sharon.heels@kirklees.gov.uk).

FOREWORD

From an idea first raised in a Labour Party policy document in 1995, anti-social behaviour orders (ASBOs) have become an integral part of the expanding legal framework to tackle nuisance and anti-social behaviour.

As with any new tool, initial take-up was slow. As local authorities and police became familiar with the processes many of the myths surrounding ASBOs were dispelled and the costs of taking out the orders better understood. Their use by such agencies has steadily increased.

Various statutory reforms to the legal framework have been made, largely in response to the demands of practitioners. The courts, too, have exercised an influence over the way in which ASBOs are prosecuted, and have had to deal with a considerable number of human rights challenges particularly in relation to interim ASBOs.

The second edition of this bulletin reflects on how we have learned from experience, and incorporates all the legislative amendments and the impact of recent case-law.

Equally, it reflects the growing confidence in how and when to use ASBOs. They are not and never have been a panacea, but rather another option available to tackle anti-social behaviour. Practitioners understand that early intervention is critical, which is reflected in the development of interim ASBOs. Housing Associations and Housing Actions Trusts can now apply for ASBOs, although there are still funding issues to be resolved. Post-conviction ASBOs are beginning to have a real impact as the police recognise their potential. Similarly, housing providers are warming to the use of ASBOs in the county court.

Practitioners have warned that, unless and until urgent prosecution of breaches of orders is common practice, their value may be undermined. The CPS has recently appointed a nationwide team of Special Prosecutors specifically to deal with the anti-social behaviour, who have the power to apply for ASBOs.

Practitioners also know that ASBOs cannot be judged by numerical data alone. Part of their success has been in bringing partner agencies together in Problem Solving Groups.

The Social Landlords Crime and Nuisance Group has been keen to promote the use of ASBOs since their introduction. We campaigned for amendments, based on what those who were using, or trying to use, them were telling us. However, there are still improvements to be made, why should a re-run of the initial hearing be allowed on appeal, for example? ? Guidance on sharing costs across partner agencies would be welcome.

ASBOs can, and do work to protect communities and prevent thuggish, bullying behaviour. As a part of an incremental process they are both proportionate and reasonable. They are neither draconian nor onerous. They are a useful tool, have assisted in changing lives, providing exit strategies and drawing boundaries.

This timely special bulletin provides analysis of the legal framework in which ASBOs operate, as well as practical know-how on all aspects of ASBOs, from formulating protocols and creating multi-agency working groups to preparing and presenting the case in court and dealing with breaches.

Tim Winter
National Organiser
Social Landlords Crime and Nuisance Group

PREFACE

We would like to express our continued thanks to our colleagues at Kirklees Metropolitan Council and Zenith Chambers for their ongoing assistance with the issues surrounding anti-social behaviour.

Since the first edition of this bulletin there have been a number of significant changes and refinements to the law and practice in ASBOs. These have come both by way of legislation and case law. We have done our best to update the bulletin to include all of these developments up to 31 July 2004. The decision in *Stanley v London Borough of Brent* with regard to publicity of ASBOs remains outstanding at the date of publication despite having been heard in July 2004. When the judgment is handed down, appropriate amendments will be available from Anesh at Zenith Chambers for any who are interested in updating that section of this bulletin (**9.11** et seq).

Finding and correcting mistakes in the previous edition and proof reading this edition has been a lengthy task and our sincere thanks also go to the publishing team at Jordans, Adrian Phillips at Barnsley Metropolitan Borough Council, West Yorkshire police, Leeds City Council (in particular, Gill Marshall) and Nicola Phillipson of Zenith Chambers for all their assistance with this second edition.

Anesh Pema and Sharon Heels
August 2004

CONTENTS

About the authors	v
Foreword	vii
Preface	ix
Table of Abbreviations	xv

Chapter 1 ANTI-SOCIAL BEHAVIOUR IN THE COMMUNITY

A definition of 'anti-social behaviour'?	1
Non-legal remedies to combat anti-social behaviour	1
Remedies in court	2
Possession proceedings	2
Injunctions	3
Criminal proceedings	3
Solutions offered by the Crime and Disorder Act 1998	4
Sex offender orders	4
Parenting orders	5
Child curfew schemes	5
Child safety orders	6
Acceptable behaviour contracts	6
Advantages of ASBOs	6
Disadvantages of ASBOs	7
Cost	7
Bureaucracy	7
Criminalisation of anti-social behaviour	7
Choosing the appropriate solution	7
Home Office Guidance	8
The Anti-social Behaviour Act 2003 – the main changes	8

Chapter 2 THE PROBLEM-SOLVING GROUP AND CONSULTATION

Introduction	11
Consultation	11
Statutory requirements	11
Consultation with other agencies	14
Home Office recommendations	14
Protocols	15
Data protection and information exchange protocols	15
Accessing 'personal data'	15
Information exchange	16
Relations with other bodies	17
Crown Prosecution Service	17
The courts	18
The defendant	18

Chapter 3 APPLICATIONS FOR ANTI-SOCIAL BEHAVIOUR ORDERS	
Where can an application be made?	19
When can an application be made?	19
'Relevant authority' – who can apply?	19
Who can be the subject of an application?	20
'Has acted in an anti-social manner ...'	21
'Caused or was likely to cause harassment, alarm or distress to one or more persons not of the same household as himself'	22
Aggregation	23
'... necessary to protect relevant persons from further anti-social acts by him'	25
Burden and standards of proof	26
Necessity for ASBO after interim order	28
Defences and disregards	29
Summary	29
Chapter 4 EVIDENCE	
Home Office Guidance	31
Sources of evidence	31
Documentary evidence	31
Disclosure	33
Previous convictions	34
Lay witnesses	35
Professional witnesses	35
Covert surveillance	36
Videos and CCTV	36
RIPA 2000 considerations	37
Hearsay evidence	38
Use of hearsay evidence	38
Adducing hearsay evidence before the court	39
Hearsay notices	39
Case-law	40
Chapter 5 APPLICATIONS TO THE MAGISTRATES' COURT	
Court forms	43
Service of court forms and evidence	44
Chapter 6 ANTI-SOCIAL BEHAVIOUR ORDERS IN THE COUNTY COURT AND ON CRIMINAL CONVICTION	
County court	47
ASB Act 2003	47
Practice and procedure	48
Application to join a non-party	49
Interim orders	49
Service	50
Orders on criminal conviction	50
Case-law – *R (C) v Sunderland Youth Court*	52
Case-law – *R v P*	54
Guidelines for fairness in post-conviction order applications	55
Chapter 7 FIRST COURT APPEARANCES	
Magistrates' courts	57

Directions on adjournments	58

Chapter 8 INTERIM ORDERS
Interim orders without notice	61
Practice	65
Summary	66
County court	66

Chapter 9 HEARING OF THE MAIN APPLICATION
Magistrates' court	67
County court	69
On criminal conviction	69
Publicity and reporting restrictions	70
Costs	71
Magistrates' court	71
County court	72
Crown Court	72
Enforcement of costs orders	72

Chapter 10 TERMS AND DURATION OF AN ORDER
Terms of the order	73
Practical considerations for applicants	75
Exclusion zones	75
Other specific terms	76
Practical considerations for defendants	77
Grounds for challenging the order	77
Negotiating and bargaining	77
Appeals	77
Vary and discharge	77
Duration of the order	77

Chapter 11 POST-ORDER PROCEDURE
Service of the order on the defendant	79
Service of an ASBO on the police and witnesses	80
Applicants' considerations	80
Defence considerations	81
Effective monitoring	81
Applicants' considerations	81
Defendants' considerations	82
Monitoring and recording information relating to ASBOs	82
Variation and discharge of order	83

Chapter 12 APPEALS AGAINST ANTI-SOCIAL BEHAVIOUR ORDERS
Appeals by the defendant	85
Magistrates' courts' decisions	85
Notice of appeal and time-limits	85
Format of Crown Court appeal hearing	85
Case stated	86
Appeal from the Crown Court	86
Appropriate venue for appeal	87
Appeals by the applicant body	88

	Appeals from the county court	89
	Appeals from post-conviction orders	89

Chapter 13   BREACH OF AN ANTI-SOCIAL BEHAVIOUR ORDER

General principles		91
	Breaches by young people	92
	Who can prosecute?	92
Sentencing		93

Chapter 14   ANTI-SOCIAL BEHAVIOUR ORDERS AND YOUNG PEOPLE

Assessment of young people's needs and circumstances		95
	What form should the assessment take?	98
Applications against children in the care of local authorities		98
Service of court forms		101
Court procedure		101
Which court?		101
Sentencing		102
Other available orders		102
	Individual support orders	103
	Breach	104
Conclusion		104

Chapter 15   FUNDING

The applicant	105
The defendant	106

Appendix 1   LEGISLATION (as amended)

(A)	Crime and Disorder Act 1998	109
(B)	Civil Evidence Act 1985	131
(C)	Magistrates' Courts (Hearsay Evidence in Civil Proceedings) Rules 1999, SI 1999/681	139
(D)	Magistrates' Courts (Anti-social Behaviour Orders) Rules 2002, SI 2002/2784	143
(E)	Civil Procedure Rules 1998, SI 1998/3132, Parts 19, 25, 65, with Supplementing Practice Directions	150

Appendix 2   PRECEDENTS

(A)	Draft ASBO application	161
(B)	Draft ASBO	163
(C)	Application for interim anti-social behaviour order	165
(D)	Interim anti-social behaviour order	167
(E)	Orders on conviction	
	I Crown Court post-conviction order	169
	II Suggested precedent for post conviction order in the magistrates' court	171
(F)	County court anti-social behaviour order	173
(G)	Specimen court service level agreement	175
(H)	Hearsay notice	181

Appendix 3   HOME OFFICE CODE OF GUIDANCE   183

Appendix 4   USEFUL CONTACTS   237

TABLE OF ABBREVIATIONS

1999 Rules	Magistrates' Courts (Hearing Evidence in Civil Proceedings) Rules 1999
2002 Rules	Magistrates' Courts (Anti-social Behaviour Orders) Rules 2002
ABC	acceptable behaviour contract
ALMO	arm's length management organisation
ASB Act 2003	Anti-social Behaviour Act 2003
ASBO	anti-social behaviour order
BTP	British Transport Police
CDA 1998	Crime and Disorder Act 1998
CDRP	Crime and Disorder Reduction Partnership
CPR	Civil Procedure Rules 1998
CPS	Crown Prosecution Service
DPA 1998	Data Protection Act 1998
HRA 1998	Human Rights Act 1998
ISO	individual support order
ISSP	intensive supervision and surveillance programme
LEA	local education authority
MCA 1980	Magistrates' Courts Act 1980
MCR 1981	Magistrates' Courts Rules 1981
PNC	Police National Computer
PRA 2002	Police Reform Act 2002
RIPA 2000	Regulation of Investigatory Powers Act 2000
RSL	registered social landlord
YOT	Youth Offending Team

CHAPTER 1

ANTI-SOCIAL BEHAVIOUR IN THE COMMUNITY

1.1 This chapter looks at what is meant by the term 'anti-social behaviour' and examines the various methods of dealing with such behaviour which should be considered before applying for an anti-social behaviour order (ASBO).

A definition of 'anti-social behaviour'?

1.2 Before an ASBO is chosen as the appropriate solution, an applicant must be satisfied that the alleged conduct is in fact 'anti-social behaviour'. However, anti-social behaviour is *not* defined in the current Home Office Guidance beyond repeating the statutory definition.[1] Examples of the types of behaviour which would appropriately trigger an application for an ASBO are, however, given. These include:

- verbal abuse;
- harassment;
- assault;
- graffiti;
- excessive noise;
- drunk and disorderly conduct;
- throwing missiles;
- vehicle crime; and
- prostitution.

Further examples of the types of behaviour that should be dealt with using ASBOs and acceptable behaviour contracts (ABCs) are given in the current Home Office Guidance.

1.3 Other sources of assistance in classifying what is or is not anti-social include nuisance clauses in tenancy agreements, and definitions or examples in case-law or statute.

1.4 The Home Office consultative document of 2002 'Tackling Anti-Social Tenants' considered whether there should be a statutory definition of what is anti-social behaviour. However, no definition has been brought into being and some practitioners believe a valuable opportunity to regulate or clarify this area has been lost. Unless and until that occurs, applicants should satisfy themselves that the allegations in the complaints constitute anti-social behaviour and not just an example of conflicting lifestyles. A distinction needs to be drawn between petty, low-level nuisance and persistent and serious misconduct.

Non-legal remedies to combat anti-social behaviour

1.5 The reasons, causes and remedies for anti-social conduct are complex and diverse. The most appropriate solution is not always court action. Other options can be equally or more effective. The key principle is for the lead agency to engage with other relevant agencies as soon

---

[1] See Crime and Disorder Act 1998 (CDA 1998), s 1(1)(a), (b).

as possible to contain, tackle and solve the problem. The following agencies may be called upon:

- social services can assist with challenging behaviour from young people in a number of ways – by supporting parents, or providing lessons in parenting skills, or seeking court proceedings for care or supervision orders;
- the council's housing department (or other similar social housing providers) can assist by enforcing nuisance clauses in tenancy agreements against unruly tenants and, to reduce the opportunities for conflict, by enforcing a sensible allocations policy and other planned housing strategies;
- schools can assist with issues of discipline, control and truancy; they can also provide focused teaching and strategies to identify and address learning difficulties, failure to deal with which can, in some instances, lead to anti-social conduct;
- the youth offending team (YOT) can help young people within and outside the youth criminal justice system by engaging formally and informally with them to change their behaviour from what is perceived as anti-social – this can include diversionary schemes (eg such as organised sports activities or supervising court sentences);
- the health authority can assist with health or behavioural problems;
- the council's environmental health department can help with noise or public safety issues;
- the council's planning department can help with breaches of planning control.

Remedies in court

Possession proceedings

1.6 Any landlord can seek to evict a tenant for breach of the terms of a tenancy agreement or seek a demotion of a secure tenancy to the level of an introductory one. For registered social landlords (RSLs), there is greater expectation to use nuisance clauses in tenancy agreements to control anti-social tenants. Tenancy agreements can be varied to tighten nuisance clauses.

1.7 Although current law does not allow those affected by tenants' behaviour to sue the landlord for failing to control them,[1] this developing area of law may one day impose a duty of care.

1.8 For possession proceedings to succeed there must be grounds for possession (breach of tenancy agreement, or a statutory possession ground) but the court also has a wide-ranging discretion to decide if it is reasonable to grant possession in each case.

1.9 Another option for RSLs is to grant introductory or starter tenancies to new tenants. If there is a breach of tenancy in the first year, the landlord can take steps to end the tenancy. Court possession proceedings must be brought in the normal way but the court has limited discretion. Provided the landlord has followed internal procedures correctly (including acceding to a tenant's request for review of the decision to regain possession), the court *must* grant a possession order.

1.10 In a consultation exercise, alternative means of strengthening the response to nuisance tenants were explored. The options included allowing the landlord to decide on the issue of possession; demoting tenancies by turning a secure tenancy into an introductory tenancy; and allowing the courts to grant possession for serious, persistent anti-social behaviour when injunctions are sought. The Government's response in the shape of new legislation is set out at **1.43**.

---

[1] See *Hussain v Lancaster City Council* [2001] QB 1, and *Mowan v London Borough of Wandsworth* [2001] LGR 228.

1.11 Possession proceedings are more drastic, and potentially less effective in dealing with anti-social behaviour. Possession proceedings can displace households for the behaviour of an individual, and affect only certain premises for a limited time, which ends when possession is regained. There are many examples of evicted households moving to new accommodation within the area, exposing the same community to the behaviour that initially gave rise to the eviction. ASBOs provide the means for targeted control of individuals with terms tailored to deal with specific misconduct. Importantly, an ASBO does not affect the family home, only the perpetrator of the anti-social behaviour.

Injunctions

1.12 Injunctions are a discretionary remedy in the county court, which can be used to control a person's behaviour. They can be an effective tool against those aged 18 or over and for those with the mental capacity to understand what they are doing and how to change their behaviour. Breach of an injunction can result in a prison sentence of up to 2 years and/or an unlimited fine for contempt of court. This law has been modified by the Anti-social Behaviour Act 2003 (ASB Act 2003) and the principle changes are discussed at **1.42**.

1.13 A cause of action is required to bring proceedings. In respect of anti-social behaviour, the following causes of action will be relevant:

- breach of tenancy agreement;
- trespass to land;
- trespass or assault to the person;
- preventing criminal activity;[1]
- a Housing Act 1996, s 153A injunction with or without powers of arrest (a specific injunction available to the local housing authority to restrain anti-social conduct, threats and violence on or near its housing stock): see **1.44**.

1.14 Interim injunctions are also available. They provide protection to those in need in the period before a trial is heard. The evidential burden to obtain an interim injunction is not as great as that required for the main hearing. The new interim ASBOs were styled on interim injunctions.

1.15 ASBOs may be applied for in a greater number of situations, for a longer period of time and over a wider geographical area. However, injunctions can provide a quick, simple, but short-lived remedy. Breach of an injunction will not result in imprisonment for those under 18 years of age[2] and therefore, apart from the threat of a fine, injunctions are a relatively toothless remedy for young persons.

Criminal proceedings

1.16 The criminal law remains an option for more serious complaints of misconduct. The following is a non-exhaustive list of crimes relevant to this area:

- assault (including common assault, assault occasioning actual bodily harm and aggravated assault);
- grievous bodily harm; wounding;
- intimidating or harassing a witness in civil proceedings (Criminal Justice and Police Act 2001, ss 39–41) – similar provisions apply for witness intimidation in the criminal courts;
- Protection from Harassment Act 1997 prosecutions;

---

[1] See *Nottingham City Council v Zain* [2001] EWCA Civ 1248, [2001] 1 WLR 607; and Local Government Act 1972, s 222.
[2] See *Harrow London Borough Council v G (a child)* [2004] EWHC 17 (QB).

- public disorder and breach of the peace offences;
- violent disorder; affray;
- taking a vehicle without consent and associated criminal vehicle-related activities;
- criminal damage;
- theft, robbery and burglary;
- possession of an offensive weapon;
- drunk and disorderly behaviour;
- drugs offences.

1.17 ASBOs were introduced in part to tackle the perceived gap in the criminal law to deal with the full range of anti-social conduct. ASBOs were initially viewed as easier to pursue than criminal prosecutions, as the standard of proof often applied was the civil standard (i.e. on the balance of probabilities). Now that the standard of proof for ASBOs is the criminal standard (see Chapter 3), criminal sanctions should not be discounted in favour of ASBOs without due consideration. Bail conditions, which apply to criminal charges, can be imposed for the protection of witnesses and the community, although obviously the bail conditions will lapse on sentence (or acquittal).

Solutions offered by the Crime and Disorder Act 1998

1.18 The Crime and Disorder Act 1998 (CDA 1998) introduced new remedies and wide-reaching changes to the criminal law. This included the removal of the presumption of lack of criminal intent for children aged 10 and over, and more varied sentencing options such as detention and training orders and reparation orders.

1.19 Sections 5–6 of the CDA 1998 identify those who are responsible for formulating crime reduction strategies. These are local authorities, the police and, from a date to be appointed, will include the fire authority and primary care trusts or health authorities. These bodies set local priorities for the reduction of crime and disorder after consultation with the local community. They must also co-operate with other bodies, such as the probation service and RSLs, when formulating strategies.

1.20 CDA 1998, s 16 gives the police power to remove truants to designated premises. It was used with success by North Yorkshire Police in York city centre, where town centre shoplifting was reduced by 30% by targeted use of this power during one school term. Other targeted initiatives achieve similar success. This power has been extended by s 75 of the Police Reform Act 2002 (PRA 2002) to include the British Transport Police (BTP).

1.21 CDA 1998, s 17 imposes a statutory duty on the police and local authority to exercise their various functions with due regard to the likely effect of them and to do all that they reasonably can to prevent crime and disorder in their area.

Sex offender orders

1.22 CDA 1998, s 2 gives the police the power to apply for sex offender orders. Sex offender orders can be made where a person is a sex offender and the police have reasonable cause to believe an order is necessary to protect the public from serious harm. Sex offenders' conduct can be regulated by orders similar in terms to an ASBO (e.g. non-association and exclusion zones). The PRA 2002 introduced a new interim sex offender order. The Sexual Offences Act 2003[1] introduced the sexual offences prevention order, which allows the court to impose or

---

[1] Sections 104–113.

the police to apply for an order prohibiting a defendant from specified acts for a minimum period of 5 years where it is necessary to protect the public from serious sexual harm. Interim orders are also available.

Parenting orders

1.23 CDA 1998, s 8 introduced parenting orders. Designed to impose compulsory parenting classes and, in some cases, conditions for parental supervision (e.g. ensuring the child attends school), they are triggered by a number of matters such as a criminal conviction against a young person, or the imposition of an ASBO. Breach is prosecutable and punishable by a fine of, currently, up to £1,000.

1.24 Experience from the pilot schemes shows the greatest success has been with parents who are willing to learn and change; it gives them access to resources which may not otherwise have been available. In addition, it emphasises the need for parents and guardians to take responsibility for their children. Parenting orders are viewed by the Home Office Guidance as a complementary tool to help the conditions of the ASBO be met and so reduce the chances of breach. These orders are supervised by a 'responsible officer', who can be from social services, education, YOT or probation. The Home Office Guidance encourages the responsible officer to work closely with the parent in the event of breach to improve compliance before prosecution steps are taken. This has been extended by the ASB Act 2003, and is discussed at **1.49**.

Child curfew schemes

1.25 Local child curfew schemes were introduced by CDA 1998, ss 14–15. Local authorities (but see **1.26**) were given the power, after due consultation with the police and those specified in the scheme, and for the sole purpose of maintaining order, to ban children under 10 years of age from specified places for limited periods (not exceeding 90 days) unless accompanied by a responsible adult. Breach of an order permits the police to take the child home unless there is reasonable belief that the child would suffer significant harm there. Breach imposes a duty on the police to notify the local authority. Under s 47(1)(a)(iii) of the Children Act 1989, the local authorities have a duty to make 'such enquiries as they consider necessary to enable them to decide whether they should take any action to safeguard or promote the child's welfare'. Because of this, the police will have new powers to disperse groups in the ASB Act 2003 (see **1.50**).

1.26 There was a very limited initial take-up of child curfew schemes by local authorities because of practical problems such as identifying those under 10 years of age, and establishing whether or not accompanying adults are responsible for the child. In 2001, the scheme was extended to those under 16, and gave the police (in addition to the local authority) power to impose a ban under CDA 1998, s 14(1).[1] However, such practical problems persist and the remedy has been rarely used, although such schemes as have been implemented have had a high profile, and the police and local authorities have reported successful results, e.g. in Seaford.

1.27 To address the problem of youth 'gangs' that instil fear in some elements of the community, other methods such as greater visible use of CCTV, youth diversionary schemes or community-based activities which bring the youths and those who fear them together to promote a greater understanding of each other may be more effective.

---

[1] Inserted by Criminal Justice and Police Act 2001, s 48.

Child safety orders

1.28 Child safety orders are available against those under 10 years old and were introduced by CDA 1998, ss 11–13. The local authority can apply to the family proceedings section of the magistrates' court which can make an order if it is desirable. Triggers for this application include anti-social behaviour or conduct which would amount to a criminal offence had the child been of prosecutable age. If a child safety order is made, the young person comes under the supervision of a social worker of a member of a YOT. Some have already discounted this remedy as adding little to existing child protection measures such as supervision orders or care orders.

Acceptable behaviour contracts

1.29 First introduced in Islington in North London, acceptable behaviour contracts (ABCs) are seen as an alternative to ASBOs. They are essentially a contract of good behaviour between the police and/or members of the local authority, other partner agencies and the person who has been involved in anti-social behaviour.

1.30 ABCs can be made with anyone aged 10 and over, although they were designed specifically to deal with young persons under the age of 18. For children under 10, the parents of the child should be asked to sign up to a parental responsibility contract. Parental responsibility contracts (not to be confused with parental responsibility agreements under the Children Act 1989) are based on the same principles as ABCs.

1.31 ABCs often contain the same or very similar terms to those found in an ASBO application. They are a voluntary recognition by alleged perpetrators of their misconduct, and a set of agreed terms to help stop it. The ABC, where appropriate, should come with the offer of support to enhance its prospects of successfully abating the anti-social behaviour.

1.32 ABCs have no legal effect or sanctions for breach. They may, however, be cited in a later ASBO application. Where an ABC has been breached an ASBO may often be the only remaining solution. The ABC usually lasts for 1 year, although this can be shortened or extended, depending on the circumstances. It is good practice to post a clear warning on the face of the document that breach of the contract may ultimately result in the relevant agency seeking an ASBO. For young people, ABCs are most effective when couched in terms they can understand.

1.33 The current Home Office Guidance contains extensive information on the ABC process.[1] The Guidance deals with the relationship between ASBOs and ABCs, and emphasises that ASBOs and ABCs are *not* in competition with each other.[2]

1.34 The experience of many local authorities has shown that ABCs can address anti-social behaviour in certain people. For the perpetrator of repeated and serious anti-social behaviour however, nothing short of an ASBO from the outset may be appropriate. The use of ABCs has been extended by the ASB Act 2003 in the context of contracts with parents (see **1.49**).

Advantages of ASBOs

1.35 Alternatives to ASBOs have been explored earlier in this chapter. The following is a checklist of the principal advantages of ASBOs:

---

[1] See current Home Office Guidance reproduced in Appendix 3, pp 215–221.
[2] See ibid, p 187.

- they do not depend on the status of a defendant as tenant to apply;
- they are not locality-specific – other remedies (e.g. some injunctions) are tied to certain locations or their vicinity, whereas ASBOs can apply throughout England and Wales;
- they can have a long duration and a wide-ranging application – ASBOs last for a minimum of 2 years and may last indefinitely;
- they can apply to anyone aged 10 and over.

Disadvantages of ASBOs

Cost

1.36 A common criticism of ASBOs is that they are expensive to obtain compared to other remedies. As well as legal costs, there are the hidden costs of the time of the officers involved in the process. This is dealt with in greater depth in Chapter 15.

Bureaucracy

1.37 To satisfy the necessity test and requirements to consult partner agencies, some discount ASBOs as too slow and complex. Although there can be more work in the ASBO process, systems should be streamlined instead of discarding ASBOs altogether. Properly prepared ASBO applications can provide a speedy and lasting remedy to the problem of anti-social behaviour.

Criminalisation of anti-social behaviour

1.38 Some view ASBOs as fundamentally wrong in that criminal penalties flow from acts which in themselves do not amount to criminal behaviour, for example being in breach of an exclusion zone. This can be addressed by having proper safeguards in place to justify the imposition of an ASBO in each case. Safeguards can include representation from all quarters on the ASBO decision panel (e.g. YOT when young people are ASBO candidates). This ensures that the correct balance and thought processes precede each application and the terms sought.

Choosing the appropriate solution

1.39 The most effective key to combating anti-social conduct is to choose the right solution from all available options as quickly as possible. The following are useful pointers in choosing the appropriate solution:

- early intervention can prevent a problem developing or worsening;
- if court action is inevitable, injunctions are available as a 'short, sharp shock';
- possession proceedings can be used for serious or persistent or multi-faceted household problems where the only practical solution is for one party to leave;
- ASBOs are available for persistent or serious misconduct to target specific terms against a specific defendant over a potentially wide area for a potentially long time;
- the criminal law is available as well as or instead of other remedies to punish and rehabilitate.

Home Office Guidance

1.40 To help practitioners with ASBOs, the Home Office has issued written Guidance. The first was issued in March 1999; the second came out in June 2000. The third and latest was published on 12 November 2002 and replaces the earlier two. It is a considerable improvement on its forerunners, and is more practical. The Guidance does not have the force of law. However, the court may have regard to it when interpreting law on ASBOs. Any public body, such as the police or local authority, must take proper and reasonable notice of any Guidance or their decisions can be challenged by judicial review. The full text of the current Guidance is reproduced in Appendix 3.

The Anti-social Behaviour Act 2003 – the main changes

1.41 The ASB Act 2003 introduces changes to remedies for dealing with anti-social behaviour, covering a range of matters from noise and graffiti to high hedges, the closure of premises used for drugs, and nuisance behaviour.

1.42 Social landlords are required by 30 December 2004 to prepare, publish and review policies and procedures for tackling anti- social behaviour. A summary must be available free of charge. The full policy document must be available for inspection at the landlord's main office or on request for a fee. Whether an actionable duty will be created if a landlord does not follow its own policies and procedures remains to be seen.[1]

1.43 From 30 June 2004 registered social landlords, as defined in Part 1 of the Housing Act 1996, can apply to the county court for a demoted tenancy order in respect of assured and secure tenancies. Where there is evidence of anti-social conduct by a tenant and/or a resident or visitor to a tenant's home and it is reasonable to make an order, the court can create a demoted tenancy for a period of one year. Existing terms, for example, rent, remain the same. If a landlord during that year applies to the court for possession of a demoted tenancy for *any breach of tenancy*, the scheme operates in a similar way to the introductory tenancy regime. The court *must* grant possession provided proper internal procedures for taking and reviewing the decision to take possession have been followed.[2]

1.44 The ASB Act 2003 replaces the current anti-social behaviour injunction provisions of the Housing Act 1996 from 30 June 2004. The changes allow *all* registered social landlords to take out this form of injunction where there is evidence of anti-social conduct, which is defined as conduct capable of causing nuisance or annoyance to any person and which directly or indirectly relates to or affects the housing management function of a relevant landlord. Other provisions prevent the unlawful use of premises and breach of tenancy agreement also by injunction.[3] It will also be possible to exclude tenants from their homes.

1.45 Powers of arrest can be attached if the conduct includes the use or threat of violence or there is a significant risk of harm to the relevant category of person, depending which injunction is being applied for.

1.46 Powers of arrest will also be available for an injunction brought under s 222 of the Local Government Act 1972 where there is the threat of or actual violence.[4]

---

[1] See ASB Act 2003, s 12.
[2] See ibid, ss 14–17 and Sch 1.
[3] See ibid, ss 12–13.
[4] See ibid, s 91.

1.47 The changes to the injunction provisions were introduced to overcome problems in case-law that arose under the Housing Act 1996 regime which demanded a nexus between the conduct complained of, the persons the injunction was designed to protect and the correct application of Housing Act legislation to protect others. A new test of 'conduct which directly or indirectly relates to or affects the housing management functions of a landlord' was introduced to remedy these problems. This term itself is imprecise and is likely to lead to similar satellite litigation.

1.48 The courts must have regard to the past, present and future effect on the community of anti-social behaviour when exercising discretion in possession proceedings brought under Ground 2 of the Housing Act 1985 (as amended by the Housing Act 1996) and Ground 14 of the Housing Act 1988 (the statutory grounds for nuisance possession for secure and assured tenancies respectively).[1]

1.49 The concept of parenting orders and contracts has been extended. Local education authorities (LEAs) and schools can enter into parenting contracts with parents of pupils excluded on disciplinary grounds. YOTs can enter into parenting contracts with parents of young people displaying anti-social or criminal-like behaviour. LEAs, schools and YOTs can also apply to the magistrates' court for a free-standing parenting order now.[2] A court must make a parenting order where it makes an ASBO against a person under 16, or give reasons for not doing so in open court.[3]

1.50 The police can disperse groups of two or more persons where there has been evidence of anti-social behaviour. Believed by some to be mainly used to tackle youth nuisance, other provisions against those under the age of 16 include fixed penalty notices for unruly children or for parents of truants,[4] and power to return children of under 16 who are out in a public place after 9 pm to their home or to a place of safety if not accompanied by a responsible adult over the age of 18.[5]

1.51 Other provisions give powers to the police and the magistrates' courts to close premises associated with class A drugs and serious public nuisance for a maximum period of 6 months.[6]

1.52 Changes to firearms legislation make it generally illegal for imitation firearms to be carried in a public place. The age limit for owning a firearm has also been increased to 17.[7]

1.53 The local authority has extended powers to close noisy licensed premises for up to 24 hours and can serve fixed penalty notices for fly tipping and graffiti. Graffiti remedial notices to tackle property defaced by offensive or detrimental images can also be served; a local authority scheme to deal with high hedges where local neighbours cannot resolve their differences is also introduced.[8]

1.54 The ASB Act 2003 introduces individual support orders (ISOs), which are discussed in detail at **14.34** et seq.

---

[1] From 30 June 2004.
[2] See ASB Act 2003, ss 18–22 and 25–29.
[3] Ibid, ss 18–29.
[4] Ibid, ss 23 and 30.
[5] Ibid, ss 30–36.
[6] Ibid, ss 1–11.
[7] Ibid, ss 37–39.
[8] Ibid, ss 65–84.

CHAPTER 2

THE PROBLEM-SOLVING GROUP AND CONSULTATION

Introduction

2.1 The framework for dealing with ASBOs has been in place since 1999, when the first Home Office Guidance was published. Many problem-solving groups are now well established. For authorities yet to form such groups, it will not be sufficient to adopt the structure of existing groups without tailoring them to local practices and procedures. The experience of established groups shows that it is essential to monitor practices and procedures and be prepared to review, refine and, if necessary, rewrite operational systems in the light of experience. For the defendant, it is important to understand not just the legal framework in which ASBOs operate, but also how the local decision-making process works, and to examine whether the group is operating within its own defined policies and procedures.

2.2 This chapter looks at the consultation requirements placed on anti-social behaviour problem-solving groups, protocols for partnership working, data protection issues that arise from handling sensitive personal data, and relationships between the anti-social behaviour problem-solving groups and other bodies such as the courts.

Consultation

Statutory requirements

2.3 Before a summons for an application for an ASBO can be issued, CDA 1998, s 1E[1] requires there to be consultation between the 'relevant authorities'. The statutory consultation requirements can be summarised as follows:[2]

(a) the council must consult with the chief officer of police for the area;[3]
(b) the chief officer of police must consult with the council;[4] and
(c) RSLs, the BTP, Housing Action Trusts and county councils must consult with *both* the police and the council for the area.[5]

2.4 The relevant council for consultation is the one which has responsibility for the address at which the defendant lives or would appear to reside.[6] It is intended that every local authority and police force should have a designated person who can be consulted, which appears to have been largely carried out in practice.

---

[1] Police Reform Act 2002 (PRA 2002), s 66.
[2] CDA 1998, s 1E, inserted by PRA 2002, s 66.
[3] Ibid, s 1E(2).
[4] Ibid, s 1E(3).
[5] Ibid, s 1E(4).
[6] Ibid, s 1E(3).

2.5 Consultation should not be confused with consent. The purpose of consultation is to inform other agencies of intended applications and to exchange information. There is no requirement to have the consent of the other relevant agencies – only that they should have had the opportunity to comment. However, in reality, if there is a lack of agreement, the application would have to be very carefully reconsidered before proceeding to a hearing.

2.6 The only document that should be filed with the court is a signed document of consultation. There is no need to indicate whether or not an agreement was reached or otherwise. There may be a temptation to file notes from case conferences together with the information and comment forms which many local authorities send to the various interested professional bodies. This is unnecessary and should not be done. Similarly, the case conference notes should not be filed or disclosed. These are prepared at a meeting in the anticipation and contemplation of the application and need not be disclosed. If support from other agencies or authorities is forthcoming and thought necessary, statements can be provided.

2.7 The wording of the statute clearly states that consultation with the police shall be with the chief officer of the police force. In practice, this never happens, and a subordinate officer, usually an inspector or lower rank, takes on the duties of consultation on behalf of the police. The notice of consultation is, therefore, not generally signed by a Chief Constable and this led to challenges to the validity of consultation certificates, and, thus, the entire applications. The case of *The Chief Constable of West Midlands Police v Birmingham Justices*[1] deals decisively with this argument. A district judge (crime) had held that the delegation by the Chief Constable of his or her powers to consult for ASBOs to persons of rank lower than a superintendent by internal memorandum was incapable of satisfying the requirements of the Act. In quashing the decision of the district judge, Sedley LJ held that:

(a) all but the most important powers of the Chief Constable could be delegated;
(b) the power could be delegated to an officer for whom he or she is answerable;
(c) it was not necessary to rely on implied delegation; and
(d) it was not for the courts to say that the Chief Constable's choice of the level or person to whom the power was delegated was right or wrong, unless that choice was irrational or otherwise beyond his or her powers.

2.8 In this case, it was not determined whether or not the sergeant involved had actual authorisation to act. Therefore, this remains a point which the defendant can legitimately seek to challenge. Conversely, the applicant should ensure that this issue has been properly addressed before the application is made. The Divisional Court did not consider the consequences of failing to consult. Whilst it could be argued that the omission was not fatal to the application, the use of the word 'shall' in the Act would seem to be a condition precedent and render the application void. However, in the unreported case of *McClarty & McClarty v Wigan MBC*,[2] the High Court considered the meaning of consultation in more depth. In this case, two applications for ASBOs were made, with the lead being taken by the housing management company, which was wholly owned by the council but was set up as an arm's length management organisation (ALMO). Before the circuit judge there was evidence of consultation by a tenancy relations manager of the ALMO with a council employee duly authorised by the council to consult on ASBO applications. That person then consulted with a duly authorised person at the police. An appeal was lodged on the previously unargued point that the circuit judge did not have jurisdiction to grant an ASBO, as consultation had not been properly complied with. By the hearing before Mr Justice Beatson, evidence had been filed showing that many months prior to the applications being made, the defendants had been

---

[1] [2002] EWHC 1087 (Admin).
[2] (Unreported), 30 October 2003, Mr Justice Beatson.

referred to a Positive Action Team, where officers from both the council and the police (and both duly authorised to consult) were present. The group met fortnightly and discussed the defendants' case every 10 weeks. The group attempted but failed to solve the problem and an application was to be approved. However, before the meeting to authorise formally an application for an ASBO, a chance to issue such an application arose during a hearing in the principal proceedings and was taken. On the day of the application (and not as previously told to the circuit judge), the tenancy relations manager called both the police and council officers 'as a courtesy to senior officers in both organisations' and they agreed to seek the orders. In fact, whilst an interim order was to have been requested, final orders were made.

2.9 Mr Justice Beatson noted that, notwithstanding the Home Office Guidance, there was no certificate of consultation produced or filed. The appellants argued that consultation required a genuine invitation to give advice and a genuine consideration of that advice with sufficient time to achieve both.[1] The appellants argued that there was no adequate consultation in this case: calls by the ALMO to the council and police could not constitute consultation between the police and council. The referral to the Positive Action Team could not constitute consultation, as there was no proposal to seek ASBOs at that time. They also argued that there was a failure to seek comments from the YOT or notify the social services department to obtain a s 17 assessment.

2.10 The judge was highly critical of the manner in which consultation had been arranged by the tenancy relations manager of the ALMO and made clear that they had no locus to bring ASBO proceedings. He also was critical of the lack of recording, note or minute-taking at the Positive Action Team meetings and the council's seeming lack of awareness of the Home Office Guidance. He highlighted the lack of structure in the consultation process and noted that where an authority could not show that there had been co-ordination between the specified agencies, it may find that the court could not be satisfied that the order was necessary. He advised the council to review its procedures and consider their adequacy, given that the ALMO was not part of the council, but a separate company.

2.11 The court also found that the telephone call by the tenancy relations manager could not constitute consultation, because, first, this was done, in his words, as a 'courtesy' and, secondly, he was not employed by the council and could not consult with anyone for the purposes of the Act's requirements. On the issue of whether consultation was a condition precedent, however, the judge held:

> 'I have concluded that in the context of the 1998 Act as amended, the requirement in section 1E to consult is fulfilled by substantial compliance even though there may not have been strict compliance. This is because the purpose of section 1E or one of the purposes is to ensure co-ordination between agencies which have authority to institute proceedings in particular before the institution of court proceedings. Such co-ordination may be achieved in a number of ways. The Home Office Guidance indicates that one of these is by partnership working arrangement such as the Positive Action Team.
>
> ...
>
> ... the obligation to consult is not to consult those who would be primarily affected by an order but it is to consult other public bodies with authority to institute proceedings for Anti-social behaviour orders. Nothing before me suggests that the police, the party to be consulted in these proceedings which were to be launched by a local authority consider that there has been no or inadequate consultation.'

---

[1] See *R v Secretary of State for Social Services ex parte Association of Metropolitan Authorities* [1986] 1 WLR 1 per Webster J at p 4.

The court held that the participation of the authorised police and local authority representatives at the Positive Action Team meetings when the defendants' position was considered over many months (albeit every 10 weeks) substantially complied with the obligation to consult. This, however, should not be encouraged, as the meaning of substantial compliance is not clear and is open to construction and argument. A recognised system of authorisation to consult and proper panel meetings is preferable. Producing a certification of consultation should not be difficult and should be in a simple form, capable of proof.

Consultation with other agencies

2.12 A case-by-case decision should be made as to which agencies, other than those defined in s 1E of the CDA 1998, should contribute to the decision-making process. Appropriate bodies can be asked to make contributions, either in writing or in person. Such bodies may include:

- the Probation Service;
- an RSL (if not the main applicant);
- the health authority;
- Community Action Groups;
- social services or the YOT (essential where the defendant is a minor);
- housing departments (where the defendant is a council tenant); and
- other council departments (e.g. environmental services).

2.13 The group needs to be able to discuss and, if appropriate, put into action alternative remedies. This is more likely to occur if all relevant bodies are present at meetings. If alternative remedies are not discussed and considered, it can be argued that the decision-making process was flawed and that it was not a reasonable or proportionate decision to apply for an ASBO. The decision-making of a public body can also be subject to judicial review on the grounds that its actions are 'unreasonable'.[1]

2.14 Alternatively, the defence may argue that the court should not make an order because it was not 'necessary', as there were other means to protect the public which were more appropriate and were not considered before the ASBO application was made. Whilst the legal advice that a group receives will be privileged, minutes or a written record of the decisions of the group and the resulting action plan should be kept in each case. The failure to keep such records has been the subject of judicial criticism.[2] Examination of the decision summary is an essential part of the defence preparation.

Home Office recommendations

2.15 The current Home Office Guidance makes the following recommendations with respect to consultation and group dynamics:

- a fully co-ordinated approach is essential – 'effective defence of communities' rests with all agencies working together;
- one specific person in the lead agency should take overall responsibility and manage and co-ordinate the case, and liaise with other agencies to take necessary actions within set time-scales;
- a suggested protocol for partnership working is provided (see **2.16**);
- the consultation process ensures that relevant information about a possible defendant is obtained from all partner agencies;

---

[1] For a definition of 'unreasonable', see *Associated Provincial Picture Houses v Wednesbury Corporation* [1948] 1 KB 223, [1947] 2 All ER 680.
[2] *McClarty & McClarty v Wigan MBC* (unreported), 30 October 2003, Mr Justice Beatson – see further **2.8**.

- the purpose of consultation is not to secure agreement between all partner agencies but to give all parties an opportunity to comment in order to reduce conflicting actions being taken by different agencies in a case;
- no one agency has the right to veto another's application; and
- case conferences are meant to allow reservations and any alternative proposals to be 'discussed carefully', but with the overriding need to bring the anti-social behaviour to an end quickly.

Protocols

2.16 The Coventry Crime and Disorder Reduction Partnership (CDRP) is used as a role model of partnership working in the current Home Office Guidance. Essential features of this scheme include:

- a wide-ranging membership, comprising most agencies suggested at **2.12**, but also the courts and the Crown Prosecution Service (CPS);
- defined protocols that also allow for the receipt of views from outside the main group;
- the use of case conferences to facilitate information exchange and discussion – these can be requested by any agency – should be held within 2 weeks of a case referral, and should end with an action plan recorded by the lead officer; and
- the appointment of one lead officer to manage all aspects of the case.

2.17 It is not necessary for problem-solving groups to set up elaborate or complicated protocols before they become operational. Protocols should set out the framework in which the group should operate. If available to the general public, and it is recommended that they should be, such protocols will be essential reading for the defence. The defence should examine whether the group is working within its protocols when reaching decisions. The second set of Home Office Guidance of June 2000 contained extensive guidance on how to set up local protocols. However, the current Guidance does not include such advice, but sets out the Coventry CDRP as a model to follow.

2.18 Protocols should be revised regularly to take account of best practice and new legislation, (e.g. the Human Rights Act 1998 (HRA 1998) and the PRA 2002). They should be flexible enough to take proper account of the views of the defendant and the interested parties.

2.19 If a defendant requests an opportunity to be heard prior to a final decision being made, this request should ordinarily be granted. Failure to give the request and any subsequent submissions serious consideration could potentially result in an application for judicial review.

Data protection and information exchange protocols

2.20 As evidence is gathered by the ASBO problem-solving group, this will almost inevitably raise issues of the proper use of the defendant's personal information by other agencies. A proper balance must be achieved between the two, often conflicting, principles of a person's right to privacy and the need to protect the public.

Accessing 'personal data'

2.21 The Data Protection Act 1998 (DPA 1998) provides an individual with the right to access his or her 'personal data' held by another. 'Personal data' means data which relate to a living individual who can be identified:

'(a) from those data, or
(b) from those data and other information which is in the possession of, or is likely to come into the possession of, the data controller,

and includes any expression of opinion about the individual and any indication of the intentions of the data controller or any other person in respect of the individual.'[1]

2.22 On payment of a fee – currently, £10 – a request by a person to access his or her personal data must be processed within 40 days, provided it has been properly made. This is defined as when it is accompanied by the correct fee, the material required to be disclosed has been properly identified and the person whom the data is about is either making the request or has given consent to do so to another.

2.23 It is good practice for the defence to consider making such a request to the local authority and the police. It may only reveal what will be disclosed as part of the applicant's evidence; however, it may also reveal information that can be used to support an argument that an ASBO was not necessary, or to establish a 'disregard' defence. For example, it may reveal that the defendant has had a difficult upbringing, with no support from social services, despite parental requests for assistance.

2.24 A defendant will often receive advance warning that he is being considered for an ASBO, either because he receives a warning letter from the anti-social behaviour problem-solving group, or because he is approached by the YOT to conduct an assessment of needs. Potentially, therefore, the defendant has an opportunity to influence the decision-making process by giving reasons for his or her behaviour or providing acceptable assurances as to his or her future conduct. However, if the group proceeds with an application for an ASBO and refuses to hear the defendant, this may provide grounds for attacking the process as a whole.

2.25 The defendant may complain to the Information Commissioner if he or she believes that the provisions of the DPA 1998 have been breached. The Commissioner can now award compensation for breach and non-compliance can result in criminal sanctions. For more details, refer to the Information Commissioner's website (www.dataprotection.gov.uk).

Information exchange

2.26 CDA 1998, s 115 states:

'Any person who, apart from this sub-section, would not have power to disclose information –

(a) to a relevant authority, or
(b) to a person acting on behalf of such an authority,

shall have *power* to do so in any case where the disclosure is necessary or expedient for the purposes of any provision of this Act.'

'Relevant authority' is defined as the chief police officer, a local authority, a police authority, a local probation board in England and Wales and a health authority/primary care trust.

2.27 Section 115 gives a power, not a duty, to give disclosure. The decision on what and how to disclose remains with the person holding the data. The 'purposes in the Act' are any of the provisions in the CDA 1998 and can include local crime audits, YOT work, ASBOs, sex offender orders and parenting orders. When coupled with the general statutory provision of s 17, this creates the potential for far-reaching disclosure.

---

[1] Extract from Data Protection Act 1998, s 1.

2.28 Information sharing is addressed in part by the Home Office Guidance. Where a body is an agent of a relevant authority for the purposes of s 115, the 'body so acting' must have consented to act and had authority to do so. Authority can be implied, be in writing or given orally and can be general or case-specific. The Guidance also suggests that information-sharing protocols should be negotiated in advance, and provides helpful website addresses. Queries should be directed to the Information Commissioner. Anti-social behaviour working group protocols should be freely available to the public.

2.29 In order to carry out disclosure lawfully, the principles of data protection principles must be followed. These include processing information fairly and lawfully, keeping information only for as long as is necessary, and ensuring that it is secure. This will only cause problems in the processing of personal data for particular cases, as opposed to depersonalised data for use in crime statistics. Unless consent has been given by a possible defendant to disclose his or her personal information to others, the best advice to applicants is to consider carefully how much personal information is needed in each case and if it can be justified under s 115 or the data protection exemptions for the prevention of crime. If in doubt, seek expert advice or consult the Information Commissioner, with a request for advice within a certain time-scale so as not to delay the ASBO process.

2.30 The defendant and his or her legal advisers will wish to ensure that the defendant's rights to privacy in general are preserved and also that evidence has been obtained properly and fairly for the purposes of an ASBO application. If material has been released or obtained in an unauthorised way, it may be argued that this evidence should not be used in court.

Relations with other bodies

Crown Prosecution Service

2.31 The CPS is responsible for the prosecution of alleged breaches of an ASBO (although local authorities are also authorised to bring a prosecution since 31 March 2004[1]). They also may have a greater part to play in obtaining ASBOs with the introduction of the post-conviction ASBO However, applicant authorities may find it helpful to consider the following practices in relations with the CPS:

- Agree a procedure with the CPS as to what information should be provided and to whom, which should include the precise nature of the information to be provided to the CPS when it is prosecuting the breach of an ASBO.
- Invite the CPS to all ASBO problem-solving group meetings. If CPS attendance is not practicable, send minutes or case action plans. The CPS should be asked to advise where it has concerns about the prosecution of particular terms of an ASBO, and may also be given information about forthcoming cases.
- Inform the CPS of any case which relies upon an incident of anti-social behaviour which is also being prosecuted as a criminal offence. This ensures that the CPS gives particular attention to the matter, rather than offering a bind-over or agreeing not to proceed in exchange for a guilty plea on another, more serious, charge unrelated to anti-social behaviour.
- Develop named liaison officers and contacts between the CPS and the problem-solving group. The co-location of CPS officers in police stations may assist here.
- Utilise the designated anti-social behaviour expert prosecutors.

---

[1] See **13.6**.

The courts

2.32 The procedures for presenting applications and appeals are dealt with in later chapters. However, meetings with court officials to agree standard procedures to deal with ASBO applications are advised. The offer of training by applicants to magistrates and their clerks on ASBO matters is usually well received.

2.33 The current service level agreement for West Yorkshire agreed by the police, magistrates' courts and local authorities within the area is set out in Appendix 2(F) as a model of good practice. If an agreement has been made, it should be available on request to the defence, so that they have the opportunity to consider the agreement and to argue against the application on any of the points set out in the agreement. Constructive criticisms made by defendants' solicitors should be given equal consideration in any review of a service level agreement.

The defendant

2.34 It should not be forgotten by either the authorities making the application or by the defendant or his or her legal advisers that preventative work with the defendant remains an option throughout the whole ASBO process. Before an application is made, other methods of dealing with anti-social behaviour should be considered and rejected as less appropriate. If a defendant accepts an offer of help, it would be difficult to satisfy the necessity test unless the defendant continues to behave in an anti-social manner. Depending on how the defendant responds to the voluntary work with agencies such as social services or the YOT, the applicant must decide whether to proceed with the ASBO application or to withdraw it, provided some acceptable guarantees as to future conduct and/or continued participation with agencies are given. This can often be achieved by entering into a carefully worded ABC. If the defendant fails to respond, then it is likely to be necessary to proceed with an application, although the applicant should remain open to any genuine and sustained change in the defendant's behaviour and/or willingness to work with the agencies.

CHAPTER 3

APPLICATIONS FOR ANTI-SOCIAL BEHAVIOUR ORDERS

3.1 The ASB Act 2003 has amended the CDA 1998 in several important ways; however, the legal basis under which applications are made is unchanged.

Where can an application be made?

3.2 An application for an ASBO may be made to the magistrates' court, sitting in its civil jurisdiction, or to a county court in appropriate cases.[1] Criminal courts on conviction can also make ASBOs against defendants.

When can an application be made?

3.3 An application may be made by a relevant authority if it appears to that authority that:

(a) the person has acted, since the commencement date,[2] in an anti-social manner – that is to say, in a manner that caused or was likely to cause harassment, alarm or distress to one or more persons not of the same household as himself; and
(b) such an order is necessary to protect relevant persons from further anti-social acts by him.[3]

'Relevant authority' – who can apply?

3.4 An application for an ASBO may only be made by a 'relevant authority'. Whereas under the original wording of the 1998 Act, an application could only be brought by a local authority or the chief officer of police for an area, the PRA 2002 amended the CDA 1998[4] to expand the definition of relevant authority to allow applications by the Chief Constable of the BTP[5] and any RSL.[6] The amendments contained in the ASB Act 2003 have resulted in the further addition of county councils for England[7] and housing action trusts.[8]

3.5 The local authority for the purposes of ASBO applications is the council for the local government area, which includes a district or London borough, the City of London, the Isle of Wight and the Isles of Scilly in relation to England, and a county or county borough for Wales.[9]

---

[1] See Chapter 6.
[2] 1 April 1999.
[3] CDA 1998, s 1(1)(a) and (b).
[4] Ibid, s 1A, as inserted by PRA 2002, s 61(1) and (2); see Appendix 1(A).
[5] The force of constables appointed under s 53 of the British Transport Commission Act 1949.
[6] Defined by CDA 1998, s 1(1)A(d) as any person registered under section of the Housing Act 1996 as a social landlord who provides or manages any houses or hostels in a local government area.
[7] Ibid, s 1A(aa), inserted by ASB Act 2003, s 85(1) and (2)(a).
[8] Ibid, s 1A(aa), inserted by ASB Act 2003, s 85(1) and (2)(c).
[9] CDA 1998, s 1(12).

3.6 The ever-increasing trend towards stock transfer of housing by local authorities has led to a need to expand the range of bodies which may apply for ASBOs. A number of local authorities no longer have any housing stock, and it was perceived that their inclination to take out ASBOs would be limited by this. The Home Office Guidance is at pains to state that the extension of those capable of bringing applications does not compel RSLs or the BTP to do so. It goes on to make clear that the police and local authority remain jointly responsible under s 17 of the CDA 1998 to develop and implement strategies for tackling anti-social behaviour and disorder in the local area.[1] It would seem that this is highlighted to disabuse those local authorities who have transferred their housing stock from the view that anti-social behaviour caused by social housing tenants or on such estates is no longer their concern. The addition of housing action trusts is welcome and recognises the recent trend in social housing.

Who can be the subject of an application?

3.7 One of the significant advantages of an ASBO is the wide range of its application. An ASBO may be obtained against any person who is aged 10 or over,[2] provided certain statutory criteria are satisfied (see **3.2** et seq). In the original Guidance issued by the Home Office, it was stated that it would be rare for an order to be made against a child aged either 10 or 11. This caveat is not included in the most recent Guidance and perhaps reflects the use of ASBOs since the commencement of the Act. Whilst the courts were initially reluctant to make orders in respect of 10- and 11-year-olds, as applications became more common, it became apparent that children of that age were often being considered for orders by panels. The first order in respect of a child of 10 was in Leeds in 2000 and, thereafter, there have been a number of others. It seems unlikely, however, that the absence of the proviso in the new Guidance will lead to a sudden increase in applications against 10- and 11-year-olds. The limitations on punishment alone would militate against them. ASBOs have been increasingly used in proceedings against young persons, often where local authorities have taken action against gangs or when targeting anti-social disorder in a particular area.

3.8 An ASBO is not dependent on the defendant being a tenant, whether of social or private housing. It is available against any person, whether house owner or hostel inhabitant. The defendant may not have a home at all. For instance, there are a number of ASBOs which have been obtained by local authorities against beggars who seek money in an aggressive or harassing way. A different course was taken by Manchester City Council, which used its powers under s 222 of the Local Government Act 1972 to bring an injunction against a beggar to ban him from the city centre. The use of s 222 against 'non-aggressive' beggars may be more prevalent now that the ASB Act 2003 has strengthened the injunction's effect by allowing the court to make a power of arrest when making injunctions which prohibit actions which are capable of causing nuisance or annoyance.[3]

3.9 The application for an ASBO is not limited by any notion of locality or nexus between the defendant's home and the scenes of his or her anti-social behaviour. Indeed, the current Home Office Guidance refers to ASBOs as being highly relevant to misconduct in public spaces, such as parks, shopping centres, transport hubs, etc. The lack of a need to show a connection between the defendant's behaviour and his or her home or a housing management function of the landlord is a significant attraction of an ASBO over remedies such as injunctions (e.g. Housing Act 1996, s 153A) (see **1.44**). ASBOs are, therefore, widely available against almost any person and experience has shown that the courts have been willing to make applications in very wide

---

[1] See current Home Office Guidance, reproduced in Appendix 3, p 192.
[2] CDA 1998, s 1(1).
[3] Section 91 of the ASB Act 2003.

circumstances. The presumed boundaries of ASBOs may have been extended somewhat, however, in a case brought by Camden Borough Council which sought ASBOs against music advertising executives of Sony UK to prevent fly posting, which the council believed the company to be condoning. At the final hearing, however, the company gave a pledge to stop the practice, which the council accepted, withdrawing the proceedings.

'Has acted in an anti-social manner ...'

3.10 The definition in s 1(1)(a) bears some relation to s 5 of the Public Order Act 1986. However, an important difference should be noted. There is no need for the anti-social behaviour to have *actually* caused any person harassment, alarm or distress. Nor is there any need for the conduct to have happened within sight or hearing of a person who might suffer harassment, alarm or distress. The only stipulation is that the conduct was likely to cause harassment, alarm or distress. There is no need to prove that the defendant *intended* his or her conduct to cause harassment, alarm or distress – only that it did or was likely to do so. There is little doubt that the definition has been widely drawn to ensure that orders are available in the greatest variety of cases.

3.11 As there is no need for evidence from the persons who were caused harassment, alarm or distress, orders can still be obtained with the use of the professionals as witnesses. In this case, the behaviour would be proved by hearsay evidence or by live evidence from professionals, such as police or housing officers. The current Home Office Guidance goes so far as to say that this was a specific intention of the draftsman.[1] The Home Office Guidance provides examples of behaviour which it considers can be the subject of an order and they include behaviour which one might not have associated with the strong measure which an application for an ASBO is often seen to represent. The examples include writing graffiti, begging, prostitution, vehicle crime, fouling the street with litter and drunken behaviour in the street.

3.12 Whilst the Act itself only refers to the relevant authority having to prove that the acts complained of occurred after the commencement date of s 1, there is, however, a time bar which applies at least to applications in the magistrates' courts. In considering an application for an ASBO, the magistrates' court is acting in its civil capacity and a complaint must be laid before it within 6 months from when the acts relied on occurred.[2] Provided a complaint is laid within the 6-month period, there is no impediment to serving the defendant outside that period or of having a hearing after it. It is, therefore, imperative that when an application is being considered, one of the first steps to undertake is to draw up a chronology of events so that from the outset incidents likely to be cited in the application will not become time-barred. This is particularly important when criminal proceedings have been taken in relation to one or more of the incidents.

3.13 Many ASBO applications are delayed due to pending or coexistent criminal proceedings. Although this matter is not dealt with in the current Home Office Guidance, it must be right that the view expressed in the original Guidance that an ASBO application should not include evidence which is due to be heard in the course of criminal proceedings remains valid. To do otherwise would be to prejudice the defendant in the criminal hearing and risk a breach of his or her right to a fair trial. It is important, however, to ensure that applications are not unduly delayed whilst awaiting the outcome of criminal proceedings. Consideration should be given to proceeding with the application without those allegations or, alternatively, to issuing an application to remove any concerns about time-limits and applying for an interim order[3] until the criminal trial is concluded. In appropriate cases, it may also be advisable to reach an

---

[1] See current Home Office Guidance, reproduced in Appendix 3, p 188.
[2] Magistrates' Courts Act 1980, s 127.
[3] See Chapter 7.

agreement with the CPS for them to withdraw the criminal matter so that it can be dealt with in the ASBO application. This is often appropriate where the offence to be tried in the criminal courts is a minor one, for which the punishment is unlikely to be significant. However, the effect of its proof at the ASBO application would be likely to result in an order being made. Care must, however, be taken that the CPS are advised to inform the defendant that whilst the criminal charge is being withdrawn, the conduct in question will be included as grounds for an ASBO application.

3.14 There is no minimum number of incidents which has to be proved to obtain an order. However, it is likely that unless the incident is a serious one, a single incident will not be sufficient. There is no restriction, however, to raising and, indeed, proving incidents which fall outside the 6-month period to support an application based on limited incidents within that period. The original Home Office Guidance suggested that a 'pattern of behaviour' had to be shown. The phrase is reproduced in the current Home Office Guidance, with reference to the use of earlier incidents to establish such a pattern.[1] In practice, it is generally very helpful to the court to provide a second schedule of those incidents which are capable of proof, whether by hearsay evidence or otherwise, but occurred outside the 6-month period. This ensures that the court has a convenient and clear list of the incidents which the relevant authority alleges the defendant has committed. Usually, those incidents include the previous convictions of the defendant, although it is good practice to provide an up-to-date antecedent history within the bundle of evidence supplied to the court. If any of the convictions are within the 6-month period, it is advisable to provide the court with the statements which gave rise to the conviction (if available) and any basis of plea which was accepted by the court. For convictions outside the 6-month period, where the incidents are public order offences or offences against the person, the court may well wish to know about the facts giving rise to the conviction, as this may assist in determining whether an order is necessary.

'Caused or was likely to cause harassment, alarm or distress to one or more persons not of the same household as himself ...'

3.15 If it is to be asserted that the defendant's actions actually caused harassment, alarm or distress to a person, then that needs to be proved by evidence. This would ordinarily be done by way of direct evidence from the person or persons who were affected or by hearsay evidence from a professional witness who can show the reaction of the person affected and/or speak to that person about it.

3.16 If, however, the allegation against the defendant is that his or her conduct was *likely* to cause harassment, alarm or distress, then, clearly, a direct witness of the effect cannot be called. Rather, the court will hear evidence of the conduct of the defendant and then be asked to conclude that this conduct was likely to cause harassment, alarm or distress. The question then arises – what must the applicant show to the court to establish such a likelihood?

3.17 The issue was examined in detail in the case of *The Chief Constable of Lancashire v Potter*.[2] The administrative court was asked to consider an appeal by way of case stated against the decision of the deputy district judge, who had refused to make an ASBO against Potter. The Chief Constable had brought the application against Potter, alleging that she had acted as a prostitute in an area of Preston. He called evidence which was almost exclusively hearsay evidence from two police officers that there was a problem with prostitution in the area, of which residents and visitors had complained. Potter had convictions for prostitution outside the 6-month period and had been seen regularly in the area, and, on occasion, had been seen to step

---

[1] See current Home Office Guidance, reproduced in Appendix 3, p 200.
[2] [2003] EWHC 2272 (Admin), [2003] 42 LS Gaz R 31, [2003] All ER (D) 199 (Oct).

forward and look into moving motor cars to attract attention. Potter did not appear and so the evidence was uncontroverted. The district judge, however, noted that there was no evidence that she had actually caused harassment, alarm or distress, or any direct evidence from local residents (the evidence was hearsay evidence from anonymous sources). Having applied his mind to the weight to be applied to hearsay evidence, he decided that he could not be sure that anyone had actually been caused harassment, alarm or distress and that he did not feel it fair, in the absence of real examples, to find that simply being a prostitute was likely to cause harassment, alarm or distress.

3.18 Lord Justice Auld considered various permutations, including that which has been used in the family law jurisdiction for findings of facts in child abuse cases, but discounted them and came to the conclusion that:

> '[32] Accordingly, as to the meaning of "likely" in this context, my view is that a higher threshold of likelihood is called for than, for example, that of "a real possibility" arising in the context of the safety of children under the Children Act 1989. It is true that the making of an anti-social behaviour order is not a criminal sentence, and serves only to prohibit in specified ways further anti-social behaviour of the sort giving rise to it. However, breach of such an order is a serious matter and can lead to a substantial term of imprisonment or fine. I would give "likely" the meaning in this context of "more probable than not". That meaning, it seems to me, is much the same as that of the Divisional Court in *Parkin v Norman* [1983] QB 92, [1982] 2 All ER 583, [1982] 3 WLR 523, which concerned a charge of insulting behaviour "likely" to occasion a breach of the peace. McCullough J, giving the judgment of the Court consisting of Donaldson LJ and himself, emphasised that the test was whether the conduct in question was "likely", not "liable", to have that effect.'

Lord Justice Auld went on to emphasise the need for the court not to confuse incidents which actually caused and those likely to cause harassment, alarm or distress:

> 'The case demonstrates the importance for a court when dealing with the issue of likelihood in this context of avoiding at least two pitfalls critical to its final decision. The first is not to confuse the second and third constituents of the s 1(1)(a) condition so as to require proof to the criminal standard that a defendant's conduct has actually caused someone harassment, alarm or distress when considering the alternative, whether it is likely to have caused that result. It is in that respect, it seems to me, that the Deputy District Judge, in the passages from his paras 6(Q) and (R) of the statement of case that I have set out and emphasised in para 19 above, fell into error. The thrust of those passages is that he rejected the likelihood alternative because the evidence was wanting as to any instances of actual harassment, alarm or distress ...'

3.19 The second pitfall concerns the standard of proof to be applied and is considered later in this chapter. However, the effect of the above seems to mean that the court will require the applicant to prove (to the appropriate standard) that the defendant's conduct could more probably than not have caused harassment, alarm or distress. To do this, the applicant does not need to provide evidence of any actual persons who may have been subjected to the same – only that the conduct of the defendant could do so.

Aggregation

3.20 *Potter* is also the only higher court authority on whether the defendant's conduct has to be taken alone or whether it can be aggregated with others. In *Potter*, the applicant called evidence of prostitution, as a whole, causing problems for the residents. There was evidence that used condoms were left in the area and that some prostitutes were getting into cars of single men and refusing to leave until given money. Neither of these 'aggravated conducts' could be proved against the defendant. The defendant was not, in any real sense, acting in concert with the other prostitutes frequenting the area. The deputy district judge accepted that the presence of the defendant would contribute to the problem of kerb-crawling, etc, to a small degree and that the activities, as a whole, of the prostitutes represented a problem to the residents; however, by the nature of the activity, prostitutes tended to congregate in an area but not to operate in concert. He therefore discounted the effect of the prostitutes as a whole and any 'aggravated conduct', as this could not be proved to have been caused by the defendant.

3.21 Lord Justice Auld observed, in agreement with the deputy district judge, that:

> 'Street prostitution in residential areas, whatever the extremes of behaviour by individual prostitutes, is clearly capable, when considered as a whole and depending on the circumstances, including the number, regularity and degree of concentration of activity, of causing or being likely to cause harassment, alarm or distress to others in the area. It is a question of fact whether any individual prostitute, by her contribution to that activity and its overall effect, has caused a "problem" which is caught by s 1(1)(a). Proof of such a fact need not depend on the attribution to her of proved "aggravated conduct" of other prostitutes that might, considered on its own, constitute harassment, alarm or distress.'

What Lord Justice Auld, however, also stated was that having found that the actions of the defendant had caused or had been likely to cause the problems arising from prostitution in the area in the sense of her contribution to it, it was inconsistent of the judge to then not find that she had caused, in the same sense, harassment, alarm or distress, as the 'aggravated behaviour' had not been proved to her own actions. He disapproved of the concept of 'aggravated conduct', considering that the only test was whether it was proved that there was conduct, whether committed individually or with others, that had caused or been likely to cause harassment, alarm or distress. He went on, crucially, to state:

> 'Section 1(1)(a) does not require proof of intent to cause any such effects, or, where the conduct of a number of persons is involved that a sole defendant was acting in concert with them. Nor, where harassment, alarm or distress are caused by the conduct of a number of people, including the Defendant, does it require proof that the Defendant's conduct on its own should have been of a sufficiently aggravated nature to cause harassment, alarm or distress or, if not, that she should have in some way shared responsibility with the others for their aggravated conduct. Section 1(1)(a) is concerned simply with a defendant's conduct and its effect, whether looked at on its own or with the conduct of others.'

3.22 The first part of the above quote affirms the statutory wording that the intention of the defendant in his or her actions is irrelevant to determining its effect. Where the decision goes further is that, whilst given in the context of a case involving prostitution and its effects, it has implications for the wider application of aggregation of conduct in ASBO proceedings. Lord Justice Auld specifically states that proving the first part of the statutory test does not require proof of joint enterprise but, further, that if the conduct of many people is causing the harassment, alarm or distress, then the defendant's conduct alone does not need to cause harassment, alarm or distress. Broader application, however, comes when the defendant is not a prostitute but a member of a group whose actions, as a whole, cause harassment, alarm or distress. Often, it is hard to say which person did what or even to prove that the defendant who can be proved to be present did any specific act. The most common examples are where a witness can give evidence that he or she was verbally abused by a group which included the defendant but cannot say what, if anything, he said, or where the witness has been subjected to stone throwing which came from a group of youths but the thrower is unidentifiable. The decision would seem to mean that the defendant's conduct, in being part of the group which verbally abused the witness or threw stones, will be sufficient to establish s 1(1)(a). The only caveat must, of course, be that the defendant's conduct has always to be considered individually as well. So, for instance, where the defendant walked away from the gang which performed the above actions, it could properly be argued that he had distanced himself from them and their conduct. Where, however, the defendant simply rejoins the group and continues, this would be harder to argue. Aggregation of a defendant's conduct with that of others must be considered very carefully, however, and care must be taken by the court to ensure that only where the group's actions as a whole cause (or are likely to cause) harassment, alarm or distress are they taken into account. Similarly, as Lord Justice Auld stated, the court must then concern itself with the defendant's conduct and its effect, taken on its own and/or with the conduct of the others in the group. The judgment remains, however, a very useful examination of what the court is permitted to consider when assessing whether the statutory test is made out and will undoubtedly make it easier to prove anti-social behaviour where gangs or groups of offenders are involved.

'... necessary to protect relevant persons from further anti-social acts by him'

3.23 Even if it has been proved that the defendant has acted in an anti-social manner, the court *must* go on to consider whether an order is necessary to protect relevant persons from further anti-social acts. This test found in s 1(1)(b) was amended by the PRA 2002, which also added a definition of 'relevant persons' which is found in s 1B of the CDA 1998. For an application by a local authority, relevant persons are those falling within the local government area of that council and, similarly, within a police area for an application by a Chief Constable or a county council.

3.24 Where the application is by the BTP, 'relevant persons' means:

(1) persons on or likely to be on policed premises in a local government area; *or*
(2) persons in the vicinity of or likely to be in the vicinity of such premises.

3.25 Where the application is by an RSL of housing action trust, 'relevant persons' are:

(1) persons who are residing in or who are otherwise on or likely to be on premises provided or managed by that authority; or
(2) persons who are in the vicinity of or likely to be in the vicinity of such premises.

3.26 It would seem unlikely that any application which either a BTP, RSL or housing action trust would wish to bring would fail for inability to show that relevant persons needed to be protected. The only potential problem may be for an application by an RSL to a housing action trust where the defendant's conduct was aimed at a particular person or family who have since left the area. In those circumstances, unless it could be shown that other persons were likely to become victims of similar behaviour, there would not be a relevant person to protect. In practice, however, it would be highly unlikely that an ASBO would be sought, as, where the anti-social behaviour was so focused on one person or family, an injunction may well be a better solution. If, however, the actions of the defendant affected persons not proximate to his or her home but the affected persons were RSL or housing act trust tenants, there is no bar to an application. It would, however, be important to provide the court with either a statement or a plan, showing the properties in the affected area which were provided or managed by the RSL or housing act trust. This plan will also have some significance if an exclusion zone is sought.

3.27 In seeking to show that an order is necessary, there are no time-limits as to the evidence which may be relied upon. Incidents which have occurred over a period of time are extremely relevant in establishing that an order is necessary. Clearly, the longer the period over which the conduct has continued, the more likely it is that an order is necessary. Evidence from residents or victims, often in the form of hearsay evidence, about the effect of the conduct on them and their fears if no action is taken, is particularly effective in showing to the court that an order is needed, with the difference in the standard of proof to establish necessity (see below). The statements of the professionals in the case should always contain details of statements given to them by residents or members of the public about the defendant's conduct. They should also provide details of relevant statistics (e.g. the number of applications for transfer of housing that cite anti-social behaviour as the reason for applying or the number of vacant, un-let properties in the area). This type of evidence was used to very good effect in a series of applications by Leeds City Council to show the extent of the problems in a particular area. The evidence provided to the court included the cost of cleaning graffiti, repairing vandalism damage, attending malicious fires, and collection and disposal of drug users' hypodermic needles.

Burden and standards of proof

3.28 The burden of proof, both evidentially and legally, is on the applicant, save where the defendant seeks to show that his or her alleged anti-social conduct was reasonable in the circumstances. In such a situation, it is suggested that the defendant bears an evidential burden to adduce evidence in support of his or her contention, but not a legal one to prove it to any standard. Whether the applicant then bears the burden of disproving it (e.g. self-defence in criminal trials) remains unresolved.

3.29 The standard of proof to which the applicant must establish the case has caused a number of problems which have now been resolved and are settled law. It is now clear, beyond doubt, that ASBO proceedings are civil proceedings and, therefore, all the civil rules on the admissibility of evidence (including hearsay) apply. However, the standard of proof to which the applicant must prove that the defendant has acted in an anti-social manner is a criminal standard (i.e. beyond a reasonable doubt). This is the ruling of the House of Lords, as given by Lord Steyn[1] in October 2002. The reason for the higher standard of proof is one of pragmatism. The Court of Appeal in the *McCann* case[2] had suggested that, whilst there was a sliding scale in respect of the standard of proof in civil cases, it would be advisable for magistrates to apply the criminal standard for uniformity. This view was approved by Lord Steyn.

3.30 Lord Steyn also went on to make clear that the standard of proof to be applied to proving the first part of the statutory criteria in s 1 has *no* application to the second part of the test (i.e. whether an order was necessary). He said:

> 'The inquiry under section 1(1)(b), namely that such an order is necessary to protect persons from further anti-social acts by him, does not involve a standard of proof: it is an exercise of judgement or evaluation.'

This was a welcome clarification of the legal test to be applied, as there had been a rising number of cases in which argument had been raised about whether it was actually possible to prove beyond a reasonable doubt that an order was necessary. The court, in deciding whether an order is necessary, should therefore take into consideration all the evidence presented to it and reach a *reasoned* decision as to the need for an order. It is important to note that the applicant is not required to show that all other steps and possible methods to regulate the defendant's behaviour have been tried. It is sufficient to show that other means have been considered and that an ASBO has been decided as the most suitable. This 'message' is repeated in the current Home Office Guidance on a number of occasions.

---

[1] *R (on the application McCann and others) v Crown Court at Manchester; Clingham v Kensington and Chelsea Royal Borough Council* [2002] UKHL 39, [2002] 3 WLR 1313, [2002] 4 All ER 593, HL.
[2] *R v Manchester Crown Court ex parte McCann* [2001] EWCA Civ 281, [2001] 1 WLR 1084.

3.31 Whilst it is clear from *McCann* that where the applicant alleges that the defendant has committed acts which have actually caused harassment, alarm or distress, he or she must do so to the criminal standard, i.e. so that the court is sure, the question arose in *Potter* as to what should be the standard of proof where the allegation was only that the actions of the defendant *were likely to cause* harassment, alarm or distress. Lord Justice Auld considered the meaning of the word 'likely' in the statute. He discounted any notion that he could distinguish *McCann* to impose a lower standard of proof, stating:

> '[28] It might be open to this Court to focus in a way that the House of Lords did not in *McCann*, on the possibility of a lower than criminal standard of proof of the likelihood of a defendant's conduct having caused harassment, alarm or distress. However, in my view, it would be a futile exercise. "Proof", to whatever standard, of a likelihood is necessarily a different mental exercise from that of proving a fact in the sense that something has actually happened. It might be described as an evaluative exercise of a similar kind to that in s 1(1)(b), notwithstanding that s 1(4) requires *proof* of it, as well as the condition in s 1(1)(a). Or it might, true to that requirement, be characterised as proof of a speculative outcome.'

And, further, that:

> '[33] As to the standard of proof required, probably the fairest and simplest solution is to say that a court, in conducting what is necessarily an evaluative exercise on this issue a well as that under s 1(1)(b), must, on the evidence before it, be sure to the criminal standard, that a defendant's conduct has caused the likelihood in the sense I have indicated. It seems to me that, whether that is a matter of proof and/or of evaluation, is no more a matter for philosophical analysis or agonising by courts than, say, a magistrate or a jury having to decide to the criminal standard whether an accused's conduct was dishonest or intentional or reckless. As I have said, determining whether conduct had a likely effect is a frequent demand made on lay and professional decision-makers in our courts in all sorts of criminal offences.'

3.32 The practical application of the two aspects of *Potter* is that the court must (where considering an allegation that the defendant's actions were likely to cause harassment, alarm or distress) be sure that the conduct would more probably than not cause harassment, alarm and distress. The court has, therefore, to be careful when doing so not to confuse the likelihood of harassment, alarm or distress being caused by the defendant's conduct ('more probable than not') with the standard of proof required to establish that likelihood ('sure'). In practice, as Lord Justice Auld observed, courts are well used to determining such issues and do so in the context of other jurisdictions. In the majority of cases, this should not prove difficult, as conduct such as violent behaviour, abusive language and dangerous driving will almost inevitably be likely to cause harassment, alarm or distress. The more difficult areas concern the effects of prostitution, begging and other less directly 'offensive' conduct on the part of the defendant. The deputy district judge in *Potter* applied too strict a test and should have considered the lower test, described above. The case was remitted for him to apply the proper test.

3.33 The issue of whether it was necessary to make an order where the conduct complained of had stopped prior to the application was considered in the case of *S v Poole Borough Council*.[1] The court also rejected any possible argument by the defendant of 'double jeopardy' by the use of the incidents for which there had been a previous criminal conviction.[2] In *S v Poole Borough Council*, the defendant, a youth aged about 15, was alleged to have been involved in anti-social behaviour for about 18 months, running up to just prior to the application for an ASBO. The hearing in the magistrates' court had not occurred until 5 months had passed and a further 7½ months went by before the Crown Court hearing. There were no alleged incidents in that

---

[1] [2002] EWHC 244 (Admin), (unreported), February 2002.
[2] See further **4.18**.

time, and the defendant's representatives argued that there was no necessity for an order, as there had been no anti-social behaviour for over a year. The Crown Court upheld the making of an order and the defendant appealed by way of case stated. Lord Justice Stephen Brown, in rejecting the argument in the Divisional Court, said:

> 'With the best will in the world, that is to my mind a hopeless argument. It must be expected that, once an application of this sort has been made, still more obviously once an ASBO has been made, its effect will be to deter future misconduct. That, indeed, is the justification for such orders in the first place. It would be a remarkable situation were a defendant, against whom an order has rightly been made, then able, on appeal to the Crown Court, to achieve its quashing because in the interim he has not disobeyed it; rather the very effectiveness of such an order would to my mind justify its continuance. The conduct on which the magistrates and in turn the Crown Court should concentrate on determining whether an order is necessary is that which underlay the authority's application for the order in the first place ... .'

3.34 It therefore follows that, with the introduction of interim orders, it will be almost impossible for a defendant to argue that the making of an ASBO is not necessary by arguing that he or she has not acted in an anti-social manner since the application was made. The period of time between the last incident of anti-social behaviour and the making of the application remains relevant, however, and the defence may raise a reasonable argument, especially if there is a sizeable gap. Of course, the need to avoid potential issues such as this makes it important for the applicant to bring an application as soon as possible.

'Necessity' for ASBO after interim order

3.35 An extension of the point in *S v Poole* occurs where it is argued that, where interim orders are made in terms which are less than the full orders applied for at the main application, the additional final order terms are not necessary, as the interim order terms have not been breached. The argument is, therefore, that the interim terms are all that is necessary to protect relevant persons from further acts of anti-social behaviour. Whilst this can be an attractive argument in some cases, where the additional terms sought are minor and do not add anything, it would seem hard to justify this argument when the statutory model and case-law are considered. First, an interim order is one which is made because there is an urgent need to protect relevant persons. It is made without any detailed consideration of the strength of the applicant's case and no findings of fact are made. Interim orders are very often made in very limited terms, with reduced exclusion zones or without non-association clauses, so that the minimal appropriate restrictions are placed on the defendant, pending his or her full trial. That is the statutory model as supported by the Home Office Guidance. To argue at the full hearing that the interim order has not been breached and, therefore, is enough to prevent further acts would fly in the face of the reasoning in *S v Poole*. The fact that an order has been made and the defendant complied with it cannot be grounds for concluding that only those terms would be necessary. If correct, the applicant would be entitled to ask for the same terms on an interim basis as a final order to prevent this argument. Further, a defendant, by complying with a limited interim order for a short period, could defeat the applicant's full order terms in every case. The defendant who complies with an interim order is in no better a position than S when he complied with the original order pending his appeal. The court should consider the necessity of the order *and* the terms as of the time of the application – not the hearing.

3.36 The introduction of interim orders has led to a further point when necessity is considered, namely whether a breach of an interim order can go towards establishing whether a final order is necessary. If the breach is one which amounts to anti-social behaviour, e.g. verbal abuse or violent conduct, there can be little doubt of its relevance. Indeed, it would be likely to make an order hard to resist in many cases. If, however, the breach is one which contravenes the interim order but is not anti-social per se, e.g. entering an exclusion zone, can it be argued that this should be considered by the court as to necessity? There are reported cases on this issue, however, where it has been argued at first instance and the courts have taken the view that the breach of the interim order shows the defendant's attitude to the orders and failure to accept responsibility for his or her actions, even at that late stage. Therefore, the courts' approach seems to be that any breach of an interim order, however minor, is relevant. This approach is borne out by the attitude of the sentencing courts in respect of breaches of interim orders. Custodial penalties are not uncommon, even for minor first breaches, with the view being taken that failure to comply with exclusion zones, for instance, is more serious than the actual acts of the defendant due to the history of anti-social behaviour which resulted in the interim order being made. It is also likely that there is a deterrent element to the sentencing, including the fact that the order being breached is a court-made order. Stronger punishment than would be the case for the actual act giving rise to the breach is necessary to maintain the court's authority and integrity.

Defences and disregards

3.37 Neither the statute nor the Home Office Guidance provides any specific defences for a defendant to rely upon. Therefore, in order to defeat an application, a defendant will have to counter the applicant's evidence in relation to either the first or second limb of the test in s 1(1) of CDA 1998. With respect to the alleged anti-social conduct, CDA 1998, s 1(5) states that the court must disregard any conduct which was reasonable in the circumstances. It is hard to imagine how this could apply to many situations, save for instances of self-defence or defence of property or other persons.

Summary

3.38 In summary:

- ASBOs can be brought by the police, the local authority, an RSL, the BTP, a housing action trust or a county council.
- ASBOs can be brought against defendants aged 10 years or over.
- There is a two-stage test: (i) have acts caused or are they likely to cause harassment, alarm or distress; and (ii) is an order necessary?
- Stage (i) has to be proved to the criminal standard of proof.
- Stage (ii) is an exercise of judgement and discretion and not a standard of proof.
- Hearsay evidence may be relied on at all stages.
- The defendant's individual conduct may be aggregated with that of others in certain situations.
- Criminal convictions may be used to prove either stage.

CHAPTER 4

EVIDENCE

4.1 As with all court proceedings, evidence is the key to a successful outcome. This chapter will cover the general techniques of evidence-gathering, which are particularly important to ASBO applications. Whether the reader seeks to secure an ASBO or defeat one, persuasive and comprehensive evidence is of crucial importance.

Home Office Guidance

4.2 Applicants are encouraged not to produce over-elaborate or excessively voluminous court files. Instead, they are asked to select their material to 'strike a balance and focus on what is most relevant and necessary to provide sufficient evidence for the court to arrive at a clear understanding of the matter'. This is something which is easier for the Home Office to state than to comply with. Whilst bringing less material to court saves money, the burden of proof is a criminal one and the order often perceived as draconian. Achieving the balance is a difficult process and it is far better to lean towards more evidence than less.

4.3 A list of available sources of evidence is provided, including:

- breach of an ABC;
- witness statements of officers attending incidents or those affected by the behaviour;
- evidence of complaints recorded by the police, housing providers or other agencies;
- statements from professional witnesses (e.g. council or truancy officers or health visitors);
- video or CCTV evidence (effective where resolution is high; alternatively, high-quality still images can be used);
- supporting statements or reports from other agencies (e.g. probation reports);
- previous successful relevant civil proceedings (e.g. eviction for similar behaviour);
- previous relevant convictions;
- copies of custody records of previous relevant arrests; and
- information from witness diaries.

In this chapter we shall examine sources of evidence, covert surveillance and hearsay evidence.

Sources of evidence

Documentary evidence

4.4 Applicants *and* defendants should be fully aware of all relevant documents. Chapter 2 deals more fully with effective information exchange between agencies and how the defendant may access various records. However, the following section should provide a useful checklist of what documents may be available from various agencies.

(i) Housing services

4.5 The files of the housing department should contain comprehensive information in respect of each tenancy, including allegations of nuisance made by or against the defendant. Further, the file should record housing management matters, such as copies of warning letters sent to the defendant and notices before possession proceedings are issued. Interviews with the defendant should also be recorded, detailing the allegations and responses.

4.6 For the applicant, the file can provide useful background information if past nuisance has been recorded. This can establish a pattern of anti-social behaviour and previous, unheeded warnings. For the defence, if there has been a lack of proper housing management, it can be argued that an ASBO is not necessary, as the defendant has not been given the opportunity to change his or her behaviour, or it may provide mitigating circumstances.

(ii) Social services

4.7 The social services department encompasses a wide variety of services, including work with young people, mental health and, in some authorities, the YOT. Documentation from their files can be used in support of or against an application. For the applicant, it can prove, for example, that, despite work having been done with a child, anti-social behaviour continues. For the defendant, the file may show that parental requests for support from the department have been ignored. Failure to provide such support can lead to awkward internal questions, especially if the local authority is also the statutory parent. In appropriate cases, a defendant's representative may successfully argue that an ASBO is not necessary if he or she can demonstrate that other, more appropriate actions should have been taken.[1]

4.8 A request for the production of social services files is often met with resistance. In relation to a child, if care proceedings have begun, permission of the court is needed before documentation can be used.[2] The case of *Re M (Care Proceedings: Disclosure: Human Rights)*[3] contains useful observations on the application of the rules in practice. In other circumstances, disclosure should, in theory, be relatively straightforward.

4.9 Applicants need to appreciate the background against which social services operate. Often, they work with Area Child Protection Committees, in which there is a culture of free and frank disclosure of information, and case discussions are held with parents or alleged perpetrators. More guidance on how these committees work in partnership with other agencies is contained in the Home Office document, 'Working Together to Safeguard Children'. The child protection process may be undermined if that information is subsequently used against a person as part of a court case. Therefore, a framework must be established for departments to come to a workable solution so as not to compromise either party's position. In the event of a lack of internal agreement, there should be a protocol for resolving internal difficulties.

4.10 Defendants and their legal advisers should consider requesting access to files or documents, provided that the request does not constitute 'a fishing expedition'. Defendants might seek access to minutes of meetings about the child, action plans to address the child's needs and any special issues concerning the child which can provide support for arguments that alternatives that are short of an ASBO should be pursued. Often, those involved in social services conferences are given access to minutes of meetings or action plans where they have been present, provided this does not contravene the Family Proceedings Rules (FPR) 1991, r 4.23.

---

[1] See *R (on the application of AB and SB) v Nottingham City Council* [2001] EWHC Admin 235, [2001] 3 FCR 350.
[2] FPR 1991, r 4.23.
[3] [2001] 2 FLR 1316.

(iii)   Environmental services

4.11   Evidence of previous convictions or successful applications for seizure of equipment can assist in building a case against a defendant. Similarly, in eviction cases, especially those cases concerning noise complaints, such records may reveal useful information for the defence. If a complaint has been investigated, what have those investigations shown? For instance, the records may show that the use of monitoring equipment failed to prove a statutory nuisance. Such evidence might deliver a blow to the credibility of the complaints.

(iv)   Education/school records

4.12   Documentation from educational sources can potentially help both applicant and defendant. The applicant may be assisted by information which establishes a pattern of misconduct throughout a defendant's schooling. Conversely, the records may reveal a system that has failed the defendant, e.g. by not exploring the possibility of specialist units, pupil referral or home tutoring, in order to try and address the defendant's conduct. The defendant may be able successfully to contend that such avenues should have been explored before recourse to the courts.

(v)   Police

4.13   Documentary evidence from the police can include previous convictions (see **4.17–4.20**), as well as police information which is not normally disclosed. Pocketbook entries of police officers can stand as evidence and printouts of calls made to the police can provide corroborative evidence of complaints, but these are of limited use if they do not identify the perpetrator or nuisance in detail. Where individuals, other than the defendant, are referred to in evidence, the defence may claim that it is discriminatory to take action against one individual and not others.

4.14   The police can also provide analyses of crime patterns. Such information can provide an indication of crime hotspots involving a particular defendant. A detailed plan can be produced to demonstrate the complaints made to the police and to highlight the areas in which the anti-social behaviour has taken place. These plans are often very useful in showing to the court the extent of a defendant's behaviour.

Disclosure

4.15   While the applicant should know the evidence available in the files, it is necessarily more difficult for the defence to identify and obtain the relevant documents. The checklists given earlier in this chapter can assist in identifying sources of evidence but obtaining them can be difficult. In ASBO proceedings, magistrates have the ultimate power to regulate their own procedure. There are no specific rules for disclosure of documents in civil proceedings in the magistrates' court. The Criminal Investigations and Procedures Act 1996, with its detailed provisions for disclosure, does not apply to ASBO proceedings, which are civil in nature. Unfortunately, the Civil Procedure Rules 1998 (CPR 1998), which govern civil actions, do not apply to the magistrates' courts. Disclosure is mentioned in the current Home Office Guidance.[1] It recommends that checks on witness support and intimidation should be made by agencies before any evidence in a case is disclosed. It states that the witness's express permission should be given before any evidence is disclosed, but evidence not disclosed cannot be relied on. The

---

[1]   See current Home Office Guidance, reproduced in Appendix 3, p 205.

magistrates' courts should, however, be encouraged to adopt the CPR 1998 as far as possible. Direct application of the CPR 1998 will follow in any application for an ASBO in the county court. CPR 1998, r 31 places an obligation on both parties to disclose relevant documents on which they rely and those which adversely affect their own case or support the case of the opposition. Only a reasonable search need be made for such documents. In dealing with disclosure, the parties should bear in mind the overriding objective of dealing with cases fairly, justly, reasonably, proportionately and efficiently (CPR 1998, Part 1).

4.16 Currently, the best way for the defence to obtain access to undisclosed documents is to request them. If the applicant does not accede to the request, an application should be made to the relevant court for disclosure of the documents, relying on the procedures in the CPR 1998 and Art 6 of the European Convention for the Protection of Human Rights and Fundamental Freedoms (ECHR), in that the defendant would be denied a fair trial if refused access to the relevant documents. The applicant may argue that some or all of the information is privileged if prepared in the contemplation of actual or pending litigation. How far the arguments will go or which will prevail is as yet untested in the magistrates' courts. When the county court has the power to grant ASBOs, it is hoped that there will follow a standardisation of procedure between both courts to bring greater clarity to this area. It would seem inappropriate not to utilise the clear rules on disclosure and other procedural steps set out in the CPR 1998.

Previous convictions

4.17 Evidence of previous convictions can be invaluable to applicants because no witnesses are required to prove the incident. As a matter of course, checks should be made for relevant convictions for use in an ASBO application. Proof of convictions can be introduced in court in one of two ways – either by exhibiting police records of convictions to a statement from a police officer or by requesting certificates of conviction from the appropriate magistrates' court or Crown Court. It is, however, very important for an applicant to file the statements of the complaints in the criminal conviction, or at least a summary of the facts. Otherwise, the bare fact of the conviction may not tell the whole story.

4.18 The use of criminal convictions was challenged in the case of *S v Poole Borough Council*.[1] The defendant sought to argue that facts which were used to found a criminal conviction should not be used to obtain an ASBO. Lord Justice Simon Brown, giving the judgment of the Divisional Court on a case stated from the Crown Court, disagreed, and stated:

> 'It seems to me to be perfectly proper to use the same material to base a criminal conviction and then, in civil proceedings, to support an order that was akin to an injunction. Indeed it would seem to me to be positively eccentric to omit reference to part of the conduct which undoubtedly contributed to the public mischief when it came to seeking to deter it in the future.'[2]

4.19 The court clearly approved the use of previous convictions as evidence in related nuisance proceedings. Previous convictions can, therefore, be used by applicants to establish the first limb of an ASBO (i.e. harassment, alarm or distress, if they involve offences of this nature). Experience shows that, faced with numerous relevant (and recent) previous convictions (e.g. assault, burglary and theft), the defence's ability to argue against all parts of the application is seriously undermined. A practical approach to these problems may well be for the defence to make limited concessions and seek to negotiate. For example, in exchange for such concessions, the defendant could attempt to negotiate with the applicant not to proceed with some of the allegations or to relax the terms of the ASBO. Alternatively, the first limb of the test could be conceded and the issue of necessity contested alone.

---

[1] [2002] EWHC 244 (Admin), (unreported), February 2002.
[2] Ibid, para [16].

4.20 Consideration should also be given to the provisions of the Rehabilitation of Offenders Act 1974. If a conviction has become 'spent' under the provisions of this Act the defendant shall be treated for all purposes in law as a person who has not committed the offence.[1] A conviction is spent if the period appropriate to that form of sentence has expired.[2] Once it has, a person cannot be asked questions which may indicate that that person has committed that offence.[3] It follows that a person may not have to answer questions in cross-examination that would lead to the disclosure of spent convictions. Whilst the defendant may seek to rely on these provisions in relation to his or her own previous convictions, there is an exception under s 7(3). If a court is satisfied, in the light of any considerations which appear to it to be relevant, that justice cannot be done in the case except by admitting or requiring evidence relating to a person's spent convictions, that authority may admit or, as the case may be, require the evidence in question. It seems likely that a very strong argument can be made by the applicant that previous convictions showing anti-social behaviour by the defendant *are* necessary to do justice in an ASBO application. The point has yet, however, to be tested.

Lay witnesses

4.21 Witnesses who suffer nuisance can provide documentary evidence in the form of diary sheets or log sheets, or letters of complaint. They can also provide compelling evidence of harassment, alarm or distress, in the form of witness statements and, better still, live evidence. Lay witnesses are, however, often reluctant to give evidence for a variety of reasons, including fear of reprisals or intimidation after the court process. Support, encouragement and protection by the police or through injunctions are very important in securing lay witnesses' co-operation and attendance.

4.22 The points that have been made in relation to the applicant's lay witnesses apply equally to the defence witnesses, although, naturally, much of the focus of court intimidation and process concerns the applicant's witnesses.

Professional witnesses

4.23 Professional witnesses are increasingly used in the context of ASBOs. These can range from council officers, police officers, health authority employees or professional surveillance personnel. Professional witnesses may themselves have been harassed, alarmed or distressed by the defendant, and they may provide information about the defendant's past conduct in order to establish the necessity test.

4.24 The current Home Office Guidance encourages the use of anonymous statements as evidence. The courts, however, do not seem to accord such statements very much weight. Therefore, professional witnesses will often be used in order to spare lay witnesses the ordeal of court attendance, whilst permitting the voice of the local community to be heard in the proceedings. This is achieved by the professional witnesses' referring in their statements to the comments made by local residents. Such comments will, of course, be hearsay (hearsay provisions are dealt with at **4.43–4.56**).

4.25 Professional surveillance firms may be used for such purposes. However, as they can be expensive and results cannot be guaranteed, they should be given very specific tasks, to ensure value for money and effective results in court.

4.26 Professional witnesses can also be used by the defence but, for reasons of finance, often are not. However, access to the same information or statements may be available, using the

---

[1] Rehabilitation of Offenders Act 1974, s 4(1).
[2] Ibid, s 5(1).
[3] Ibid, s 4(1)(b).

same tactics explored in the disclosure of documents. The defence can ask if any professional surveillance firms have been engaged and, if so, what the results were. If their findings are adverse to the applicant's and helpful to the defendant's case, they should be disclosed. As this is still an untried concept, it is not known how far the court will go in ordering disclosure for reasons of trial fairness when balanced against arguments of privilege.

4.27 There is nothing to prevent the defence from approaching council employees (or similar), e.g. the family social worker, a YOT worker, a teacher, etc, for witness statements to support their case. The response to such a request may differ from authority to authority. A typical reaction is often to refuse the request so as not to compromise the applicant's case. If the defence feels that the person approached would be likely to assist the case but feels compelled to refuse to give a statement, a witness summons can be served, to require that person's attendance. However, there is a risk that, in such circumstances, the witness may not give helpful evidence at trial. This risk can be reduced, but not removed, by interviewing the witness outside the court, prior to calling him or her.

Covert surveillance

4.28 Covert surveillance can often reveal the truth of the situation or at least provide dispassionate, independent, corroborative evidence of nuisance.

Videos and CCTV

General

4.29 Video or CCTV footage can provide compelling evidence in court. Indeed, it is specifically mentioned in the Home Office Guidance as an example of what evidence can be included in a case. It notes that such evidence is effective where resolution is high, and that high-quality still images can be used. In one of the first ASBO applications taken by Liverpool City Council, such evidence was adduced of a defendant's jumping up and down on cars, which proved incontrovertible evidence of harassment, alarm or distress. CCTV footage has now been used to significant effect in the multiple-defendant ASBOs obtained in Leeds and by many other applicants. On a practical note, it is important to provide the court with statements from people identifying defendants on the video. This is often best done by using a still taken from the video, so that the court can readily follow the identified person as he or she appears in the video.

4.30 More and more lay witnesses have access to home video cameras. The use of such equipment should be encouraged, as neighbours are able to monitor the area over a far longer period than could be done by professional witnesses. However, the defendant can also use home video footage to undermine the case against him or her. If the allegations centre on the intimidating behaviour of the defendant, and footage shows the local community happily interacting with him or her, that will undermine the case. Also, if the defendant captures footage of the applicant's witnesses engaging in similar exploits to those levelled against the defendant, this can be raised as explaining the defendant's conduct as reasonable or, in relation to the necessity test, that the claimant's witnesses did not receive protection from the defendant, but the converse.

Using video footage

4.31 If video footage is to be used, the other party should be notified as soon as is practicable, and given the opportunity to view it, to avoid any unnecessary court adjournments. Whoever is adducing video evidence should provide the other side with a copy, or should arrange for private viewing facilities at their office. If the receiving party insists on viewing the original or it is not possible to obtain copies, it should be released only on the solicitor's undertaking to hold it to order, return it on demand and keep it safely. There are no rules in the magistrates' court that deal with the presentation of video evidence in civil proceedings. Applicant authorities and defendants are, therefore, left with the general powers by which the magistrates control their own procedure. In the county court, the position is governed by CPR 1998, r 32.1. This states that the court may control evidence as it sees fit. It can regulate the nature and way in which evidence is presented, and can even exclude evidence that is normally admissible. It can require a party to give evidence by videotape. However, under CPR 1998, r 32.1(6), the court should not let any party hold back evidence to ambush a witness. Video evidence undermining a claimant's case should be disclosed at an early stage. However, following *Rall v Hume*,[1] the fact that video evidence is disclosed late in the day is not always sufficient to justify its exclusion.

4.32 It is important to notify the court as soon as possible, to ensure that the correct equipment is available at court. No assumption should be made about the nature of the technical facilities available at court. Tapes should be wound to the relevant place to save court time. A chronology may assist in identifying individuals or events, unless self-evident.

4.33 As ASBO applications are civil proceedings, there is no strict need to preserve the chain of evidence, as in criminal proceedings. Often, rightly, there is little point in challenging the continuity of evidence but it is useful for the applicant body to be able to prove, if called upon, that the equipment was in good working order and in whose possession the video was before being used in evidence in court.

Using CCTV footage

4.34 In practice, CCTV footage is only available to the police or local authority. The quality of the tapes is generally very clear and, thus, may avoid the additional financial outlay of using professional surveillance firms. Where this is available, still pictures can be taken from the tapes and often provide telling pieces of evidence.

4.35 The defence should be given the opportunity to view the tapes. The operation of CCTV is heavily regulated by codes of practice issued by the Information Commissioner to ensure fairness and compliance with data protection and human rights legislation. A detailed examination of these codes is beyond the scope of this book, but more information about them can be obtained from the Information Commissioner's website.[2] The defence should check to see if these operating guidelines have been followed, to ensure that evidence obtained cannot be challenged or undermined by operational irregularities.

4.36 Effective planning and gathering of evidence by applicants can reduce or remove the necessity for witness evidence. For example, ASBOs targeted at controlling conduct in areas covered by CCTV, such as city centres or train stations, can benefit from such planning if the operatives are tasked with targeting and recording anti-social conduct.

RIPA 2000 considerations

4.37 The Regulation of Investigatory Powers Act 2000 (RIPA 2000) provides a framework for the effective authorisation and conduct of 'directed surveillance' by local authorities and the police. This is defined as surveillance which is 'covert but not intrusive', and is part of a planned operation which is likely to result in the acquisition of private information, which is

---

[1] [2001] 3 All ER 248.
[2] www.dataprotection.co.uk.

not an 'immediate response to events or circumstances', and where it is not reasonably practicable to obtain prior authorisation.

4.38 Surveillance is defined in s 48 of RIPA 2000 as including monitoring, observing or listening to persons, their movements, their conversations or various other activities or communication. Communication is, itself, widely defined to cover anything comprising speech, music, sounds, visual images or data of any description. An example of directed surveillance in an ASBO context is where evidence is covertly gathered by installing secret cameras, trained on a person's home, to obtain evidence of nuisance allegations in and around his or her home and estate as part of a planned investigation.

4.39 The RIPA 2000 also impacts on local authorities and the police when they permit the use of what s 26(8) refers to as a 'covert human intelligence source'. This is where a personal or other relationship is established or maintained for the covert purpose of using that relationship to obtain or provide access to any information to another, or covertly disclosing information obtained because of that relationship to another (e.g. where professional surveillance firms pose as local neighbours and befriend an alleged perpetrator to gather evidence of anti-social conduct or nuisance in the community).

4.40 Appropriate officers within the police and local authority can authorise others within their related public bodies to carry out surveillance operations for planned aims and for set periods of time. The request for authorisation must persuade the authorising officers that it is necessary on one or more specific grounds, such as national security or for the prevention or detection of crime. Considerations of proportionality are also built in. Similar grounds are, of course, available in Art 8(2) of the ECHR to reconcile interference by a public body with interference in a person's right to respect for his or her private and family life, home and correspondence.

4.41 If covert surveillance is carried out relying on a RIPA 2000 authorisation, according to s 27(1), it makes conduct pursuant to it 'lawful for all purposes'. The exact application of this is unclear, as there is little defining case-law in this area. Applicant authorities can rely on RIPA 2000 authorisations to meet any challenge to the fairness of evidence gathered and relied on as part of the application. The defence may, however, attempt to challenge the parameters of 'lawful for all purposes' or seek to challenge whether the authorisation was proportionate and necessary or whether the conduct carried out went beyond the bounds of that which was authorised. The prospects of success of such an application are doubtful. It remains unclear whether this would lead to exclusion of the evidence.

4.42 The police have wider powers to intercept communications contained in RIPA 2000 by the use of interception warrants, and can obtain access to communications data about a subject. For example, lists of email subscribers can be obtained and also the key to encrypted electronic data using other provisions of RIPA 2000. Since 5 January 2004, local authorities also have limited powers to access certain types of communications data. The issues in relation to these matters are varied and beyond the scope of this book, and unlikely to be directly relevant to ASBOs.

Hearsay evidence

Use of hearsay evidence

4.43 The court system in England and Wales is adversarial and the rules of evidence are dictated by this doctrine. Persons who have directly witnessed the events giving rise to the application normally give evidence of those events. Their evidence is then tested and challenged through cross-examination by the opposing party. The court then adjudicates on where the truth lies.

4.44 Hearsay evidence is the term given to evidence that the court is asked to accept when the person who directly witnessed events is not giving evidence. The evidence, therefore, cannot be tested in the same way as when a live witness is available to be cross-examined. Hearsay falls into two categories: first-hand or multiple hearsay. Hearsay is not generally admissible in criminal proceedings, but, as has been confirmed by the House of Lords in *McCann*,[1] ASBOs are civil proceedings. Therefore, hearsay evidence is generally admissible.

4.45 The admissibility of hearsay evidence in civil proceedings is governed primarily by s 1(4) of the Civil Evidence Act 1995,[2] which states that evidence shall not be excluded purely on the grounds that it is hearsay. Those provisions apply to magistrates' courts and, therefore, ASBOs by virtue of the Magistrates' Courts (Hearsay Evidence in Civil Proceedings) Rules 1999.[3]

4.46 The 1999 Rules often allow, in the context of ASBOs, applicants (and defendants) to introduce anonymous statements, statements from missing witnesses and those who are too afraid to come to court (e.g. for fear of reprisals).

Adducing hearsay evidence before the court

4.47 There are several types of hearsay evidence. These may be summarised as follows:

- a statement identifying the witness, signed and dated by him or her, giving a direct account of events – this is the best form of hearsay, especially if accompanied by a statement that the witness is too afraid to attend court;
- an anonymous statement in which the witness states the reasons for not attending;
- direct evidence from a professional witness, telling the court what an identified (or even anonymous) witness has told him or her and why that witness will not attend court.

Hearsay notices

4.48 These are the means used to put the other side on notice of the intention to adduce hearsay evidence and can be used as a tactic to give greater weight to hearsay evidence. If hearsay evidence is to be used, notice should be given to the other party. The requirements under the Civil Evidence Act 1995 are less onerous than those under the 1999 Rules, and seem difficult to reconcile.

4.49 Under the 1999 Rules,[4] a party wishing to rely on hearsay evidence must give the other party 21 days' written notice by serving a hearsay notice. This notice must also be filed with the court. The court may, however, reduce or increase the period of notice required either on application by a party[5] or its own motion.[6] Applicants should avoid delay, and should, therefore, make such an application when the papers are issued. The court clerks will need to have proper reasons if they are to shorten deadlines (e.g. the witnesses are suffering current nuisance and there is a real risk that some witnesses will become too afraid to give evidence if the matter is delayed in coming to court). It should, however, be noted that, by virtue of s 2(4) of the Civil Evidence Act 1995, failure to comply with notice requirements will not affect the actual admissibility of the hearsay evidence but will adversely affect the weight to be attached to it. In considering weight, the court will have regard to the various points at s 4(2) in particular. These

---

[1] *R v Manchester Crown Court ex parte McCann* [2001] EWCA Civ 281, [2001] 1 WLR 1084.
[2] See Appendix 1(B).
[3] SI 1999/681 (L3), set out at Appendix 1(C).
[4] Ibid, r 3(1).
[5] Ibid, r 3(2).
[6] Ibid, r 3(3).

include whether it would have been reasonable and practical to produce the maker of the hearsay evidence, whether the statement was made contemporaneously with the events described, and whether the person involved had any motive to conceal or misrepresent matters.

4.50 Under the 1999 Rules, a hearsay notice must:

'(a) state that it is a hearsay notice;
(b) identify the proceedings in which the hearsay evidence is to be given;
(c) state that the party proposes to adduce hearsay evidence;
(d) identify the hearsay evidence;
(e) identify the person who made the statement which is to be given in evidence; and
(f) state why that person will not be called to give oral evidence.'[1]

4.51 A single hearsay notice may, however, deal with the hearsay evidence of more than one witness. A sample hearsay notice also appears at Appendix 2(G).

Case-law

4.52 The first case to consider the question of admissibility of hearsay evidence in ASBO proceedings was *Clingham v Kensington and Chelsea Royal Borough Council*.[2] In this case, the defendant appealed by way of case stated against the decision of the district judge in the magistrates' court to admit evidence of complaints of anti-social behaviour when the witnesses to the acts complained of were not being called. This comprised police officers giving live evidence of what they had seen *and* also what others had told them the defendant had done. The district judge had initially ordered proper hearsay notices to be served but, at the hearing, decided that the evidence was not hearsay evidence at all and admitted it as of right without any notices being required. The defendants appealed the decision.

4.53 Schiemann LJ, giving the judgment of the Divisional Court,[3] referred first to the Civil Evidence Act 1995 and then to the 1999 Rules. He held that the evidence was hearsay and, therefore, both the Act and the Rules applied. The primary consequence of failing to serve the notice was that this had to be considered in assessing the weight to be attached to it. The judge, however, left open whether there would be other consequences. What is clear is that the court accepted that hearsay evidence was admissible and should not be excluded simply because it may have little or negligible weight. It was a matter for the court to determine whether the weight was sufficient to make an order, having regard to all the circumstances. This view was reinforced in the House of Lords' decision in the conjoined appeals of *Clingham* and *McCann*, which confirmed that hearsay evidence is admissible in ASBO applications. Lord Steyn, giving the judgment of the House, said:

'Having concluded that the proceedings in question are civil under domestic law and Article 6, it follows that the machinery of the Civil Evidence Act 1995 and the Magistrates' Courts (Hearsay Evidence in Civil Proceedings) Rules 1999, SI 1999/681, allow the introduction of such evidence under the first part of section 1 ... .'[4]

'... use of the Civil Evidence Act 1995 and the rules in cases under the first part of s 1 are not in any way incompatible with the HRA ... .'[5]

---

[1] Magistrates' Courts (Hearsay Evidence in Civil Proceedings) Rules 1999, r 3(4).
[2] *R (on the application McCann and others) v Crown Court at Manchester; Clingham v Kensington and Chelsea Royal Borough Council* [2002] UKHL 39, [2002] 3 WLR 1313, [2002] 4 All ER 593, HL.
[3] (2001) *The Times*, 20 February, DC.
[4] *R (on the application McCann and others) v Crown Court at Manchester; Clingham v Kensington and Chelsea Royal Borough Council* [2002] UKHL 39, [2002] 3 WLR 1313, per Lord Steyn at para [35].
[5] Ibid, at para [36].

'... hearsay evidence will often be of crucial importance. For my part, hearsay evidence depending on its logical probativeness is quite capable of satisfying the requirements of s 1(1).'[1]

4.54 The 'other consequences' which the Court of Appeal in *Clingham* referred to may well be a reference to an application by the defence to require hearsay witnesses to be called.[2] When acting for the defendant, it is essential that hearsay evidence is challenged immediately and the court is asked for permission to require the witness's attendance. If this is not possible or it is refused, submissions should be made to the court that the evidence should carry little or no weight, as there has been no opportunity to challenge the witness. Further, it can demonstrate that there was direct evidence available to the applicant which it has failed to adduce. The defence can also take issue with the applicant body's proffered reasons for the evidence being hearsay. Ultimately, however, it is for the court to decide whether the reasons are genuine and what weight to give to the evidence.

4.55 There are cases in the county courts where immediate possession orders have been made, relying on the direct evidence of previous convictions and the hearsay evidence of a housing officer alone.[3] How far the court will apply this to ASBO proceedings, where the consequences are potentially more draconian, is open to real dispute. The most likely result is that, unless there are previous convictions (which are incontrovertible and do not therefore require proof), hearsay evidence alone is unlikely to be sufficient in the vast majority of ASBO applications. This, however, cannot be an absolute rule and, with the right evidence, an application based solely on hearsay may well succeed.

4.56 The current Home Office Guidance expressly refers to hearsay evidence. It classifies such evidence as 'vital' to protect those in the community who are fearful of reprisals. It refers to the different forms of hearsay covered at **4.47** and offers the advice that hearsay evidence must be relevant, and include specific details of dates, places, times and actions. This advice is simple and obvious, but remains true and important when deciding what evidence to submit in an application.

---

[1] *R (on the application McCann and others) v Crown Court at Manchester; Clingham v Kensington and Chelsea Royal Borough Council* [2002] UKHL 39, [2002] 3 WLR 1313, per Lord Steyn at para [37].
[2] Magistrates' Courts (Hearsay Evidence in Civil Proceedings) Rules 1999, r 4 – on 7 days' notice.
[3] *Leeds City Council v Harte* (1999) *Current Law Cases* 4069.

CHAPTER 5

APPLICATIONS TO THE MAGISTRATES' COURT

Court forms

5.1 The Magistrates' Courts (Anti-social Behaviour Orders) Rules 2002 (the 2002 Rules) previously dictated that any application for an ASBO or interim order had to be in the form which is at Schedule 1 to the Rules; however, this was amended in June 2003 so that the application 'may' be in such form.[1] The Rules also previously provided mandatory forms for the summons, ASBO and interim ASBO order. This requirement was removed by amendment to the 2002 Rules at the same time. Whilst there is no requirement to follow set forms, many courts have approved formats for such forms, and it is suggested that it is appropriate to follow these unless there are good reasons not to do so. A sample draft ASBO application is set out in Appendix 2(A), a sample draft ASBO in Appendix 2(B), and a sample draft interim order application at Appendix 2(C).

5.2 When laying the complaint, the applicant body should ensure that the following documents are filed with the court and served on the defendant:

- summons;
- ASBO application;
- draft order;
- certificate of consultation;
- list of previous convictions;
- information to the defendant on how to obtain legal advice;
- hearsay notices;
- evidence in support;
- case summary; and
- a clear warning to the defendant that it is an offence to pervert the course of justice and that witness intimidation in civil proceedings is a criminal offence[2] and can lead to prosecution.

5.3 In order to keep delays to the minimum, in practice, it is advisable for the applicant body to give the defendant a letter in which not only is he or she told of the right to legal advice and representation but which also includes addresses and telephone numbers of the Citizens Advice Bureau, local Law Centre and advice where legal representation can be obtained (e.g. the Law Society). The letter should finish with a large typeface warning that the defendant must seek legal advice immediately and that failure to do so may result in the hearing proceeding without his or her having legal representation. This letter can be of real importance when opposing an application to adjourn by the defendant. Where the letter has been personally served (there is no reason why it cannot be served with the papers) and includes the above warning, it would be hard to argue for an adjournment if there has been delay by the defendant.

---

[1] The 2002 Rules, SI 2002/2784, r 4(1) and (5), as amended by SI 2003/1236. The 2002 Rules are set out at Appendix 1(D).

[2] Criminal Justice and Police Act 2001, ss 39–41 (note that the Home Office Guidance citation is wrong).

5.4 Whilst it is usual to serve the evidence which the applicant body relies upon with the summons, it is not always appropriate to serve all the available evidence at this time. On occasions, where it is feared that the defendant may intimidate a witness or there is a reasonable prospect that he or she will accept an order being made, statements from lay persons can be withheld. It may, however, be that if all the evidence is served the defendant will concede the making of the order and save the witnesses giving evidence in any event. If the defendant seeks to contest the application, that evidence can be served at that time. If not, the defendant need never know that there were other witnesses willing to come forward, thus protecting them from possible reprisals.

Service of court forms and evidence

5.5 Save in the case of service of interim ASBOs, the 2002 Rules provide that any summons, or copy of an order or application required to be sent under the Rules, can be served either:

- in person; or
- by post to the last known address.[1]

If sent by the latter method, it is deemed to have been received unless the defendant proves otherwise. In practice, however, it is unlikely that a court would reject a defendant's assertion that he or she had not received notice unless there was good reason to disbelieve the defendant. As a matter of pragmatism, it is suggested that service, certainly of the initial summons and documents, should always be effected by personal service, unless impracticable to do so. A certificate of service can then be lodged with the court. New evidence or documents can then be sent by post if personal service is not straightforward.

5.6 If possible, when serving the original summons, it would be wise to serve an indexed and paginated trial bundle on the defendant and on the court. It should be remembered that four copies may be needed for the court and a further one brought to the hearing for any witnesses. Whilst many magistrates' courts have now had experience in ASBO applications, it is unfortunately rare that lay magistrates at least, have read much, if anything, of the bundle before the trial. It is therefore important for the applicant to send a letter with the trial bundles, reminding the clerk that, as the magistrates are sitting in their civil capacity, they should be given the bundle to read prior to the hearing – preferably the day before. If they can read the papers in advance, valuable time will be saved at the hearing, as witnesses' evidence-in-chief will be significantly shorter, as can be the opening.

5.7 If the defendant is under 18 years of age, a person with parental responsibility or the defendant's guardian must also be served with at least the summons. If the child is being 'looked after' by the local authority or there is a care order in place, the local authority social services social worker may be served instead of the parent.

5.8 By virtue of r 7(2) of the 2002 Rules, the summons, order, applications, etc, shall also be sent by the justices' chief executive to the applicant body and to any relevant authority whom the applicant body was required by s 1E of CDA 1998 to consult with. Rather oddly, r 7(2) then goes on to state that, where appropriate, these authorities shall be invited to make observations and be advised of their right to be heard at the hearing. The 2002 Rules were drafted after the current Home Office Guidance and it is noticeable that there is no mention of this rule in it. It is most unusual that, having filed a certificate of consultation, which the Guidance says should not indicate whether they consent, the court should be able to ask these authorities to comment on the application. Still stranger is the notion that they have the right to be heard at the

---

[1] Rule 7(1).

application hearing. Where the power for this right to be heard arises is not clear, and it is hard to see why that right should exist. Finally, there is no assistance as to when the court may think it appropriate to invite observations or advise authorities of this right to be heard. The strong likelihood is that the court will do it in all cases, to ensure uniformity, until some guidance is given either by case-law or amended Guidance. What can be said for the moment is that if the magistrates' courts are to routinely ask relevant authorities for comments, it would be a brave applicant who applied without the support of all.

CHAPTER 6

ANTI-SOCIAL BEHAVIOUR ORDERS IN THE COUNTY COURT AND ON CRIMINAL CONVICTION

County court

6.1 Following the amendments brought about by the PRA 2002, an application for an order akin to an ASBO could be commenced in the county court.[1] Whilst not strictly an ASBO, the criteria and punishments are the same and therefore are referred to as ASBOs in this book. The circumstances in which such orders could be brought were, however, far too restrictive and of very limited practical use. Essentially, an application for an ASBO could only be brought by a relevant authority[2] and only in two instances:

(1) where the relevant authority was already a party to the principal proceedings to which the intended defendant was a party;
(2) where the relevant authority was not a party to the principal proceedings but considered that it would be reasonable to make an application against a party to them.

6.2 The use of the section was therefore limited to cases where a person was already being proceeded against (e.g. for possession) and it was thought appropriate to obtain an ASBO to regulate that person's behaviour beyond those possession proceedings. Applications could not be brought under this section against a child unless he or she had a tenancy and was the subject of the proceedings. This meant that, where possession proceedings were brought against a person as a result of, or in part due to, the behaviour of a partner or child who was not a tenant, there was no power for the court to join the partner or child or make an ASBO against them. This led to the expensive and potentially embarrassing position whereby ASBO proceedings against the partner or child were commenced in the magistrates' court and ran alongside the county court possession proceedings. This could have led to inconsistent findings of fact and was certainly an unwelcome complication.

ASB Act 2003

6.3 In response to the criticism raised as a result of the above problems, a number of changes were introduced by the ASB Act 2003.[3] Now, where the relevant authority is a party to the principal proceedings and considers:

(a) that a person who is not a party to the proceedings has acted in an anti-social manner; and
(b) that the person's anti-social acts are material in relation to the principal proceedings,

---

[1] CDA 1998, s 1B is added by PRA 2002, s 63.
[2] See Chapter 3 for definition.
[3] Section 85(1), (5), (6) of the ASB Act 2003, inserting s 1B(3A)–(3C) into the CDA 1998 and amending s 1B(5) of that Act.

it may apply to join that person to the principal proceedings and apply for an ASBO (or then apply to join another person to defend such an application). However, a person may not be joined unless the anti-social acts complained of are material to the principal proceedings. This prevents applications where only one incident is material to the possession proceedings and the remaining allegations have no bearing on them but the relevant authority wishes to obtain an order. The current Home Office Guidance suggests that the county court will be able to make an order only where the principal proceedings involve evidence of anti-social behaviour and, indeed, its use will predominantly, if not exclusively, be in association with possession proceedings. This amendment will have most effect when it is feared that, if a possession order is made, the defendant will simply move into privately rented accommodation, close by, without abating the alleged anti-social behaviour. By the use of this section, in appropriate circumstances, it would be possible to apply for an ASBO in general terms but, more particularly, perhaps, to prevent the defendant from returning to live within a particular area or estate and/or harassing named persons (e.g. witnesses in the possession proceedings).

6.4 In relation to adult defendants, the above amendments came into force on 31 March 2004.[1] However, the power to join defendants who are under 18 years of age is not expected to come into force until 1 October 2004. It will then be piloted in 11 county courts[2] for an 18-month period.

6.5 In considering an application, the court has to be satisfied that the conditions in s 1(1) are fulfilled.[3] Formal consultation must be established before making any application for an order in the county court.[4] Interim orders can be applied for,[5] and the order must be for a minimum of 2 years, cannot be discharged in that period without the consent of the applicant and carries on breach the same punishment as an ASBO.[6]

Practice and procedure

6.6 The procedure is governed by the newly implemented CPR Part 65 and the Practice Direction which accompanies it. The rules state that where the application for an ASBO is being made by the party who is the claimant in the main proceedings, the application *must* be made in the claim form.[7] Where the applicant is the defendant in the main proceedings the application notice must be filed with the defence.[8] This may well occur where a claim for disrepair is initiated and the council seeks possession of the property.

6.7 If an application for an ASBO is not raised in the claim form, and the applicant becomes aware of circumstances which lead it to apply for one, this application must be made as soon as possible by an application notice.[9] Any such application should normally be on notice.[10]

6.8 Any application for an ASBO in the county court must be accompanied by written evidence and *must* include evidence that consultation has been complied with.[11] It is also important that both applications to join and applications for ASBOs should be accompanied by

---

[1] SI 2004/690, art 2(b)(ii).
[2] Bristol, Central London, Clerkenwell, Dewsbury, Huddersfield, Leicester, Manchester, Oxford, Tameside, Wigan and Wrexham.
[3] CDA 1998, s 1B(4).
[4] Ibid, s 1E(1)(b).
[5] Ibid, s 1D(1)(b).
[6] Ibid, s 1B(7).
[7] CPR, r 65.22(1)(a).
[8] Ibid, r 65.22(1)(b).
[9] Ibid, r 65.22(2).
[10] Ibid, r 65.22(3).
[11] Ibid, r 65.25.

evidence showing the connection between the principal proceedings and the application to join/for an ASBO. ASBOs made in the county court should be made on Form N113.[1] This form is for final orders only, but the initial paragraph referring to the test in s 1(1) can be deleted, and wording that the court found it 'just to make an interim order pending the hearing of the main application' can be inserted. Further, the sentence which begins 'Unless both parties consent ...' , just over halfway through the order, should be deleted, as this applies only to full orders. It is hoped that a practice form will be available shortly, with these or similar amendments included.

Application to join a non-party

6.9 To use the powers granted under s 1B(3B) of the amended CDA 1998 to join a party to the principal proceedings to obtain an ASBO against them, application must[2] be made:

- at the same time as and in the same application notice in which the ASBO application is made out;
- in accordance with CPR, r 19.1;
- as soon as the applicant considers that the criteria in s 1B(3A) are made out.[3]

This means that the application has to be brought complying with CPR, rr 19.2 and 19.4, i.e. that permission of the court is required and that the order joining the person must be served on all relevant parties. The application notice must contain the applicant's reasons for claiming that the person's acts are material to the principal proceedings and details of the acts alleged.[4] This would be necessary in any event as CPR, r 19.2(2) requires the court to be satisfied that it is desirable to add the party to resolve all matters in dispute or that there is a connection issue which the court should resolve. Applications to join non-parties can be made without notice but should normally be made on notice.[5] Unless there was a very urgent need for an interim order without notice it is hard to foresee circumstances when notice would not be given.

6.10 Where the relevant authority is not a party to the principal proceedings, e.g. if an ALMO is bringing a possession action, but wishes to apply for an ASBO, it must apply in same way as above, but must apply to become a party in accordance with CPR Part 19. Again, applications should be made as soon as the authority becomes aware of the principal proceedings and should normally be made on notice and with evidence of why the authority needs to be joined to the action.

Interim orders

6.11 Applications for interim ASBOs in the county court must be made in accordance with CPR Part 25, which provides that any application must be made with supporting evidence in witness statements, and that if it is made without notice (applications should normally be made on notice[6]), then the statements should explain why notice has not been given.[7] The court may grant an interim order without notice if it appears to it that there are good reasons for not giving notice.[8]

---

[1] See Appendix 2(F).
[2] See CPR, r 65.23(1).
[3] See **6.3**.
[4] CPR, r 65.23(2).
[5] Ibid, r 65.23(3).
[6] Ibid, r 65.26(2)(b).
[7] Ibid, r 25.3(3).
[8] Ibid, r 25.3(1).

6.12 Where the application is made on notice then the notice and evidence in support must be served as soon as practicable after issue and in any event not less than 3 days before the hearing of the application.[1] The applicant is responsible for filing a draft order and bringing to the court a copy of the order on a computer disk.[2]

Service

6.13 Unlike ASBO orders granted in the magistrates' courts, orders granted by the county court, whether interim or full, must be served on the defendant personally.[3]

Orders on criminal conviction

6.14 Any criminal court, on conviction of a person of a relevant offence, can make an order to prohibit the defendant from doing anything specified in the order.[4] The order, whilst made by the criminal court, is a civil order with the same effect as an ASBO. The order may be made by the magistrates' court, youth court or Crown Court. Again, for convenience, these orders will generally be referred to as ASBOs.

6.15 ASBOs on conviction were introduced by the PRA 2002 but have proved to be a difficult vehicle by which to make an application. The ASB Act 2003 brought a complete change to the legislation with the introduction from 31 March 2004 of new subsections 1C(3), (3A) and (3B). Now the court may make an order only if the prosecutor asks it do so or if the court thinks it appropriate. This would seem to remove any role for the local authority, county council or other relevant authority in making applications or submissions unless they are the prosecuting authority, for instance for breach of a noise abatement notice. The Home Office has stated that local agreement and protocols with the court can allow relevant authorities to ask for an order themselves. However, this would seem to be contrary to the statute, which refers to a prosecutor. Although the hearing as to whether to make a post-conviction order is a civil one, a relevant authority cannot in any way be described as a prosecutor in those circumstances. It would seem strange if an agreement between the court and the applicant could override a statute if the defendant (not party to the agreement) objected and referred to the statutory wording as regards *locus standi*.

To make an order the court has to be satisfied that:

(1) the offender has acted in an anti-social manner (i.e. has acted in a manner which caused or was likely to cause harassment, alarm or distress to one or more persons not of the same household as the offender);[5] *and*
(2) an order was necessary to protect persons in any place in England and Wales from further anti-social acts by him.[6]

6.16 The first part of the test mirrors CDA 1998, s 1(1)(a), but the second part is far wider as there is no need to show that the order is necessary to protect 'relevant persons' rather than simply 'persons in England and Wales'.

---

[1] CPR PD 25, para 2.2.
[2] Ibid, para 2.4.
[3] CPR PD 65, para 13.1.
[4] CDA 1998, s 1C, as added by PRA 2002, s 64.
[5] Ibid, s 1C(2)(b).
[6] Ibid.

6.17 The court may only make an order if it sentences the offender in respect of the relevant offence or conditionally discharges him or her. A relevant offence is one which is *committed* after the coming into force of PRA 2002, s 64 (i.e. 2 December 2002).[1]

6.18 The decision as to whether an order is to be made follows the criminal trial (or plea) and is based on the evidence which was heard in the criminal proceedings but also any additional evidence which is presented by the prosecution and defence. CDA 1998, s 3A is inserted by the ASB Act 2003 to make this point clear, as it appeared that, notwithstanding the Home Office Guidance, many courts refused to consider any matters outside the offence before them. To further clarify this point, s 3B now provides that it is immaterial whether the evidence which the prosecution lead would have been admissible in the proceedings in which the defendant was convicted. Again this should have been an obvious matter not requiring statutory force, as the decision as to whether to impose an order is a civil hearing entirely distinct from the criminal proceedings.

6.19 It would seem sensible for relevant authorities to work closely with the police and CPS, as it may well be that valuable time could be saved if an application for an order could be made following the defendant's conviction in the criminal courts. It is submitted, however, that it will be very difficult to prove that an order is necessary unless the relevant authority is in a position to provide the court with evidence to establish the second criteria. Whilst the changes to the primary legislation now make it plain that the courts must consider the evidence put before them, there continue to be problems with applying for orders in this way. Pilot schemes and protocols now in place in many areas allow a relevant authority to work with the CPS to present the appropriate evidence. If, however, the defendant denies the evidence in those additional packs he must be permitted to test it and have a contested hearing. Therefore a full hearing is required, making it no different from that which would have occurred if a free-standing application had been made, although there is likely to be reluctance on the part of busy criminal courts to embark on lengthy consideration of contested evidence in relation to other incidents of anti-social behaviour which have not been the subject of the criminal proceedings.

6.20 The applicant authority may be disadvantaged in waiting and supporting this application in that it will not be able to give direct instructions to the prosecutor, who is unlikely to be an expert in the field of anti-social behaviour orders or civil proceedings. The Government has recently unveiled a scheme to have designated anti-social behaviour prosecutors. However, they cannot cover all courts and presumably will not cover Crown Court hearings. They are also not ASBO specialists which would require in our view more specialist knowledge. Whilst it is to be hoped that the new procedures will lead to smoother processes and to the making of post-conviction ASBOs, where appropriate, there seem to be more reasons why the prudent relevant authority would be better advised to pursue the application itself in the civil courts.

6.21 In any event, it may not be wise for a relevant authority to simply wait for a criminal conviction in order to request an order. This could prove to be a significant problem if the person was not convicted (or was convicted of a more minor offence), or the court refused to make an order, as the evidence of this incident (and/or others) was more than 6 months old. The suggested best practice is for a relevant authority to proceed to make its own free-standing application but to seize the opportunity of shortening the process if the defendant is convicted prior to the application being made in the normal way. The prospects of obtaining an order will be far greater if the criminal conviction related to significant anti-social behaviour which could satisfy the criteria at s 1(1)(a). However, another option is to await the outcome of the criminal proceedings and seek to make an application at that time. This has the advantage of reducing

---

[1] SI 2002/2750, art 2(a)(vii).

the costs but has the risks discussed above. Further, if no application has been made, the defendant could properly argue that there is no need for an order if there have been no incidents since the criminal offence took place. This argument would not be open to him if an application had already been made.[1]

6.22 Any order which is made will come into force on the day on which it is made. However, the court may state that the requirements of the order will be suspended until the defendant is released from custody.[2] This would seem to mean that the court may direct that the order, whilst having a duration of, say, 3 years, will only start to run on the defendant's release from custody.

6.23 An order made under CDA 1998, s 1D must be made for a minimum of 2 years and cannot be discharged within the 2-year period from which the order begins to run.[3] This means that the order cannot be discharged even with consent. However, a defendant can apply to vary the terms within that period. Breach of an order carries the same punishment on breach as the breach of an ASBO.

Case-law – R (C) v Sunderland Youth Court

6.24 There are two important cases to be considered in relation to post-conviction ASBOs, one in relation to practice and procedure, and the other more fundamental, with possible ramifications for all ASBOs. The first case is that of *R (on the application of C (by his mother and litigation friend, C)) v Sunderland Youth Court*,[4] where a defendant appeared before the youth court after being convicted of number of offences and having a very poor criminal record. Having given notice of his intention to do so, the CPS prosecutor expressly reminded the sentencing court of its power to impose an ASBO. The Bench declined to do so, imposing community penalties and a parenting order. The defendant subsequently was convicted of one, and pleaded guilty to another, charge. Both the offences pre-dated the previous sentencing date. After the above convictions, the CPS invited the court again to consider making a post-conviction order. There was a further report from the Sunderland Youth Offending Service, which indicated that the defendant was complying fully with his Intensive Supervision and Surveillance Programme (ISSP) (positive comments were made) and a recommendation for a reparation order was made.

6.25 The magistrates returned from their deliberations and stated that they were making an order, and the chairman indicated that his wing member had been able to give more detail about one of the offences than the prosecutor had (it is assumed that the wing member was, coincidentally, on the Bench that heard the trial). The exact nature of this detail was never specified. The order that was made was vague and contained no geographical restrictions, and was served on the defendant's parents, in a format that was consistent with a s 1 ASBO and not a post-conviction order.

6.26 Prior to giving judgment on the subsequent judicial review, Mr Justice Sullivan was asked for an adjournment, to prepare a preliminary point as to whether orders under CDA 1998, s 1C were civil or criminal in nature. He concluded that this was not a point that he needed to determine and declined to do so. It is surprising that the point caused the court or parties any real concern, as it would seem inevitable that this aspect is a civil hearing which follows the separate criminal sentencing. This is expressly stated in the Home Office Guidance, to which the judge was seemingly not referred.

---

[1] See *S v Poole Borough Council* [2002] EWHC 244 (Admin), (unreported), February 2002.
[2] CDA 1998, s 1D(5).
[3] Ibid, s 1D(8).
[4] [2003] EWHC 2385 (Admin), (2004) Crim LR 75.

6.27 Mr Justice Sullivan held that the court had failed to act fairly in its procedure, both in relation to its reasons and in relation to the terms of the order purportedly made:

> 'Whatever may be the extent of the general duty upon magistrates to give reasons for their decisions, in the particular circumstances of this case, fairness to the claimant required the court to give him an explanation, however brief, as to why it was now considered appropriate to make an order under section 1C. Consistency in the exercise of discretionary powers is an important aspect of fairness. If, having had the matter fully explained to them on 8 May, the magistrates decided not to make a section 1C order, then absent any further evidence justifying the making of such an order, it would not be prima facie reasonable to make one on 12 June. The only change of circumstances since 8 May was the two matters for which the claimant was being sentenced on 12 June.' (para [27])

6.28 Further, the absence of a formal application meant that a court had to have greater regard to fairness to the defendant in its procedure:

> '... if no application is made to the magistrates for an order, there is a danger that the defendant may suffer unfairness because he will not be in a position to know the case that he has to meet under section 1C. The nature of the case may be obvious from the surrounding context, e.g. where the defendant has just been convicted, and is about to be sentenced, for a string of anti-social offences. But that was not the case here, particularly having regard to the decision on 8 May. Elementary fairness requires a court, if it proposes to make an order of its own motion, to indicate the basis on which it provisionally considers an order may be appropriate, and the material on which it proposes to rely so that the person potentially liable can make meaningful submissions as to why the order should not be made at all or should not be made in the form provisionally proposed by the court. That did not happen in the present case.' (para [31])

6.29 The judge went on to criticise the seeming reliance on 'detail' provided by the wing member which was never explained and the lack of any record of the details of the order made by the court. He observed that it was an unfortunate lacuna in the statutory scheme that there was no requirement for service of an order made under s 1C. Further, the absence of any geographical restriction to the prohibitions without any reasons was also criticised. Lord Justice Brooke re-emphasised the need for a fair procedure, but both he and all counsel (including Treasury Counsel for the Home Office) in the case seemed to be surprisingly unaware of the standard form for post-conviction orders which appeared at Sch 4 to the 2002 Rules.[1]

Comment

6.30 The case of C is a good example of the potential problems which can arise in post-conviction orders unless care is taken. The use of evidence packs where such orders are envisaged will greatly assist. However, it is imperative that the prosecutor and court clerk are alive to the potential problems which can arise. It is important to ensure that the defendant is given the opportunity to respond to all the matters which the prosecutor wishes to rely upon and, if an order is made, the court record should be checked by both legal representatives before the hearing is concluded. The terms should also be read out to the defendant and the consequences of breach explained. Whilst not strictly necessary, it is suggested that it would be prudent for a court and prosecutor to serve on a defendant a formal note of the order before he leaves the court. There can be no good reason why a post-conviction order cannot be served on the defendant. The requirement to use the form which previously appeared at Sch 4 to the 2002

---

[1] Now repealed by Magistrates' Courts (Miscellaneous Amendments) Rules 2003, SI 2003/1236, rr 88, 89(2), with effect from 20 June 2003.

Rules has been removed; however. the form itself with suitable amendments is still a useful precedent.[1]

Case-law – R v P

6.31 The second case to be considered is that of *R v P*.[2] The facts bear careful consideration in order to place the judgment in context. On first blush, it would appear to present serious difficulty to most post-conviction order applications and even, potentially, to free-standing applications.

6.32 In *P*, the defendant was 15 when he committed 12 offences over a 6-day period. The offences were mostly theft and robbery of mobile phones from people in public places. The defendant acted alone and, whilst serious threats were made, no actual violence was used. The judge at the Crown Court imposed a 4-year custodial sentence and also a 2-year post-conviction order, suspended until his release. The defendant appealed to the Court of Appeal against both matters.

6.33 The Court of Appeal first of all reduced the sentence to one of 3 years, to take into account his guilty pleas and troubled youth. Turning to the imposition of the post-conviction order, Mr Justice Henriques, giving the unanimous decision of the court, held that the judge was empowered to make the order he did and to suspend it until his release from custody. He cited with approval the comments of Mr Justice Sullivan as to fairness of procedure in the case of *R (C) v Sunderland Youth Court*, as discussed above. He then went on to state:

> 'whether in the particular circumstances of this case, assuming proper procedure, the judge was satisfied in making such an order having regard in particular to the fact that aged 16 this appellant would remain in custody until he was 18. Thereafter, he would remain on licence for a further year if he was convicted of any imprisonable offence committed within 2 years of his release from custody or 18 months on the reduced sentence which we are minded to substitute.'

Mr Justice Henriques then pointed out that this defendant was not a hopeless case who would not succeed in amending his behaviour. He noted the contents of the pre-sentence report and a psychiatric report which recommended psychological intervention for chronic depression and detailed the defendant's difficult childhood, which included not seeing his mother since he was 5 and being brought up by a father with acute psychiatric problems. He accepted that imposing geographical restraints may well properly supplement licence conditions and that there was public confidence in ASBOs; however, each case depended on its particular facts. On the facts of this case, it was not possible to say that an order would be necessary in the future, as custody may well prove effective and the deterrence of a return to custody for breach of licence was sufficient.

6.34 In a later passage, which is probably *obiter dicta*, Mr Justice Henriques noted that it was likely that the conduct primarily envisaged as triggering applications for orders consisted of less grave offences than street robbery. However, he expressly drew back from saying that orders would be necessarily inappropriate in cases with characteristics such as these. However, the judge observed that, where custodial sentences in excess of a few months were passed and offenders were liable to be released on licence, the circumstances in which necessity could be shown were likely to be limited, although he did endorse the suggestion that there still would be cases were geographical restraints may properly supplement the licence conditions.

---

[1] See Appendix 2(EII).
[2] [2004] EWCA Crim 287, (2004) *The Times*, 19 February.

Discussion

6.35 The case of *R v P* has resulted in a number of hearings where it was argued, in freestanding applications for ASBOs, that, as the defendant had been sentenced to a term of custody of more than a few months, an order could not be necessary. This has mostly been unsuccessful and, in the majority of cases, it is submitted, correctly so. P committed 12 offences in 6 days, had no previous convictions for robbery (he had one for assault and five for theft) and had never served a period in custody. He had had a tragic childhood and chronic depression for which there was proposed treatment, with prospects of success. If the offences had not been so serious that it was impossible to do other than impose a custodial penalty, it is likely that he would have been given a supervision order, with a condition of attendance for treatment. This is to be contrasted with the vast majority of applications for ASBOs. Often, there will have been a long period of anti-social behaviour, with a variety of types of offending. Whilst there may be a more serious matter which has been prosecuted in the criminal courts, often, the majority of incidents are either borderline or sub-criminal. It is submitted that this is not the type of case which the Court of Appeal envisaged when the comments about custody and necessity were made. As the court observed, each case must depend on its own particular facts and a properly brought, freestanding application is not likely to depend solely on a number of serious offences over a 6-day period. Had there been proper evidence before the court in *P* of other anti-social behaviour, aside from the robberies, carried out over a longer period, it is submitted that the Court of Appeal may well have considered the geographical constraints suitable, notwithstanding other matters. If the judge's dicta were to have general application beyond post-conviction orders, this could easily result in some unjust outcomes. For instance, an application could be made, alleging 2 years of anti-social behaviour over a wide area but the trial delayed for 5 months due to unavailability of witnesses, length of trial or pending criminal trials. If the defendant, in the meantime, was charged with social security fraud, pleaded guilty and was sentenced to 6 months' custody, he could avoid an ASBO being made and, by the time he was released, all the previous incidents would be lost to the time bar if a further application was made because the behaviour had started again. This says nothing of the loss in public confidence for all those witnesses who would then have no protection from any order and the expense incurred in bringing the proceedings in the first place. It is suggested that subsequent courts have rightly taken the view that *R v P*, whilst spelling out certain principles, must be considered in the light of its own particular facts, i.e. a post-conviction order application following convictions for robberies without additional evidence of other anti-social behaviour. Therefore, it is only in cases where the evidence is wholly or almost entirely limited to serious criminal offences without any history of a pattern of anti-social behaviour that the court will consider that necessity will be hard to establish. This, of course, assumes also that the defendant has not previously had terms of imprisonment so that he can still argue that the first custodial sentence will, when linked with the threat of recall under licence conditions, have a deterrent effect. Where the defendant has been to prison and continued to offend, it is suggested that this would be a difficult argument for the defence to advance.

Guidelines for fairness in post-conviction order applications

6.36 It is also important to note that the court in *R v P* set out clear general principles of fairness and procedure which the court must follow, particularly when considering whether to make post-conviction orders. The Court of Appeal stated that these principles were:[1]

---

[1] [2004] EWCA Crim 287, (2004) *The Times*, 19 February, at [34].

(a) the test for making an order is one of necessity, to protect the public from further anti-social acts by the offender;
(b) the terms of the order must be precise and capable of being understood by the offender;
(c) the findings of fact giving rise to the making of the order must be recorded;
(d) the order must be explained to the offender; and
(e) the exact terms of the order must be pronounced in open court and the written order must accurately reflect the order as pronounced.

Mr Justice Henriques also made it clear that the Court of Appeal disapproved strongly of submissions or comments being made in the defendant's absence and that it was plainly the duty of the court making any order to identify the matters relied on by the party seeking the order, to give the defendant an opportunity to dispute the allegation, and to record the findings of fact in the order.[1]

6.37 It therefore follows that the defendant's representatives must be alive to any breaches of the above principles in the procedure adopted by the court. Any breach should be highlighted at the time to ensure that no adverse comment is made of the representative if an appeal is required. Similarly it is incumbent on the prosecution to ensure that all the above matters are adhered to by the court and to ensure that the presentation of evidence and drafting of any order complies with those principles. It should be remembered that there is no power in the magistrates' court which allows drafting slips to be corrected in civil hearings save by further formal applications to amend.

---

[1] [2004] EWCA Crim 287, (2004) *The Times*, 19 February, at [32].

CHAPTER 7

FIRST COURT APPEARANCES

Magistrates' courts

7.1 The application, having been made by complaint, is heard by the magistrates in their civil capacity, as determined by the MCA 1980. The defendant is obliged to attend and the court has the power to proceed in his or her absence,[1] or may compel attendance at an adjourned hearing by issuing a warrant for his or her arrest.[2] If either course is to be adopted, the court may not do so unless it is proved, on oath or otherwise, that the defendant has been served within a reasonable time before the hearing date or has appeared in the matter before.[3] Whilst the current Home Office Guidance[4] encourages the court to continue and hear matters in the defendant's absence and suggests that adjournments should be avoided unless absolutely necessary, in practice, it has not been common for courts to proceed to make an order on the first non-attendance of the defendant. The prospects of persuading the court to do so are enhanced if there has been personal service and a clear information letter to the defendant as to the likely consequence of his or her non-attendance. Similarly, the courts are reluctant to refuse a defendant an adjournment if he or she attends on the first occasion, requesting legal representation, even if he or she has failed to make real efforts to do so prior to the hearing.

7.2 As a consequence of the difficulties related above, especially with having lay witnesses attend court unnecessarily, it is now accepted that the best practice is to request the court to list the application as soon as possible after service for a preliminary hearing, to last for no more than 2 hours. At this hearing, no lay witnesses should be asked to attend but proof of service should be available to provide to the court, and at least one professional witness to relevant incidents should be present. This approach is made even more sensible in the light of the availability of interim ASBOs (see Chapter 8). It would seem appropriate, therefore, to issue an application for an interim order to be heard at the same time, unless the interim order is to be sought without notice to the defendant.

7.3 If the defendant does not attend the initial hearing, the court can be asked to hear the application in the defendant's absence. Live evidence can be called and the remainder submitted as hearsay evidence (notices should be served with summons). Subject to satisfying the relevant test (see **8.2** et seq), an interim order will be granted. However, with regard to the final order, the defendant may well be given a further chance to attend, or a warrant for his or her arrest is made and the matter can be adjourned to a fixed date. If the defendant does attend, it can then be ascertained whether he or she objects to the making of the interim and/or final order. It may well be that if the defendant has legal representation an order can be agreed at that stage. This saves the lay witnesses attending and saves the substantial costs of a trial. If the

---

[1] MCA 1980, s 55(1).
[2] Ibid, s 55(2).
[3] Ibid, s 55(3).
[4] See current Home Office Guidance, reproduced in Appendix 3, p 206.

defendant does oppose the making of the order, the application for the interim order can proceed and the case can be listed for trial of the main issue with appropriate directions.

Directions on adjournments

7.4 If there is to be an adjournment, it is important to ensure that the court makes full and clear directions. Whilst the CPR 1998 do not strictly apply to magistrates' courts, the court has the power to control the procedure of the hearings before it, and it is widely accepted, in practice, that the substance and spirit of the CPR 1998 should apply to ASBO applications. A number of local authorities and magistrates' courts have entered into discussions about the appropriate procedure to be followed in applications for ASBOs and have prepared agreed service level agreements. An example of such an agreement is to be found at Appendix 2(F).

7.5 The most important directions to be sought are:

- requirement for defence to serve a defence statement;
- time period for the service of further evidence by the applicant;
- time-limit for the service of evidence from the defendant;
- all statements of witnesses to stand as their evidence-in-chief; and
- reporting restrictions relating to any juveniles until the conclusion of the proceedings.

Written statements of witnesses should be regarded as their primary evidence for the application, which is in accordance with the CPR 1998 and also a matter of time management. The amount of information/evidence in many statements is large and it would significantly extend the length of a hearing if professional witnesses such as housing officers had to go through each document. In any event, the statements will have already been seen and read by the magistrates prior to the hearing. It must also be noted that it would be almost impossible for witnesses to recall hearsay evidence which was taken from a file or from complaints from residents. Given the clear Parliamentary intention to be able to rely on such evidence, it would seem impossible to argue that the criminal rules should apply. It would be strange if witnesses were forced to recall the whole of their evidence in one forum and not another, especially now that proceedings can be brought in the county court.

7.6 The requirement that defendants must serve witness evidence on which they rely is a matter on which there should be more debate. Whilst it is ultimately an issue for the court to determine, it would again seem odd if the county court should order disclosure of statements in proceedings for an ASBO before it but the magistrates do not. It is unlikely, however, that a court would prevent a defendant from giving evidence at a subsequent hearing if he or she has failed to comply with the direction. It may, however, take a different view if the defendant seeks to call evidence from a number of witnesses. Whilst the applicant is allowed to call evidence to rebut the evidence called by the defendant,[1] it may be that permission to call the evidence would be refused or an adjournment granted. Defendants' representatives should challenge any such finding strongly, as Art 6 of the ECHR may weigh heavily in such an argument. The availability of interim orders also means that there would be little prejudice, save that of costs and potentially witness unavailability (or reluctance) in an adjournment.

7.7 The issue of whether any reporting restrictions should apply after the making of an ASBO is very much open to argument and is considered fully at **9.11**. Until the final hearing it would seem to us to be impossible to argue against making an order preventing publicity of an application against a minor pursuant to s 39 of the Children and Young Persons Act 1933. It would seem to be contrary to principle and good sense if the child's details were able to be published in a newspaper, pending the hearing of an application where the council may fail to

---

[1] Magistrates' Courts Rules 1981, r 14(3).

obtain an order. If, however, an interim order is made pending the final hearing, the issue is open to debate. There is an argument that, for the interim order to be effective, the terms need to be disseminated to the community at large. This point was recently considered by the High Court[1] where Mr Justice Harrison held that it should *not* be the standard practice to make a s 39 order. Each case was to be considered on its own particular facts and that involved a balancing exercise between the public interest in disclosure and the welfare of the person against whom the application was made. The fact that the order was an interim one was a factor to be put into the balance. The fact that the allegations were unproven and the defendant had not had the opportunity to put his case were weighty matters, but the nature of the allegations did reinforce the public interest in disclosure. It is submitted that it is likely, however, that in most cases the balance of public interest as against the interests of the child weighs against publicity by way of media coverage or leaflet distribution at the interim stage. There is, of course, no reason why only the witnesses concerned cannot be personally told of the interim order (and its terms) which has been obtained partly for their benefit.

---

[1] *Keating v Knowsley Metropolitan Borough Council* (unreported), 22 July 2004, Lawtel AC90600602.

CHAPTER 8

INTERIM ORDERS

8.1 Introduced by the PRA 2002,[1] interim orders are available in all applications for ASBOs save for post conviction orders, Interim orders have become a much used and valuable tool for applicants since the first edition of this bulletin and, indeed, are applied for more often than not. Their use has also become more common where a number of local authorities have sought and obtained ASBOs against multiple defendants from one area. These applications have always involved obtaining interim ASBOs, some without notice.

8.2 Interim orders may be made where the court considers it to be 'just' to make an order pending the determination of the main ASBO application.[2] An application for an interim order may be made in the form given by Sch 5 to the 2002 Rules.[3] The court must be satisfied that the requirements of consultation and necessity have been satisfied before making such an order and, once made, breach of an interim order carries the same penalties as breach of a full order. The right to apply, vary, discharge and appeal also applies in exactly the same way as on the making of a full order.[4] There is no definition given in the statute or Home Office Guidance as to the meaning of 'just' or what the standard of proof is; however, as discussed below, this has been ruled on determinatively by the courts.

8.3 Any interim order which is made will cease to have effect on the determination of the main application, including where that application is withdrawn.[5]

Interim orders without notice

8.4 Interim orders may be sought without notice by leave of the justices' clerk,[6] but leave should only be granted if the clerk is satisfied that it is necessary to do so.[7] If the interim order is granted, both the order and a summons giving a date for the defendant to attend court, must be served on the defendant personally, as soon as possible.[8] Any interim order is only effective on service[9] and, if not served within 7 days, ceases to have any effect.[10] If the defendant applies to have the interim order discharged or varied, the court *must* hear his oral application.[11] As interim orders must be for a fixed period but may be renewed,[12] it is suggested that every order which is made without notice should have a return date as soon as possible for the defendant to either challenge or accept the interim order. There is merit in having the first hearing in the

---

[1] CDA 1998, s 1D was added by PRA 2002, s 65(1).
[2] Ibid, s 1D(2).
[3] 2002 Rules, r 4(5).
[4] CDA 1998, s 1D(5).
[5] Ibid, s 1D(4), and 2002 Rules, r 5(6).
[6] 2002 Rules, r 5(1).
[7] Ibid, r 5(2).
[8] Ibid, r 5(3).
[9] Ibid, r 5(4).
[10] Ibid, r 5(5).
[11] Ibid, r 5(8).
[12] CDA 1998, s 1D(4).

main application at the same time as the return date for the interim order, as this saves both time and costs.

8.5 The lawfulness of the interim order regime came under challenge when without notice ASBOs were made in Leeds Magistrates' Court in 2003. The local authority made applications for interim without notice ASBOs against 66 individuals who they claimed were responsible for anti-social behaviour in a particular area of Leeds. The main allegations related to drug dealing but also associated anti-social behaviour, including abusive behaviour, car crime, robbery, burglary and intimidation. The clerk to the justices gave permission for the application to be made without notice, and the district judge granted the orders without notice. The orders were confirmed at an on notice hearing of the interim orders, and the defendants issued an application for judicial review, asserting that r 5 of the 2002 Rules, which introduced the without notice procedure, was incompatible with Art 6 of the ECHR (as set out in Sch 1 to the HRA 1998). Further, they contended that the test applied by the court was too low and should have required proof to a heightened civil standard and that without notice orders should only be made in exceptional circumstances, which were not met here.

8.6 The defendants argued:

(a) that Art 6 was engaged at every stage of the ASBO proceedings, including at the without notice hearing, and that the without notice procedure was incompatible with this requirement of scrupulous fairness. This was on the basis that an interim order could be made for the same terms as a final order and carried the same punishment;

(b) that the procedure in r 5 meant that the defendant was denied the right to oppose the making of the interim order by representations, etc;

(c) that the procedural safeguards were not effective, as there was no prescribed requirement for a return date, that an application to vary or discharge required 14 days' notice and that, at the application to discharge or vary, the burden would be unfairly on the defendant to prove that the order was not just;

(d) that the test to be applied by the court should have been whether there was an extremely strong prima facie case, and that without notice ASBOs should only be granted in exceptional circumstances where there was compelling urgency; and

(e) that there should be a heightened civil standard of proof, to be applied when the court considered the application, as in *McCann*.[1]

8.7 Mr Justice Owen[2] concluded that whilst Art 6(1) was engaged, this was not the situation with which the House of Lords was concerned with in *McCann*, as this was an interim order without notice. Whilst this was a hearing which necessarily did not comply with the requirements under Art 6(1) as to a fair hearing, that did not make the procedure incompatible with the Convention. He stated that:

> '[28] ... There is nothing inherently unlawful in interim injunctions made without notice. The power to make such orders is a necessary weapon in the judicial armour, enabling the court to do justice in circumstances where it is necessary to act urgently to protect the interests of a party, or where it is necessary to act without notice to a prospective defendant in order to ensure that the order of the court is effective.'

He went on to say:

---

[1] *R (on the application McCann and others) v Crown Court at Manchester; Clingham v Kensington and Chelsea Royal Borough Council* [2002] UKHL 39, [2002] 3 WLR 1313, [2002] 4 All ER 593, HL.

[2] *R (on the application of Kenny) v Leeds Magistrates' Court; R (on the application of M) v Secretary of State for Constitutional Affairs and another* [2004] 1 All ER 1333.

'[25] Furthermore the 2002 Rules provide important safeguards for the protection of a defendant, namely that an order does not take effect until served on the defendant (rule 5(4)), if not served within 7 days of being made the order will cease to have effect (rule 5(5)), it is open to a defendant to apply for the discharge or variation of an order (section 1D(4)(b)), and on such an application the defendant has the right to make oral representations (rule 5(8)), and finally that a defendant has a right of appeal to the Crown Court (section 4(1) as amended).'

8.8 This is an important point, as the safeguards under the 2002 Rules are what go towards making the without notice procedure lawful, notwithstanding the failure to comply with Art 6. Mr Justice Owen, however, went further and concluded that an interim ASBO was not, in any event, a determination of the defendant's rights within the meaning of Art 6. Determination of civil rights involved three things: (a) a decision as to whether Convention rights are engaged, (b) a decision as to whether there has been an interference with Convention rights, and (c) a decision as to whether any interference with Convention rights is lawful (i.e. whether it is in accordance with law, necessary in a democratic society, in pursuit of a legitimate aim and proportionate). Whilst a without notice order engaged the defendant's rights, the remaining matters could not be resolved on a without notice hearing and, therefore, there was no determination of civil rights.

8.9 Further, Art 6 was concerned with procedural fairness in that procedure which leads ultimately to a determination. The interim order was, by its very nature, temporary, and regulated behaviour pending a full hearing. He cited, with approval, a passage from Clayton and Tomlinson *The Law of Human Rights* (2000), at p 623, para 11.157:

'... Determination or "decisiveness" in relation to civil rights and obligations refers to the decision on the merits of a case and its finality. Proceedings which are not determinative are not subject to Article 6 guarantees. It has been held that the following are not "determinative": applications for interim relief ... .'

In essence, his conclusion was that, whilst there may be a determination at an application to vary or discharge the without notice order, the procedural safeguards in the 2002 Rules had already had effect and satisfied the requirements of Art 6(1) at that stage.

8.10 Mr Justice Owen then turned to consider the test to be applied by the court and the standard of proof. He rejected any attempt to 'put a gloss' on the wording of the statute, holding that the test was whether it was just and that there could be no requirement to prove compelling urgency or exceptional circumstances. He concluded that:

'Consideration of whether it is just to make an order without notice is necessarily a balancing exercise. The court must balance the need to protect the public against the impact that the order sought will have upon the defendant. It will need to consider the seriousness of the behaviour in issue, the urgency with which it is necessary to take steps to control such behaviour, and whether it is necessary for orders to be made without notice in order for them to be effective. On the other side of the equation it will consider the degree to which the order will impede the defendant's rights as a free citizen to go where he pleases and to associate with whosoever he pleases.'

8.11 On the issue of what standard of proof was to be applied, Mr Justice Owen declined to apply the heightened civil standard of proof settled in *McCann* (i.e. the criminal standard) and further emphasised the balancing act for the court, which was an exercise of judgment or discretion, as was suggested in the first edition of this *Bulletin*. He said:

'But as I have already observed, the House of Lords was not considering the position with regard to an application for interim relief in *McCann*. Secondly the balancing exercise involved in consideration of whether it is just to make an interim order, is an exercise of judgment or evaluation. As Lord Steyn said in *McCann*:

> "The inquiry under section1(b), namely that such an order is necessary to protect persons from further anti-social acts by him, does not involve a standard proof; it is an exercise of judgment or evaluation. This approach should facilitate correct decision making and should ensure consistency and predictability in this corner of the law. In coming to this conclusion I bear in mind that the use of hearsay evidence will often be of crucial importance."

8.12 The judge went on to cite, with approval, the Home Office Guidance in relation to ASBOs and, as this and the above test was cited to the judge, the correct test had been applied. He went on to consider the individual facts of the two defendants' cases before him, approving one but quashing another, which related to incidents only outside the relevant area, one of which, by the on notice hearing, had been shown to be a case of mistaken identity. As an important final note, he provided assistance to magistrates' courts which heard applications to discharge or vary without notice (and, presumably, on notice) interim orders:

> '[61] I do not consider that the effect of the Rules is to shift the burden to the defendant to demonstrate why an interim order made without notice should be varied or discharged. The test to be applied on such an application will be that set out in s 1D(1),(2), namely whether *"... it is just to make an order under this section pending the determination of that application (the main application)"*. In applying that test the court will necessarily consider the material relied upon by the party seeking the interim order, and will obviously take account of any evidence adduced by and/or submissions made on behalf of the defendant. The burden remains on the party seeking the order to demonstrate that it is just for there to be an interim order until the hearing of the main application.'

8.13 The defendant, M, appealed against the decision of the Administrative Court on the issues of compatibility with the ECHR and the correct test. A strong Court of Appeal of three Lord Justices, including the Master of the Rolls, heard the appeal. The unanimous judgment of the court[1] was given by Kennedy LJ, who gave succinct conclusions at [39], namely that:

(1) whilst unusual for courts to make orders without notice, they could be made where necessary and with proper safeguards. There was nothing intrinsically objectionable about the power to grant an interim ASBO without notice;
(2) the more intrusive the order, the more the court will require proof that any order is necessary and that it is necessary in the form applied for;
(3) the safeguard that the without notice order was ineffective until served was an important one, as was the fact that there was an early on notice return date or final hearing. The former was preferable (here, it was 13 days, after which the court would have power to vary or discharge the order[2]), unless the final hearing was at a very early date. At that return date, it would be open to the court to reconsider the order, either to vary or to discharge it;
(4) the defendant could apply to have the without notice order varied or discharged, and the requirement that the justices' chief executive give not less than 14 days' notice of the hearing of the application was judged a sensible and realistic procedural requirement, which did not undermine the right of the person affected to seek rapid relief. It was not a breach of Art 6 that, under r 6, it is for the defendant to seek discharge rather than a requirement on the court to list for an on notice hearing;
(5) as a without notice order could only be made when the justices' clerk was satisfied that it was necessary for the application to be made without notice, and because the order could

---

[1] *R (on the application of M) v Secretary of State for Constitutional Affairs and Lord Chancellor and another* [2004] 2 All ER 531.
[2] Ibid, per Kennedy LJ at [29].

only be made for a limited period, and when the court considers that it is just to make it, and in circumstances where it can be reviewed or discharged, as indicated above, it was impossible to say that it determined civil rights. For a time, it restricted certain freedoms, and the restriction could be enforced by sanctions, but that is the nature of any interim order, and, therefore, Art 6 of the Convention would not be engaged (at either the without notice hearing or at any application to discharge or vary);

(6) although Art 6 is not engaged, the procedure must be fair, but there was no apparent unfairness in the procedure;

(7) even if Art 6 were engaged, it would be appropriate to look at the process as a whole, bearing in mind that the application for an ASBO is a civil procedure to which an application for an interim order is ancillary, and if that approach were adopted, no contravention of the requirements of Art 6 could be discerned;

(8) the test to be adopted by a magistrates' court when deciding whether or not to make an interim order must be the statutory test: whether it is just to make the order. That involved consideration of all relevant circumstances, including, in a case such as this, the fact that the application has been made without notice. Obviously, the court must consider whether the application for the final order has been properly made, but there is no justification for requiring the magistrates' court, when considering whether to make an interim order, to decide whether the evidence in support of the full order discloses an extremely strong prima facie case;

(9) the correct test having been used in the present case, there was ample evidence to support the conclusion of the judge that it was just for an interim order to be made. The fact that no vulnerable witnesses were identified by name was of no significance when the available evidence and information were considered as a whole.

8.14 One final matter which should be borne in mind when making submissions to the court about the appropriate test to be applied is that, whilst made in the context of considering the interests of young persons at interim order applications (see, further, Chapter 14), it is clear that whilst the interests of a child are a primary consideration for the court, the interests of the public are also a primary consideration when it considers the making of an order.[1]

Practice

8.15 The test to be applied when an applicant seeks an interim order is, therefore, not a high test and, indeed, the Guidance, which was approved by Mr Justice Owen, is at pains to say that the court, when considering an application, should be aware that the full extent of the evidence may not have been obtained. The court is directed instead to consider whether the application for a full order has been properly made and whether there is sufficient evidence of an urgent need to protect the community. The Guidance suggests that an order will be appropriate where the applicant feels that persons need to be protected from the threat of further anti-social behaviour before the main hearing. To this can be added that an application would seem appropriate where there are vulnerable witnesses and there is a real risk that they will be intimidated by the defendant (and/or subjected to anti-social behaviour) before the main application is heard. Following the Leeds cases, a without notice order can also be appropriate where there is a significant problem in an area for which interim orders were urgently required

---

[1] *R (on the application of A) v Leeds Magistrates' Court and Leeds City Council* [2004] EWHC 554 (Admin), (2004) *The Times*, 31 March.

to provide some regulation of the anti-social behaviour,[1] or where without notice orders are required to make them efficacious.

8.16 When commencing an application for an interim order, it will be important for the applicant to file detailed statements providing evidence of the urgent need for an order. Hearsay evidence is likely to be more prominent in such statements and will carry more weight at the interim order application stage than may be appropriate at the final hearing. Such statements should ordinarily be compiled by the housing officers and can include matters within their own knowledge and those obtained from other sources. If exclusion areas are sought it is helpful to provide a plan showing the location of the incidents alleged in relation to those areas, and it is important to produce a statement which explains the need and extent of the exclusion area. Careful consideration should also be given to the terms which are requested at the interim application stage, taking into account the fact that the allegations have not been proved. The stronger and more serious the evidence, the easier it will be to persuade a court to make more restrictive terms. Any defence submission that the terms are not in a child's best interests will have to be positively stated and supported by evidence[2] (see further **14.6**).

Summary

8.17 We would suggest that the following principles can be discerned from the statutes and case-law which now exists on interim orders.

(a) The test to be applied is only whether it is just to make an order.
(b) 'Just' requires consideration of all the relevant circumstances, including whether the order is applied for without notice, the behaviour complained of, the terms applied for and the age of the defendant.
(c) Article 6(1) is not engaged by the making of a without notice interim order or at an application to discharge or vary.
(d) The needs of a child may be a primary consideration for the court, but so are the needs of the community.

County court

8.18 The procedure for applications for ASBOs in the county court is dealt with in more detail in Chapter 6. Applications for interim orders may also be made in county court proceedings but should be made as soon as possible within those proceedings (i.e. within the claim form if the applicant is the claimant or in the application notice in all other cases). The application must be made in accordance with CPR Part 25 and normally on notice[3]. This would seem to accept that without notice orders can in appropriate circumstances be made. We would suggest that the Court of Appeal's approach in *M* can properly be applied to all such applications. Service of an interim order (and final orders) in the county court must be personally effected.[4]

---

[1] *R (on the application of Kenny) v Leeds Magistrates' Court; R (on the application of M) v Secretary of State for Constitutional Affairs and another* [2004] 1 All ER 1333.
[2] *R (on the Application of A) v Leeds Magistrates' Court v Leeds City Council* [2004] EWHC 554 (Admin), (2004) *The Times*, 31 March.
[3] CPR, r 65.26: see Appendix 1(E).
[4] CPR PD 65, para 13.1: see Appendix 1(E).

CHAPTER 9

HEARING OF THE MAIN APPLICATION

9.1 Prior to the hearing of the main application, it is the responsibility of the applicant body to ensure that all parties have an agreed paginated bundle[1] and that the court has sufficient copies of that bundle.[2]

Magistrates' court

9.2 Proceedings are governed by the court's powers under the Magistrates' Courts Act 1980 (MCA 1980) and the MCR 1981. Rule 14 of MCR 1981 provides that before calling any evidence the applicant may address the court. It is important when opening the case to the magistrates to give a clear picture of what the applicant body alleges has happened, exactly what findings of fact the court is being asked to make and the evidence on which the authority will be relying. This is also an opportunity to ensure that the court is aware of the correct legal tests to be applied and also the duration and terms of the order being sought. For obvious reasons, it is worthwhile seeing if agreement as to the law and issues can be reached between the applicant body and the defendant's representatives prior to the commencement of the hearing. In any case where there is likely to be substantial dispute, it would be prudent for the applicant to have a skeleton argument to ensure that there is a record of the test which the court is being asked to apply.

9.3 When the applicant body comes to call its witnesses, that evidence is given on oath.[3] If the written statement is to be the witness's evidence-in-chief, it is usual for the witness to confirm that he or she has read the statement and to verify the truth of its contents. Whilst it may be sufficient to leave the witness to be cross-examined, it is often far better to ask for permission to ask a few supplementary questions. This allows the expansion of a few of the key parts of the witness's evidence and also gives the opportunity to deal with any incidents which may have occurred since the statement was made. Importantly, it also allows a lay witness to become more comfortable with the process of giving evidence in court prior to what may well be hostile cross-examination.

9.4 Cross-examination of witnesses by the defendant's representatives is often a delicate process. Whilst the points which the defendant wishes to have made need to be put to each witness, the manner in which this is done may have a decisive effect on the impression which each witness gives. It should be borne in mind that most lay witnesses will not wish to give evidence and are often vulnerable individuals. Unless there is a good reason to do so, courts are generally not positively influenced by attacking the characters of witnesses. Of course, if the witness has a criminal record, especially for dishonesty, or has an ulterior motive for giving evidence, the whole application may fall on the defendant establishing the same. It is often the case that a witness will report an incident but, on cross-examination, it transpires that he or she

---

[1] See current Home Office Guidance, reproduced in Appendix 3, pp 206–207.
[2] Four copies if being heard by lay magistrates and two if being heard in the county court or by a district judge (crime).
[3] MCA 1980, s 98.

did not actually hear or see the defendant do anything and are giving hearsay evidence for which there has been no notice. As there are usually a number of incidents which the authority will be relying on, it is important to challenge each and every incident cited in the application notice. Failure to do so will mean that the evidence is unchallenged and should be found as a fact. It will also pose problems if the defendant later asserts something about an incident or witness which is not put to that witness.

9.5 When cross-examining the professional witnesses, one tactic is to seek to undermine the process by which the application came to be made against the defendant. If doubt can be thrown on the steps that the applicant body took before applying for the order, it may be possible to persuade a court that the order is not necessary. Another line of inquiry is to seek information from the witness about the action taken against similar other persons whom the defendant may identify as being involved in the incidents. If there is a disparity in the level of action, it may again provide support for a submission that an order is not necessary. Clearly, when representing a juvenile, there is more scope to ask questions relating to the measures taken by the local authority to provide assistance and services and to discharge the various duties imposed by statute.

9.6 After the evidence for the applicant has been heard, the defendant has the right to address the court, whether or not he or she later gives evidence.[1] It is unusual for this right to be taken up unless the evidence from the applicant body has been so poor as to justify a dismissal of the case at that stage or there has been a serious procedural or evidential irregularity (e.g. failure to prove consultation which may defeat the application). In any event, the defendant may choose to give evidence or not. It is unlikely, however, if he or she decides not to give evidence, that any issues of fact will be found in his or her favour. Whilst the test on the first criteria is a criminal one, the presence of 'one-sided' evidence coupled with supporting hearsay evidence is likely to be sufficient to pass that hurdle unless it was inherently unbelievable. The issue of whether the court should make an order at all, however, may be easily argued against in the absence of evidence from the defendant. In many cases, the sole argument before the court is whether an order is necessary, as the defendant concedes some or all of the allegations made in the application notice. This is often a more successful method of resisting the making of an ASBO than for a defendant to deny various incidents and to be found to be untruthful by the court. After such findings, it is often hard to submit to the court that the defendant is unlikely to repeat such behaviour and can be believed in such assurances given that he has denied he did it.

9.7 It is open to the applicant to call evidence in rebuttal of the defendant's case; however, this is rarely done. Thereafter, the defendant has the right to a closing speech, but the court may grant leave for both parties to have a second speech. If one side is allowed a second speech, so must the other. However, if the applicant has a second speech, it must be the last to be heard.[2] This leads to the situation where, unless the defendant's representative addresses the court after the applicant's evidence, there is no second speech for the defendant's representative to make and the applicant cannot have a closing speech. In practice, this is not adopted and a more sensible approach is taken to mirror the practice in the county courts where the applicant opens the case and has a closing speech as well. In the county court, the applicant has the opening and closing speech and, as the proceedings are in the civil jurisdiction, it would seem appropriate to follow the same procedure. The only difference perhaps is that in a civil trial, if the defendant calls no evidence then the claimant gives his speech first. It is not likely that this would be appropriate in ASBO hearings.

---

[1] MCR 1981, r 14(2).
[2] Ibid, r 14(5) and (6).

9.8 It is suggested that it is important when making submissions for both applicant and defendant to clearly divide their arguments into sections. The first would be to make those points which can be made as to the law, the second as to the evidence in support of the allegations of anti-social behaviour which are sought, the third as to the issue of necessity, bearing in mind those matters proved and adduced outside the 6-month period, the terms of any order if the court were minded to make one and, finally, the duration of the same. If followed, it is likely that the magistrates will also be able to produce reasons which mirror that progression of required findings.

County court

9.9 Neither CPR Part 65 nor the accompanying Practice Direction[1] provide any guidance on the procedure in the county court and, therefore, it must be assumed that the usual principles and procedures of a civil trial will apply. This means that the applicant will in almost every case make an opening speech (the court may dispense with the need for one but in almost every case will expect one) and the statements of the witnesses will stand as the evidence-in-chief. The defendant will make the first closing speech, with the applicant having the last speech. The defendant, however, has the right to the final speech if he or she calls no evidence of his or her own. Given that applications for ASBOs have to be made ancillary to other proceedings, the evidence in support of the ASBO will be heard before the submissions are made. The situation, however, could well arise where a defendant to an ASBO application is represented separately to the defendant to the main proceedings. The defendant to the ASBO proceedings will, of course, be permitted to cross-examine witnesses and make submissions after the defendant to the main application. The applicant should, however, generally make the final speech.

On criminal conviction

9.10 The procedure is unspecified. The current Home Office Guidance simply states that an interested relevant applicant body may request the making of an order or that the court may make one of its own volition. It is submitted that, unless the facts are incontrovertible, a separate 'sentencing' hearing will probably have to be arranged for evidence to be produced for the sentencing court to decide if the criteria in s 1C(2) of CDA 1998 are satisfied. This is because there is unlikely to be sufficient time allowed for what is, in effect, a fully contested hearing, often including evidence. It is unclear what the procedure at that hearing will be. However, it seems likely that the format will be very similar to that of a normal application, although with limited evidence called. A failure to allow the defendant to challenge evidence relied on by the applicant, including allowing him or her to give evidence and call witnesses, is likely to be a breach of Art 6(1) and incompatible with the Human Rights Act 1998. For this reason, it is unlikely that a criminal court will be willing to make an order, unless it can do so without having to hear substantial evidence. Applications for ASBOs on criminal conviction including the fair procedure to be adopted are discussed in greater detail in Chapter 6.

---

[1] See Appendix 1(E).

Publicity and reporting restrictions

9.11 Publicising the making of an ASBO and its terms serves two important functions. The first is to maximise the effectiveness of the order in that breaches are much more likely to be reported if the terms are known to the wider community and, secondly, it shows that effective action will be taken against those who commit anti-social behaviour. An order against an adult can be publicised without difficulty and should be disseminated to police stations and other relevant bodies.

9.12 ASBOs made against a juvenile pose considerations of balancing the interests of the child against the public interest. The prohibition against publicity in s 39 of the Children and Young Persons Act 1933 is a discretionary one. It is very important to note that there is no *automatic* restriction on reporting and, unless an order is made, every detail may be published. Whilst it is very hard to argue that a restriction should not be imposed until the main application is heard, if an order is granted, the converse is true. The current Home Office Guidance suggests that the court should have a good reason, aside from age alone, to impose the order. However, this is not quite in accordance with the case-law which has developed. The leading authority is the judgment of Elias J, who gave a single judgment in respect of two cases,[1] which he heard separately, argued on similar points but with very different facts. The judge explored the various cases[2] which had previously dealt with the competing public and child's interests in relation to publicity after criminal conviction and applied them to the unique situation that arose in ASBOs. The main points in his decision were as follows:

- there is a conflict which must be balanced between the public interest in disclosure and the welfare of the young person who may require anonymity;
- the court should consider whether there are good reasons for naming the defendant;
- considerable weight should be given to the age of the offender and the potential damage of being identified as a criminal before adulthood;
- the court must have regard to the welfare of the child or young person[3];
- the prospect of being named in court with accompanying disgrace is a powerful deterrent and the naming serves as a deterrent;
- the public has a particular interest in knowing who in their midst has been responsible for outrageous behaviour. This is not simply 'naming and shaming', which is, in any event, a relevant legitimate factor;
- disclosure of the identity of an individual may well make an order efficacious, as the community would be aware that an order has been made and report breaches;
- there is strong public interest in open justice;
- the fact that an appeal has been made may be a material consideration;
- whilst the court need not refer to every factor above, it should briefly summarise relevant factors and the competing interests before setting out its determination;
- there is no presumption against making an order but the strong public interest is a weighty factor against upholding any claim for anonymity; and
- in general, it is not appropriate or relevant to have regard to the effect on members of the defendant's family.

9.13 Of particular note is the concern that the judge had about the lack of a fully reasoned decision by the Crown Court in the *St Albans* case. On the facts of that case, he suggested that the extreme youth of the child (an 11-year-old) should have been expressly referred to and,

---

[1] *R (on the Application of T) v St Albans Crown Court; Chief Constable of Surrey v JHG and DHG* [2002] EWHC Admin 1129, (unreported), 20 May 2002.
[2] In particular, *R v Winchester Crown Court, ex parte B* [1999] 1 WLR 788, [2000] 1 Cr App R 11.
[3] Children and Young Persons Act 1933, s 44.

further, the apparent improvement in the period after the order had been made required special consideration. For applicant authorities, this case makes it clear that it will be important to ensure that the court has a copy of the decision of Elias J and that the need for full reasons is explained. For defendant's representatives, it would seem that it is unlikely that an order can be obtained unless there are good reasons which outweigh the strong arguments of public interest and efficacy of enforcement. The latter may possibly be addressed by arguing for an order which allows the naming of the child but not disclosure of his or her address, or arguing that disclosure of the terms of the order to the wider community can be permitted but reporting in the newspapers should not. In practice, however, it is now unusual to be successful in obtaining an order if an ASBO is made. The one exception is if an appeal is to be lodged, in which case it is highly unlikely that the order will be refused. In this case, the applicant should ensure that the wording of the prohibition is such that the order will expire at the appeal hearing or if the appeal is withdrawn. This prevents the defendant from simply appealing and withdrawing the appeal to secure an order preventing publicity.

9.14 The issue of publicity using leaflets and its compliance with the European Convention has very recently been considered by the court in *Stanley v London Borough of Brent*. The Court of Appeal heard the submissions on 8 and 9 July 2004, although judgment in the case is not expected until early September. When judgment is delivered, an update to this section will be available by email from Anesh Pema at Zenith Chambers to anyone interested.

Costs

Magistrates' court

9.15 Whether the proceedings have been in the magistrates' civil capacity or following a criminal conviction, there is power to award costs. Where the application is by way of complaint, the court may, in its discretion, make an order for costs to be paid by either party to the other, as it thinks just and reasonable.[1] A legally aided defendant to a civil action in the magistrates' court is still liable to pay costs as the proceedings are deemed criminal proceedings for the purposes of such considerations.[2] If the court does make a costs order, it must specify the sum in the order.[3] The costs must be fixed by the court as part of the adjudication and may include fees for the attendance of witnesses and also legal costs but limited to those properly incurred. Any costs awarded in this way are enforceable as a civil debt.[4] Civil debts are enforced through the magistrates' court; however, a person may not be committed to prison in default unless it is proved to the satisfaction of the court that the defendant, having the means to pay the sums, has defaulted, refused or neglected to pay.[5]

9.16 A successful defendant to an application can apply for his or her legal costs to be paid from central funds under r 14 of MCR 1981. In practice, the amount is determined by the court after the defendant's legal representative has filed details of his or her costs for assessment.

9.17 On criminal conviction, the power to award costs is not clear. However, there is power for the criminal court to award prosecution costs. This does not, of course, include the costs of bringing the application for a post-conviction ASBO, which are not strictly those of the prosecution. The costs of providing the court with the additional information to pursue a post-conviction ASBO could be minimal, but could also be little different from the costs of a full

---

[1] MCA 1980, s 64(1).
[2] Criminal Defence Service (General) (No 2) Regulations 2001, reg 3(2)(b).
[3] MCA 1980, s 64(2).
[4] Ibid, s 64(3).
[5] Ibid, s 96(1).

application if the defendant contests the making of the order and requires evidence to be called on the issue of necessity or other alleged anti-social behaviour. The CPS is not a relevant authority for applications and, therefore, costs cannot be recovered as prosecution costs. This is another reason why it is most unlikely that the intention of Parliament was for post-conviction ASBO applications to be used in any but the most straightforward cases.

County court

9.18 In the county court, the power to award costs is governed by CPR Parts 43–48. The general principle is that the losing party should pay the costs of the winning party. However, similar difficulties in recovering any actual costs arise where the defendant is legally aided. If the main application has been allocated to the fast track, the costs will be assessed summarily at the end of the hearing. These applications are allocated to the multi-track; the amount of costs will be assessed at a later date.

Crown Court

9.19 When hearing an appeal from the magistrates' court sitting in its civil capacity, the Crown Court has the power to make all orders which the magistrates' court could have made. This must, therefore, include costs orders. On criminal conviction in the Crown Court, the court has the same powers to award prosecution costs, as discussed above.

Enforcement of costs orders

9.20 In the county court, unpaid costs orders can be pursued by the court's enforcement provisions. These are contained in the CPR and include the following:

- *Warrant of execution (CPR Sch 2, CCR Ord 26)* – bailiffs seize and sell the goods of the defendant (known as 'the judgment debtor') to satisfy the costs order.[1]
- *Charging order (CPR Part 73)* – the costs order can be secured by registering a charge against any property or home of the judgment debtor. The cost order can be satisfied from the net sale proceeds when the house is sold.[2]
- *Third party debt orders (CPR Part 72)* – if the judgment debtor is owed money by a third party, the applicant (known as 'the judgment creditor') can obtain an order so that the third party pays their debt to the judgment debtor direct to the judgment creditor (or as much as is necessary to satisfy the order). It is most often used against a bank where the defendant has an account. The bank pays money from the defendant's bank account directly to the applicant body, to pay off the costs.[3]
- *Attachment of earnings order (CPR Sch 2, CCR Ord 27)* – if the judgment debtor is employed, the judgment creditor can obtain an order that the judgment debtor's employer should pay the judgment creditor directly from the judgment debtor's salary, until the cost order is satisfied.[4]

---

[1] Relevant forms: N42, N323 and N326.
[2] Relevant forms: N86, N87 and N379.
[3] Relevant forms: N85, N84 and N349.
[4] Relevant form: N337.

CHAPTER 10

TERMS AND DURATION OF AN ORDER

Terms of the order

10.1 If the conditions in s 1(1) of CDA 1998 are satisfied, the magistrates' court may make an order which prohibits the defendant from doing anything described in the order.[1] Whilst the applicant body will, as matter of good practice,[2] have filed with its application the prohibitions it seeks, the court may make some, all or entirely different prohibitions. In reality, however, it is very unusual for a court to make prohibitions which have not been applied for.

10.2 The terms of the order must be negative and prohibitory in nature. They may not be positive or mandatory.[3] Clearly, this covers attempts by negative wording to impose a truly mandatory term (e.g. you must not fail to attend school). The terms which are sought should be carefully and properly drafted. There are far too many applications which include terms which are simply incapable of enforcement. For instance, one application contained the proposed prohibition that the defendant must not 'sing loudly' and another that he should not appear in public where more than two people were present. The former is imprecise and the latter would prevent the defendant catching a bus.

10.3 Another common problem is the use of inappropriate language in orders. The order is directed to the defendant, and the defendant's understanding and nature must be considered when drafting the order. In *R v P*,[4] the Court of Appeal was rightly critical of a term directed at the 16-year-old P, which read:

> 'either by himself or by instructing, encouraging or inciting any other person to engage in any conduct that tends to prevent the public from passing freely along the highway or enjoying free access to any place to which the public has access.'

10.4 Simple, plain language should be employed. Two terms rather than one overly complicated one are preferable. If necessary, professional help can be sought to formulate the terms of an order to ensure that the defendant can understand them. In a case brought by Bradford Metropolitan Borough Council, a psychologist specialising in Asperger's syndrome assisted in drafting the agreed terms of the order for a defendant with that condition and provided an additional pictorial representation to supplement the defendant's understanding of the court order. This was, however, an extreme example and, in the vast majority of cases, plain, simple, ordinary language will be sufficient. The current Home Office Guidance provides a very

---

[1] CDA 1998, s 1(4).
[2] Mandatory for county court applications.
[3] *R (on the application of M, a child) v Sheffield Magistrates' Court* [2004] EWHC 1830 (Admin), per Mr Justice Newman at [57]. The case is unreported at date of publication but available at www.bailii.org/ew/cases/EWHC/Admin/2004/1830.html.
[4] [2004] EWCA Crim 287, (2004) *The Times*, 19 February.

useful checklist of principles and practical points to be considered when drafting terms of an order. It states that the order should:[1]

- cover the range of anti-social acts committed by the defendant;
- be necessary to protect person(s) within a defined area from the anti-social acts of the defendant;
- be reasonable and proportionate;
- be realistic and practical;
- be clear, concise and easy to understand;
- be specific when referring to matters of time, if, for example, prohibiting the offender from being outside or in particular areas at certain times;
- be specific when referring to exclusion from an area, include street names and clear boundaries such as the side of the street included in the order (a map with identifiable street names should also be provided);
- be in terms which make it easy to determine and prosecute a breach;
- contain a prohibition on inciting/encouraging others to engage in anti-social behaviour; and
- protect all person who are in the area covered by the order from the behaviour (as well as specific individuals).

Furthermore, the Guidance confirms that the order may:

- cover acts that are anti-social in themselves and those that are precursors to a criminal act, e.g. a prohibition on entering a shopping centre rather than on shoplifting;
- include a general condition, prohibiting behaviour which is likely to cause harassment, alarm or distress;
- include a prohibition from approaching or harassing any witnesses named in the court proceedings.

10.5 The above list reflects what, in practice, applicants have applied for and what the courts have granted in the years following the commencement of the CDA 1998. Of note in the current Home Office Guidance are the specific references and approval of terms which seek to prevent the defendant from doing something which is already a criminal offence. It was a common argument in the magistrates' court that any term preventing the defendant from committing an act which was already a criminal offence should not be made. Whilst it would not be good practice to have numerous terms which simply relate to matters which are already criminal offences, there can be no bar. In fact, the use of ASBOs to require the defendant not to drive other than with a valid driving licence and insurance is commonly being used to target persistent joyriders. The point has been answered to a large extent by the Court of Appeal in *R v P*, where Mr Justice Henriques, giving the judgment of the court, said:

> 'Next, it is submitted that the prohibitions imposed by paragraphs 2 and 7 are redundant as they prohibit conduct which is already subject to a general prohibition by the Public Order Act 1986 and the Prevention of Crime Act 1953 respectively. In that regard we are by no means persuaded that the inclusion of such matters is to be actively discouraged. So far as more minor offences are concerned, we take the view that there is no harm in reminding offenders that certain matters do constitute criminal conduct, although we would only encourage the inclusion of comparatively minor criminal offences in the terms of such orders.' (at [30])

Similarly, a common point of contention was the application for a general term which prevented the defendant from doing what s 1(1)(a) of CDA 1998 required the authority to

---

[1] See current Home Office Guidance, reproduced in Appendix 3, p 204.

prove. The current Home Office Guidance makes it plain that there is no difficulty in the magistrates making such a prohibition and, indeed, it would seem strange if that could not be a valid term, given the statutory definition.

10.6 It is suggested that, when seeking to draft orders, the general prohibition from anti-social behaviour and the prohibition from approaching or harassing named lay witnesses who provided statements for the application is included as a matter of course. Thereafter, the prohibitions sought should reflect the incidents which have been alleged and proved. This could mean simple prohibitions against abusive or threatening language, but may also prevent the defendant from entering an area where the incidents have occurred. A common prohibition is to prevent a defendant from returning to an estate from which he has been evicted or a young person to a school from which he has been permanently excluded.

Practical considerations for applicants

10.7 Deciding suitable terms of the order is a crucial element of court preparation for applicant authorities. It is good practice to consult with witnesses and victims about the proposed terms, as it is for their benefit that the order is being sought.

10.8 Applicants should give thought to the geographical terms of the order, particularly since it is now possible for an ASBO to cover all of England and Wales.[1] Clearly, the wider the geographical area sought in the application for an ASBO, the more compelling the evidence will need to be to secure the term. Where there is reason to believe that the defendant may move, or has already moved, a wider geographical area will be more easily justified. Evidence of an itinerant lifestyle, a possible move by the defendant, or evidence showing a wide geographical spread of anti-social behaviour can be used to support such an order. The Guidance states that the applicant does not have to prove that the behaviour will occur elsewhere, but merely that it is likely to. The Guidance states that the more serious the behaviour, the more likely it will be that the court will grant a geographically wide order.[2] It is submitted that this must be correct as, having shown that an order is necessary to protect relevant persons from further anti-social acts, the likelihood of further acts has been established. It would seem a misguided argument to assert that a narrow geographical area should be imposed where an exclusion order is made, as, inevitably, there will be a displacement of the defendant into uncertain areas. The wider geographical area will be necessary to protect the relevant persons from any future anti-social behaviour. This argument is to be contrasted with that of the need for an exclusion zone which should be limited to the areas where the incidents have occurred *and* the immediate areas surrounding it, where ready displacement and continuation of the problems giving rise to the application may occur.

10.9 Specific terms, tailor-made for the situation in hand, are recommended wherever possible. Examples of specific terms are discussed at **10.12** and **10.13**.

Exclusion zones

10.10 Exclusion zones are now popular and in regular use. Commonly, they exclude a defendant from a defined zone, giving relief to specific communities. They are easy to prosecute, as it is not necessary to prove that the defendant was acting in an anti-social manner. Such schemes were pioneered in Liverpool, where minors were banned from named streets. In Kirklees, a defendant has been banned from a named street despite the fact that family

---

[1] CDA 1998, s 1B(6), as amended by the PRA 2002, with effect from 2 December 2002. See the current Home Office Guidance, reproduced in Appendix 3, p 193.
[2] See Appendix 3, p 194.

members resided there. The use of exclusion zones is often an important part of the process to curb anti-social behaviour. By denying the defendant access to the places where he or she has displayed anti-social behaviour in the past, the relevant persons in that area are being afforded a measure of direct protection. Exclusion zones will not always be appropriate but, where the acts are localised, then, even if the defendant lives in that area, the courts are willing to consider and make orders. In the multiple 'Little London' ASBOs, made in Leeds Magistrates' Court, an exclusion zone was made against all the defendants and often provided the defendants with a single route in and out of the area from their homes. The Divisional Court and the Court of Appeal did not comment adversely on these exclusions and the final orders that were made almost always included that exclusion zone.

10.11 If an exclusion zone is to be sought, then certain practical matters should be attended to by the applicant authority. First, the court should be provided with a clear, coloured map of the area from which the applicant seeks to exclude the defendant. If possible, the authority should indicate the size of the area and mark where the incidents of anti-social behaviour are alleged to have occurred. The map should also indicate the defendant's home (if within the area) and other key locations, e.g. witnesses' homes (assuming that the addresses were known to the defendant). The maps to be used with the order should, however, not be marked, save with the exclusion area being clearly marked by a coloured outline. The map should be marked with the defendant's name and its purpose, i.e. 'map to show exclusion area for 'X''. The term prohibiting entry to the exclusion zone should provide the defendant (where appropriate) with exceptions when attending pre-arranged medical appointments, schools, solicitors and when accompanied by probation or YOT workers.

Other specific terms

10.12 Other specific terms can include non-association with groups over a certain number (but see **10.2**), or with named individuals who also display anti-social behaviour when with the defendant. The use of non-association terms has rapidly increased in recent years and, indeed, where actions against youths are concerned, it is now commonplace to have such a term included in the application. The obvious purpose is to keep defendants away from others with whom they are liable to commit anti-social behaviour. The equally clear balance to be applied is that it prevents a person from having free choice over his or her associates or friends. One way to limit the restriction posed by this term is to limit the non-association requirement to public places, ie the defendant may associate with whom they like, provided it is not in public (or a place to which the public have access). This allows a measure of conformity with the ECHR in that there is no general right of freedom to associate with others protected by the Convention – only where the association is for political or demonstration ends – see *Anderson v UK*.[1] If a non-association clause is sought, then it is important to ensure that only those persons against whom there is evidence of anti-social behaviour when together with the defendant are included in the list of names. Often, this is not adhered to and there is little, if any, evidence to link the defendant to any of the persons named.

10.13 Curfews and prohibitions on drinking in public places can all be used as terms. Further examples of ASBO terms can be found on the Crime Reduction website, the details of which can be found in Appendix 3.[2]

---

[1] [1998] EHRLR 218.
[2] See current Home Office Guidance, reproduced in Appendix 3, p 194.

Practical considerations for defendants

Grounds for challenging the order

10.14 The defendant will wish to ensure that the least possible interference is caused by the terms of the ASBO. General terms not to cause harassment, alarm or distress are the least intrusive. A defendant can safeguard his or her interest by checking that the current Home Office Guidance has been adhered to, namely:

- Are the terms (sufficiently) specific?
- Are they discriminatory to the defendant in any way?
- Are they justifiable interferences with the defendant's human rights?
- Are the terms necessary, reasonable or proportionate in the light of the evidence against the defendant?
- Is the geographical area commensurate with the seriousness of the alleged anti-social behaviour and/or locations?
- Is the exclusion zone necessary? Does the defendant need access to the area for work or pass through it on a bus route?
- If an exclusion zone is necessary can the defendant reach essential services such as doctors or dentists; does he or she need to visit relatives in the area?
- Does the list of names in the non-association clause accord with the evidence of anti-social behaviour?
- Are the terms drafted in a clear and simple language that the defendant can understand?

Remember that any terms not couched as prohibitions are not permissible.

Negotiating and bargaining

10.15 The defendant may wish to negotiate with the applicant body about the terms sought. For example, the defendant can agree not to challenge part of the evidence, so long as the applicant body negotiates as to the terms sought at court. Similarly, the defendant may be willing to accept the making of an order provided certain incidents are removed and/or certain terms can be altered to make the order less restrictive.

Appeals

10.16 This issue is discussed in Chapter 12.

Variation and discharge

10.17 This issue is discussed in Chapter 11.

Duration of the order

10.18 An ASBO must be made for a minimum period of 2 years, but may be for any period of time, including an indefinite one. Ultimately, the length of the order is a matter for the court, but the Guidance suggests that the applicant body should propose a period as part of its application. We would not suggest that any proposal is made in writing prior to the hearing as this would make it difficult to reach any form of compromise with the defendant. It is often the case that if the defendant will agree to an order and prevent the witnesses (often lay) from having to give evidence, the authority can afford to be less demanding on the terms it would seek from the court and/or the duration of the order. This is both sensible and effective, and whilst the decision is for the court alone, it is usually guided by what the applicant body is willing to accept. The court will usually realise that the applicant will have a better knowledge of the strength of its evidence and witnesses' fears and not lightly interfere.

10.19 If the proceedings are to be contested, then it is appropriate for the applicant body to state in its opening remarks for what period of time it believes the order should be made. The assessment of the duration of the award will take into account all the circumstances of the case; however, the following are probably most relevant:[1]

- the severity of the anti-social behaviour proved;
- the history of the anti-social behaviour (i.e. for how long it has continued);
- the age of the defendant;
- the number of warnings and other remedies which have been attempted;
- whether there have been breaches of interim orders; and
- the effect of the behaviour on others in the community.

---

[1] See current Home Office Guidance, reproduced in Appendix 3, p 194.

CHAPTER 11

POST-ORDER PROCEDURE

Service of the order on the defendant

11.1 The 2-year duration period of an ASBO, during which no order can be discharged, except with the consent of both parties, runs from the date of service.[1] Ideally, the defendant should therefore wait in court until the order is signed by the chair of the justices or their clerk. The West Yorkshire court service level agreement advocates such an approach.[2] It is important that the magistrates are asked to sign both the order and any map which is attached. Further, when served, the court file should be endorsed to prevent future possible arguments about service in the event of a breach of the order. A number of courts have adopted the policy of requiring defendants to sign a note on the court file that they have been provided with a copy of the order. This would seem a very sensible procedure if it can be achieved. If the defendant does not wait in court after the order has been made, the court should be asked to serve the order personally,[3] as soon as possible. This will remove any doubts as to whether service has been effected. A defendant who refuses to wait to be served with the order will, however, be unlikely to be able to rely upon lack of service if he commits a breach. This mirrors the approach of the county court in relation to committal proceedings for breach of an injunction or undertaking. If a defendant is persistent in avoiding personal service of an order, it may be sufficient if the order is brought to his attention by other means, e.g. personally delivering it to a known address. If the order was read out to the defendant whilst he was in court then, provided this was noted on the court file, the fact that he did not stay to receive the order personally will not prevent a breach.

11.2 It is important that the terms of the orders which are pronounced in open court, recorded in the court register and served on the defendant are the same. It is likely, however, that the order pronounced in court will be the one accepted as correct. In *Walking v Director of Public Prosecutions*,[4] Mr Justice Stanley Burnton held that, whilst s 1(9) referred to service of the order and that this might make it appear that a written document was involved, injunctions and undertakings were often referred to in similar terms, and injunctions made in open court were effective to bind the parties. The general rule was that the order of the court was as pronounced in open court, and this applied to ASBOs. It should also be noted that there is no power in the magistrates' court to correct a error on the court documents, as the county court slip rule does not apply[5] to the magistrates' court and its power to amend errors applies only to criminal matters.[6] Therefore, extra care must be taken to ensure that the wording is correct on the order

---

[1] CDA 1998, ss 1(9), 1B(6) and 1C(8), as amended. See current Home Office Guidance, reproduced in Appendix 3, p 210.
[2] See Appendix 2(F).
[3] See current Home Office Guidance, reproduced at Appendix 3, p 210.
[4] [2003] All ER (D) 57 (Dec).
[5] See *R v Brighton Magistrates' Court* [1986] 1 FLR 426, [1986] Fam Law 134.
[6] MCA 1980, s 142.

(as read by the court), as any amendment, however obvious or simple, will require an application to vary the order.

11.3 In the interests of certainty, it is good practice for the defendant to be reminded of the terms of the ASBO in a letter from his or her own advisers or the applicant body. If the defendant is a minor, a copy of the ASBO should also be given to his or her parent, guardian or an appropriate adult. All parties should check carefully the ASBO at court to ensure that it accurately reflects the terms and duration of the order, as well as the proven incidents of harassment, alarm or distress recorded by the court. Maps should be attached securely to the order and edged or hatched, as described in the order. Interim orders made in the magistrates' court (other than without notice orders) can be served by post to the last known address[1] and, therefore, it cannot be invalid to serve a full ASBO by the same method. We would suggest that, whilst this can be done, every effort should be made to try to serve the order on the defendant personally, as well. It should be noted, however, that orders made in the county court, whether interim or final, *must* be served on the defendant personally.[2]

11.4 A certificate of service should be kept with the original order and all copies. A copy should be sent to the court which made the ASBO, for retention on the court file, as well as to the defendant's solicitor, if represented. An accompanying letter can highlight the terms of the order, and reinforce the fact that an ASBO will not be suspended pending an appeal.

11.5 Where the defendant is a minor, special considerations apply to ensure that he or she understands the terms of an order. See Chapter 14, where this is dealt with more fully.

Service of an ASBO on the police and witnesses

Applicants' considerations

11.6 Standard post-order procedure should involve serving a copy of the order on the police and relevant agencies and interested parties (eg schools or YOT). In *all* cases, *when*, and *only when*, the defendant has been served with the order (or it is clear that the terms are known to him or her) should the defendant be arrested for a breach of the order. Whilst postal service is effective for an order made in the magistrates' court (see **11.3**), we would strongly advise that the order is served on the defendant personally and a certificate of service prepared, and preferably that the defendant asked to sign a document to acknowledge receipt.

11.7 The lead agency, if not the police, should give a copy of the ASBO to the police immediately, as well as to the anti-social behaviour co-ordinator of the local CDRP[3] and any other partnership agency.[4] The police should then notify the appropriate police command area on the same working day.

11.8 Effective dissemination of ASBO information may differ according to local practice and the organisation of local police divisions. One proven method is to serve a copy on every main police division in the local authority district area by handing it in at the front desk, addressed to a named police officer who is responsible for dissemination throughout that police station or area. A copy of the ASBO should also be given to the police community safety team and local community safety police officers, as the police's local eyes and ears on the ground.

11.9 The recording of ASBOs on the Police National Computer (PNC) will assist the police in enforcing orders, which is essential to the overall effectiveness of the ASBO regime.

---

[1] Magistrates' Courts (Anti-social Behaviour Order) Rules 2002, r 7(1).
[2] CPR PD 65, para 13.1.
[3] See current Home Office Guidance, reproduced in Appendix 3, p 210.
[4] Ibid, pp 210–211.

Arrangements for this are currently being made as a matter of priority.[1] West Yorkshire police have had this capacity since 1 December 2002. By agreement in West Yorkshire, councils will provide designated police departments with details of each ASBO for the PNC record. This record will have a unique reference number. In many cases, however, the full details cannot be recorded on the PNC and therefore contact details for a holder of the full terms will be given.

Defence considerations

11.10 The defence may have a more limited role in checking that information held by the police or local authority on computer is accurate. A personal data access request under the DPA 1998 may provide this information (subject to possible exemptions from disclosure on the grounds of prevention or detection of crime), or the defence may seek an assurance from the police or other agency that any ASBO details held are accurate.

Effective monitoring

Applicants' considerations

11.11 '[O]btaining ... the order is not the end of the process. The order must be monitored and enforced.'[2] The challenge facing applicants is to promote public awareness of specific ASBOs and maintain awareness in the local population when the glare of publicity has faded. This is an essential element of breach monitoring as the local community plays a vital role in informally policing ASBOs. The Home Office recommends the promotion of awareness strategies, including an effective media strategy.[3]

11.12 Suggestions for achieving public awareness of ASBOs include leaflet drops of ASBOs obtained in the local community (used to great effect in Manchester), features on the partner agencies' websites and use of tenants' and residents' newsletters. It is also suggested that local housing officers, neighbourhood wardens and community constables are informed of all ASBOs in their area. However, any publicity will have to comply with the guidelines expected to be given in the pending case of *Stanley v London Borough of Brent* (see **9.14**).

11.13 For the local ASBO group, current orders should be a standing item for review. How this should be done is a matter for local agreement. An ASBO should last only as long as is necessary to protect the public. If the need for the order no longer exists, it should be discharged.

11.14 Effective awareness is also a necessary part of policing ASBOs by agencies' officers. Until the recording of ASBOs on the PNC is rolled out nationwide, other methods will have to be used. Some police forces use local intelligence systems, which a number have indicated they will retain in addition to the PNC system. For the first time, in 2002, tackling anti-social behaviour appeared as a key performance indicator in the National Policing Plan. This is likely to result in an increased awareness and allocation of resources to deal with the problems. Other police initiatives include retaining copies of all ASBOs in the custody suite for routine checking by the custody sergeant on processing defendants, and identifying subjects of ASBOs as a routine item on all shift briefings.

11.15 Providing staff with comprehensive training is essential to the successful use of ASBOs. Defence solicitors should not underestimate the need for specialist training. The Social Landlords' Crime and Nuisance Group is available to give training and guidance in this field.

---

[1] Current Home Office Guidance, reproduced in Appendix 3, p 211.
[2] Ibid.
[3] Ibid, p 215.

The Home Office's new Anti Social Behaviour Unit may also be willing to assist with seminars or workshops on good practice. Details of the Home Office telephone advice line and website for further information about tackling anti-social behaviour and ASBOs generally are contained in Appendix 4.

Defendants' considerations

11.16 ASBO publicity can stigmatise a defendant, especially a minor. Defendants may wish to restrict the method of publicity and awareness by asking the court to impose reporting restrictions. Publicity and reporting restrictions are dealt with in Chapter 9.

11.17 General concerns can be raised directly with applicants by defendants or other interested parties, such as human rights organisations. Applicant authorities, when acting as public bodies, must take reasonable account of objections, otherwise they could face human rights challenges or judicial review. ASBO protocols, together with media or publicity strategies, are usually public documents made available on request or on relevant websites. (See Chapter 2 for more details of protocols and policies.)

11.18 Applicants and their partner agencies should check regularly whether the defendant is complying with the terms of the ASBO. This not only protects the public, but can be used to actively consider what help can be given to the defendant. This could include the provision of youth groups, drop-in centres, mentoring schemes, sporting activities and activities in the school holidays. This can also be coupled with specific work with the defendant.

11.19 For defendants with mental health problems or drug or alcohol addictions, specialist help should be considered to address their problem. Whilst it is not permissible to make an order requiring the defendant to attend for treatment, there may be an opportunity to see if the council can provide services or treatment which the defendant needs but which has been delayed or denied before. The role of the defence should be to enquire what help is available, check whether it is appropriate for their client or challenge non-provision of appropriate assistance.

Monitoring and recording information relating to ASBOs

11.20 Local procedures should be introduced to monitor all ASBO applications.[1] The current Home Office Guidance recommends a minimum level of information to be recorded by the anti-social behaviour working group, as follows:

- the original application for an ASBO (or prosecution details if a post-conviction ASBO), including the name, date of birth, address, gender and ethnicity of the defendant;
- the ASBO details and any exclusion maps;
- date and details of any variation or discharge of the ASBO; and
- any breach action.

11.21 Additional voluntary recording may include details of victims or complainants, contributory factors such as drugs or alcohol, aggravating factors such as racial issues, and whether the anti-social conduct has ceased.

---

[1] See current Home Office Guidance, reproduced in Appendix 3, p 215.

Variation and discharge of order

11.22 Parties may make an application to vary or discharge an order for a variety of reasons, e.g. the defendant may wish to vary the terms of an order because an exclusion clause precludes him or her from visiting family members, or because of a non-association clause with friends; or the applicant may wish to extend the terms of an exclusion clause or request new terms if the defendant displaces his or her anti-social behaviour to another area. Applications to discharge ASBOs prior to the relevant date should be considered when a defendant has complied with the terms of the ASBO for a significant period of time. An assessment can be made by the relevant bodies as to whether his or her behaviour has been controlled by the orders or has been permanently changed. It is good practice to review at reasonable intervals all orders made to see if discharge is appropriate or if a variation to tighten or relax the prohibitions is necessary. An example of the need for a variation may be where the defendant's behaviour has improved so that the exclusion area, or perhaps the restriction on attending particular shops or restaurants, is no longer needed.

11.23 An ASBO, whether interim or final, can be varied or discharged on application:

- either applicant or defendant can make the application;
- an application to vary or discharge the order must be made to the court that first made the ASBO;
- a post-conviction ASBO may be heard by any magistrates' court in the same petty sessions area;
- no ASBO can be discharged within 2 years of service of the order without both parties' consent;
- a post-conviction order cannot be discharged before 2 years;
- if the defendant brings the application, the applicant body must give the court a 'considered' response to the application;[1]
- for a contested application, reasons and appropriate evidence on the ASBO's effectiveness should be given.

11.24 The procedure for applying to vary or discharge an ASBO is set out at r 6 of the 2002 Rules, which came into force on 2 December 2002. The main principles are as follows:

- any application, with reasons, must be in writing to the magistrates' court which made the order (or any magistrates' court in the same petty sessions area for post-conviction ASBOs);
- if the court thinks there are *no* grounds to vary or discharge the ASBO, it can determine the case without hearing *anyone* in person (*except* when an interim ASBO was made without notice to the defendant – the court *must* give him or her the chance to be heard before deciding on the application);
- if there *are* grounds to hold a hearing, unless the application is withdrawn, a summons for a hearing will be issued giving at least 14 days' notice of the hearing. The clerk will send a copy of the application to vary or discharge with the summons.

11.25 Where a defendant has an ASBO in place but continues a course of anti-social behaviour, the appropriate procedure for extending or varying the terms of the original ASBO is unclear. Is the length of the order a term which can be varied? Or should the authority make a fresh application? It is suggested that, as the Act refers to applications to vary the order rather than its terms, extending the end date of the order is more properly a variation application rather than a fresh application. In practice, it is submitted that the best course is to file both a r 6 application and a completed Sch 1 application, setting out the previous order and then the

---

[1] See current Home Office Guidance, reproduced in Appendix 3, p 214.

subsequent breaches and anti-social behaviour alleged. The new proposed terms can then be included in the application so that the defendant has an opportunity to respond fully to the proposed variation and/or extension.

CHAPTER 12

APPEALS AGAINST ANTI-SOCIAL BEHAVIOUR ORDERS

Appeals by the defendant

Magistrates' courts' decisions

12.1 Where the ASBO has been made by the magistrates' court, sitting either in its civil capacity or following a criminal conviction, appeal primarily lies to the Crown Court.[1] The same provisions which govern appeals from criminal matters are applied, namely rr 74 and 75 of the MCR 1981 regarding the documents to be sent to the Crown Court and rr 6–11 of the Crown Court Rules 1982 regarding the procedure and notices of appeal.

Notice of appeal and time-limits

12.2 Notice of appeal is made in writing and should be made to the justices' chief executive for the relevant magistrates' court (specimen forms can be found in *Stone's Justices Manual* (Butterworths)). A notice of appeal must be lodged no later than 21 days after the ASBO was made.[2] With the exception of post-conviction ASBOs these are appeals against the making of a civil order and, therefore, no actual grounds of appeal are needed save that the court erred in law or reached a decision that it should not have done on the weight of evidence. It would, however, seem sensible for limited grounds to be given by a defendant, if only to guide the Crown Court when it is considering the papers. Appeals against post-conviction orders are appeals against sentence and the notice of appeal should specify this along with the grounds of appeal. There is power to extend the time of filing a notice of appeal, both before and after the 21 days.[3] Any application to extend time is made to the Crown Court, to an appropriate officer, and should be made in writing, specifying the grounds of the application.[4] If the application is granted, then the Crown Court officer will give notice of this to the appellant and the magistrates' court. It is the appellant's responsibility to give notice of the extension to the other party.[5]

Format of Crown Court appeal hearing

12.3 The hearing at the Crown Court is an entirely fresh one and, by s 79(3) of the Supreme Court Act 1981, is a full re-hearing of the evidence and law. Section 79(3) is an unusual section, which states that the customary practice and procedure with respect to appeals to the Crown Court, particularly as to the extent to which an appeal was a re-hearing of the case, should

---

[1] CDA 1998, s 4, as amended; for post-conviction orders, the order is ancillary to the sentence on the criminal conviction and the right of appeal lies to the Crown Court in the same way.
[2] Crown Court Rules 1982, r 7(3).
[3] Ibid, r 7(5).
[4] Ibid, r 7(6).
[5] Ibid, r 7(7).

continue to be observed. It is regrettable that the Government ignored the feedback and complaints made by a number of applicant bodies and did not make ASBOs an exception to this 'customary practice'. It is incompatible with the repeatedly expressed desire to protect vulnerable and unwilling witnesses, to provide the defendant with a right of a re-hearing. It is hard enough to persuade witnesses to attend court, without having to tell them, when asked, that this is not the end and the witness could undergo a second cross-examination in the Crown Court. It would have been a simple step, and a considerable improvement, had there been a right of appeal which was limited to the usual appellate discretion where the decision was wrong in law or perverse. This is the usual appeal jurisdiction in the civil courts.

12.4 At the re-hearing either party may submit further evidence in support of their case. As the hearing is a re-hearing, the applicant body may rely upon any evidence of recent alleged incidents. The Home Office Guidance suggests that, when determining an appeal, the Crown Court should have before it a copy of the original application for an order, the full order and the notice of appeal. The applicant body has responsibility for ensuring that copies are sent to the court. With the greatest respect to the authors of the current Home Office Guidance, this appears to be incomplete or incorrect. It cannot be right that the Crown Court does not have before it all the evidence that was before the magistrates' court. It would be strange in the extreme if the magistrates were entitled to consider the statements from the witnesses and to accept them as their evidence-in-chief, but judges in the Crown Court were not. The invariable practice that we have adopted is that the entire trial bundle is sent to the Crown Court, together with a copy of the notice of appeal and the perfected order. It should also be remembered that most Crown Court judges have had little or no exposure to ASBOs, and few have been given the appropriate training. The common situation is that the hearing is before a Crown Court judge and two lay magistrates, who would not normally read any statements before hearing an appeal. The difference for ASBO appeals should be carefully and politely pointed out in a letter. It is also advisable to give a sensible time estimate in this first letter as, unless the case can be dealt with in a short time, it will normally be listed along with another 10–12 cases in a rolling list, which will almost inevitably lead to an adjournment and disaffected witnesses and defendant. The letter can also be produced to the court and the Department of Constitutional Affairs if a case is unnecessarily adjourned due to 'impossible' listing.

12.5 The Crown Court may, on appeal, make any orders it wishes as are necessary to give effect to its findings. It may also make any incidental or consequential orders as are just. If the Crown Court makes an ASBO, then it is treated as if it was made by the magistrates' court for the purposes of applications to vary and/or discharge.

Case stated

12.6 The defendant has the right, pursuant to s 111 of MCA 1980, to ask for a case to be stated to the Divisional Court in respect of a decision of the magistrates' court (see **12.13** for procedure). However, if the defendant does so, he then loses the right to appeal as of right for a re-hearing before the Crown Court[1] and, therefore, it would not normally be in the defendant's interests to use this avenue of appeal first, as this option remains open even if the Crown Court subsequently rules against the defendant.

Appeal from the Crown Court

12.7 Appeal from the Crown Court is only by way of case stated, pursuant to s 28 of the Supreme Court Act 1981,[2] or judicial review, pursuant to s 29(3), both of which lie to the High

---

[1] MCA 1980, s 111(4).
[2] Crown Court Rules 1982, r 26.

Court. The grounds of appeal for case stated are that the Crown Court was 'wrong in law or is in excess of jurisdiction'.[1] The principles of the remedies of the mandatory order, prohibiting order and quashing order, which an application for judicial review allows, are beyond the scope of this book. The practical difference is unlikely to be significant: to succeed in an application for judicial review, the court would have to be satisfied of an error of law or that the decision was *'Wednesbury'* unreasonable.[2] It should be noted that, as discussed in Chapter 6, appeals from the Crown Court from post-conviction orders lie only to the Court of Appeal and then only if the sentence was wrong in principle or manifestly excessive.[3]

Appropriate venue of appeal

12.8 This section is concerned with the appropriate venue for an appeal from an ASBO imposed by a magistrates' court. Whilst there are three possible choices for appeal, discussed above, it has become common for any challenge to the making of the order to result in a judicial review application. Although there are undoubtedly cases where this is appropriate, it is by no means the correct route for the majority of cases. The court in *C (by his Mother and Litigation Friend, C) v Sunderland Youth Court, Northumbria Police, and Crown Prosecution Service*[4] made it clear that there was a right of appeal under s 108 of MCA 1980 and they would not wish to encourage applications for judicial review when there was an alternative remedy to appeal against sentence to the Crown Court.

12.9 This has been further explored by the Administrative Court in the case of *R (on the application of A) v Leeds Magistrates' Court and Leeds City Council*,[5] where the defendant applied for judicial review of two decisions made by a district judge, first, when making interim without notice orders and then when renewing the orders at a later on notice renewal hearing. The application was on the basis that whilst the defendant did not dispute that there was prima facie evidence before him to justify an interim order, the judge had failed on the without notice hearing to have any regard to A's best interests as a child (held to be a primary consideration by the Administrative Court in related proceedings, after the making of the without notice orders[6]) and, at the renewal notice hearing, to have both applied the wrong test and erred in law.

12.10 Mr Justice Stanley Burnton noted that a defendant who had had a without notice ASBO imposed could:

(a) apply to the magistrates' court for the order to be discharged or varied;
(b) appear and oppose the making of a further order, as the defendant had done here;
(c) appeal to the Crown Court;
(d) appeal to the High Court by way of case stated; or
(e) apply to the High Court for judicial review. However, he considered (e) to be the least suitable option, stating:

> '30 Of these procedures, judicial review is the least suitable in a case such as the present, where it is not disputed that the evidence before the magistrates' court justified (although it did not necessarily require) the making of the order. In such a case, if the claimant establishes that the District Judge applied an incorrect test, the only relief this Court can grant is to quash the ASBO. In judicial review proceedings, the High Court cannot consider the evidence before the District Judge (or any evidence

---

[1] Supreme Court Act 1981, s 28(1).
[2] *Associated Provincial Picture Houses v Wednesbury Corporation* [1948] 1 KB 223, [1947] 2 All ER 680, CA.
[3] Criminal Appeal Act 1968, s 9(1).
[4] [2003] EWHC 2385 (Admin), (2004) Crim LR 75.
[5] [2004] EWHC 554 (Admin), (2004) *The Times*, 31 March.
[6] *R (on the application of Kenny) v Leeds Magistrates' Court; R (on the application of M) v Secretary of State for Constitutional Affairs and Lord Chancellor and another* [2003] EWHC 2963 (Admin), [2004] 1 All ER 1333.

subsequently available) and itself decide whether, applying the correct legal test, the order should be upheld, save in cases in which no District Judge properly applying the law could have come to any conclusion other than that the order should be made. Nor can the High Court vary the terms of the ASBO so as to accommodate the contentions successfully made by the claimant. The High Court cannot substitute its discretion for that of the magistrates' court.

...

32 ... Judicial review proceedings have a further disadvantage. There is often no reliable record of the reasons given by the magistrates' court for its decision. The decision of 11 December 2003 is a case in point: I shall have to refer to the evidence below. Where however a case is stated, the District Judge has the opportunity to set out the facts on which he based his decision and his reasons for making the order.

33 Parliament has specifically provided in the 1998 Act for applications to the magistrates' court to discharge or to vary interim orders and for appeals to the Crown Court. In my judgment, it follows that these are the primary routes for challenging an interim order. Appeal by way of case stated is appropriate where a legal issue arises which is suitable for determination by the High Court ...

12.11 The judge concluded that judicial review was appropriate only where there was procedural unfairness or bias (to which we would add where an urgent remedy is needed). Here the alleged failure by the district judge to apply the correct legal test to the facts before him would not, in general, be an appropriate subject for judicial review. He dismissed the argument that judicial review was the preferable remedy for the defendant, as this would, if granted, have led to a quashing of the order, thereby sparing him the breach proceedings. The judge stated that an ASBO was an order of the court and must be complied with unless and until discharged or set aside. Indeed, he considered that breach of an ASBO by a defendant who has not applied for its variation or discharge may well be good reason for the court to refuse judicial review. The judge dismissed the application for judicial review on the grounds of delay, alternative remedy and on the merits – the latter is discussed in Chapters 13 and 14.

12.12 *A* was a case involving interim orders; however, the principles set out must, as a matter of logic, apply to the making of full orders as well. What is clear is that the courts, whilst willing to exercise supervisory administrative control of the magistrates' courts in appropriate cases, consider that challenges to orders, whether interim or full orders, should be brought using the mechanism of appeal to the Crown Court for arguments on the facts or application of discretion or by way of case stated for points of law.

Appeals by the applicant body

12.13 The applicant body has only one avenue of appeal against a refusal by a magistrates' court to grant an ASBO: to apply by way of case stated to the Divisional Court for review of the decision on the grounds that the decision is wrong in law or in excess of jurisdiction.[1] The application must be made within 21 days of the decision of the magistrates.[2] The application is made with the proposed terms of the case stated for the magistrates to consider. The magistrates may refuse to state a case but only if they consider the application to be frivolous. If so, they must provide a certificate of refusal, and the applicant body may apply to the High Court for an order of mandamus to require the magistrates to state the case.[3]

---

[1] MCA 1980, s 111.
[2] Ibid, s 111(2).
[3] Ibid, s 111(6).

Appeals from the county court

12.14 Any appeal from the decision of the county court in 'bolt-on' proceedings will have to be made by reference to CPR 1998, Part 52. Here the appeals are generally to the next 'tier' of judge, namely to a circuit judge from a district judge, and from a circuit judge to a High Court judge. If, however, the case is allocated to the multi-track, then the appeal is with permission to the Court of Appeal.[1] This will not apply to the majority of county court orders, as the rule is not applicable to appeals in Part 55 possession proceedings,[2] where the appeal will actually lie to the High Court. It remains to be seen whether any alteration to Part 52 will occur but, at present, there is no right of appeal from an ASBO hearing; the appellant needs permission to appeal.[3] This permission can be granted by the court which hears the ASBO application or by the appeal court[4] but should be made initially to the court making the order.[5] The application for permission in the appeal court is generally dealt with on paper, and the appellant must show a real prospect of success or some other compelling reason why the appeal should be heard. The application must be made within 14 days of the decision of the lower court.[6]

12.15 The hearing before the higher court will be limited to a review of the decision of the lower court[7] (i.e. an appellate jurisdiction) as to whether the trial judge erred in law or fact, or there was a serious procedural or other irregularity, unless the court considers that, in the circumstances of an individual appeal, it would be in the interests of justice to hold a re-hearing. Unless it orders otherwise, the court will not hear any oral evidence or accept any evidence which the lower court did not hear. It may be possible to argue that, as an application in the magistrates' court would have allowed an appeal which would have resulted in a fresh hearing, the appellate court in an appeal from the county court application should also hear the matter afresh. It is unlikely, however, that the court will deviate readily from the usual appeal procedure in the county court.

Appeal from post-conviction orders

12.16 If the order imposed by the magistrates' court, then the appeal is one to the Crown Court, by virtue of the same statutory powers as for ASBOs made in free-standing applications.[8] However, if the order is imposed by the Crown Court, then, although not part of the criminal sentence, the correct venue for the appeal is the Court of Criminal Appeal. This has been confirmed in the case of *R v P*,[9] where Mr Justice Henriques, giving the decision of a Court of Appeal, including the Lord Chief Justice, stated:

> '36 Finally, it should be noted that whilst the making of such an order is strictly not part of the sentencing process, the appropriate venue for an appeal against the making of such an order when made in the Crown Court is plainly to the Court of Appeal Criminal Division. So much is plain from a reading of section 9(1) of the Criminal Appeal Act 1968 together with section 50(1) of the same Act.'

---

[1] CPR PD 52, para 2A.2.
[2] Although Part 65 has been added to the CPR 1998, it does not seem to affect the appeal route.
[3] CPR, r 52.3(1).
[4] Ibid, r 52.3(2)
[5] CPR PD 52, para 4.6
[6] CPR, r 52.4.
[7] Ibid, r 52.11.
[8] MCA 1980, s 108, even though the order is not a conviction or sentence.
[9] [2004] EWCA Crim 287, (2004) *The Times*, 19 February.

CHAPTER 13

BREACH OF AN ANTI-SOCIAL BEHAVIOUR ORDER

General principles

13.1 Breach of the terms of an ASBO without reasonable excuse is a criminal offence and renders the offender liable to be arrested and prosecuted. If proved, the breach is a recordable offence. Breach of an interim order is a criminal offence in the same way without distinction as to procedure or penalties.

13.2 As the breach is a criminal offence, the CPS will ordinarily prosecute all alleged breaches. Usually, the defendant will have been arrested and charged by a police officer and, therefore, the police will liaise directly with the CPS. Prosecutions for breach of ASBO terms will have to be proved to the criminal standard and will also have to pass the public interest test which the CPS applies to all prosecutions. In practice, this has sometimes led to problems owing to the lack of training and/or familiarity with ASBOs and their prosecution. On a number of occasions, the situation has arisen where evidence of a breach has been compiled and the defendant charged, only for the defendant to be bound over or the charge dropped by representatives of the CPS (sometimes as leverage to obtain a guilty plea on other offences), as they considered that the conduct was not significant and not likely to result in tangible punishment. This misconception seems to come from the view that a breach should not be proceeded with unless the defendant has caused harassment, alarm or distress on that occasion. This is not the correct approach, as any breach of an ASBO should be considered to be a serious matter and the courts are encouraged to take that view (indeed, a number of custodial sentences have been imposed for first instances of breach even though the conduct was 'merely' entering an exclusion area, with nothing more). At any breach hearing, the court's attention should be drawn to the fact that the order has been made after the defendant has embarked on a course of behaviour which has made an order necessary. Whilst a defendant who simply enters an area from which he is forbidden by the order does not necessarily cause any harassment, alarm or distress, it is contrary to the principles behind the imposition of the order for there not to be a prosecution of that breach. This would make the order irrelevant and ignores the reason for prohibiting him or her from the area in the first place. A first breach of this nature may not result in a custodial sentence (but see **3.10**) but must be prosecuted. Otherwise, that term of the order may as well not have been made. The effect of the public perception of the effectiveness of ASBO proceedings should not be underestimated if much publicised terms are breached and no action is taken.

13.3 In practice, complaints about breaches in the community are often made to the local authority or RSL officers. It is important that the officers who receive the complaints obtain as much information as possible about witnesses, as the nature of the proceedings is now criminal and, therefore, hearsay evidence will normally be excluded, save for limited exceptions. The investigation of a breach of an ASBO is an investigation of a criminal offence, and care must be taken, as an investigation will be subject to the provisions of the Criminal Procedure and Investigations Act 1996 and the Police and Criminal Evidence Act 1984. Ideally, the investigation of whether a breach has occurred and the taking of statements should be left to the police.

13.4 Care must be taken by the prosecuting authority that prosecutions are brought together if allegations of both a breach of an ASBO and a criminal offence are to be founded on the same or similar facts. To do otherwise may well be an abuse of process or lead to an instance of *autrefois convict*. Defence representatives should seek at an early stage to try to put the prosecution to an election as to charges and to challenge attempts made to bring duplicitous charges.

Breaches by young people

13.5 Unlike applications for ASBOs, proceedings for breach of an ASBO by young people are heard in the Youth Court, where the reporting restrictions are automatic[1] and are far less likely to be lifted than on the making of an ASBO. The proceedings before the Youth Court follow the same course as any criminal prosecution before that court and require the attendance of the defendant's parent or legal guardian if they are aged 15 or under. The maximum sentence of detention for a breach of an ASBO term for a young person is a 2-year detention and training order (only 12 months of this can be served in custody). A young person may only be sentenced to a detention and training order if he is aged 15 or over, or is a persistent offender and aged 12–14 years of age. A minor aged 10–11 who is in breach of an ASBO may not, at present, be sentenced to a term of detention but may be made subject to a community penalty. CDA 1998, s 1(11) applies to young people as well, preventing the making of a conditional discharge. In sentencing a person under the age of 16, the Youth Court must now consider whether a parenting order (see **1.23–1.24**) should be made and, if not, it should state the reasons why. In relevant areas it must also consider whether to make an individual support order (see **14.31**).

Who can prosecute?

13.6 If the defendant has been arrested by the police, then the CPS, through its director, has the statutory responsibility for the conduct of all criminal proceedings instituted on behalf of a police force.[2] This will mean, therefore, that any person who is charged by the police will be prosecuted by the CPS. This is what Parliament originally intended and is confirmed in the current Home Office Guidance. With the above problems arising from prosecution of breaches of ASBOs by the CPS, the CDA 1998 has been further amended by the ASB Act 2003,[3] with additional subsections being inserted into s 1 to permit a council which is a relevant authority and a council for the local government area in which the defendant resides or appears to reside to prosecute for an offence under s 1(10), namely breach of an order. This amendment came into force on 31 March 2004. Further, from 20 January 2004, where breach proceedings are brought against a young person, s 47 of the Children and Young Persons Act 1933 is to be read by virtue of the ASB Act 2003 to allow a single person, authorised by the relevant authority, to be present. This deals with the anomalous situation whereby the relevant authority could not be present in the Youth Court in any criminal proceedings. This amendment, therefore, allows representation from the relevant authority to prosecute a breach.

13.7 The CDA 1998 has been further amended[4] to allow the council for the local government area in which the defendant resides or appears to reside to bring proceedings under s 1(10) for breach of a post-conviction order. At first blush, this seems strange, as it would appear that by applying s 1(10) for the purposes of making and effecting post-conviction orders (see s 1C(9)), this would already allow a council or local government area council to bring a prosecution by

---

[1] Children and Young Persons Act 1933, s 49.
[2] Prosecution of Offences Act 1985, s 3(2).
[3] ASB Act 2003, s 85(1) and (4), amending CDA 1998, s 10, and inserting ss 10A and 10B.
[4] Section 1D(9A)–(9C), inserted by ASB Act 2003, s 86(3).

virtue of s 1(10A). A possible reason could have been the reference to 'an anti-social behaviour order' in s 1(10). However, this cannot be valid, due to the 'applying' of s 1C(9) and, if correct, then breaches of county court ASBOs cannot be prosecuted by the council as, whilst there is a similar 'applying' subsection at s 1B(7), there is no similar amendment to allow prosecution of breaches. The reason therefore would seem to be that, as s 1C(9) brings in only s 1(10), this does not include s 1(10A). It is submitted that s 1C(9A) is clumsily drafted and is unnecessary. All that was needed was to add s 1(10A) to the list of sections in s 1C(9A). This is another example of the poor drafting which affects the Crime and Disorder Act 1998 (as amended).

13.8 There is, however, an alternate way in which a body other than the CPS can bring or conduct proceedings. Section 6(1) of the Prosecution of Offences Act 1985 expressly preserves the right of any person to institute or conduct any criminal proceedings, although the Director of the CPS may take over their conduct at any time, whether or not he has a duty to do so.[1] Local authorities also have a specific reserved power to initiate proceedings under s 222 of the Local Government Act 1972, which provides:

> 'Where a local authority considers it expedient for the promotion or protection of the interests of the inhabitants of their area –
>
> (a) they may prosecute or defend or appear in any legal proceeding ... '

13.9 From a practical standpoint, however, if the police have charged a person with the breach of an ASBO term and the local authority wish to conduct the proceedings, they must seek to have the charge withdrawn and prosecution proceedings begun by the council. Caution must be taken to ensure that a not guilty verdict is not entered on the withdrawal of the police charge, otherwise the principles of *autrefois convict* will apply and no further charge can be brought. The alternative is to request that the CPS appoint someone in the local authority legal department to take over the conduct of the criminal proceedings pursuant to s 5(1) of the 1985 Act. The person must, however, be someone who holds a general legal qualification, that is to say, a person who has a right of audience in any part of the Supreme Court or all county or magistrates' courts.[2] Alternatively, some local authorities are considering investigating, and prosecuting breaches of ASBOs themselves. We would suggest it is preferable wherever possible to allow the police and CPS to perform this task as they have greater experience in this field and it is also generally more cost effective. Building good relationships with the police and CPS is therefore vital, and use should be made of the specialist anti-social behaviour Crown Prosecutors. It should, however, be noted that these prosecutors are not specialists in ASBOs and therefore, where appropriate, it may be sensible to arrange for either the CPS to instruct specialist counsel or for the local authority to take over the prosecution at that stage. If the relationship between local authority and the police/CPS is not fruitful the option does of course remain for the local authority itself to bring the prosecution.

Sentencing

13.10 On summary conviction, an adult defendant (see **13.5** for young people) can be sentenced to a maximum of 6 months and a fine not exceeding the present statutory maximum of £5,000 and, on indictment, up to 5 years' imprisonment and/or a fine.[3] It should be noted that, whilst the court has the power to impose community penalties as well as fines or prison

---

[1] Prosecution of Offences Act 1985, s 6(2).
[2] Courts and Legal Services Act 1990, s 71.
[3] CDA 1998, s 1(10).

terms, it does not have the power to impose a conditional discharge,[1] although, presumably, an absolute discharge remains available. The penalty for breach is the same, whether the breach is of a final or an interim order. The courts are likely to regard the breach of an ASBO to be a serious matter and, in the most recent Magistrates' Courts Sentencing Guidelines,[2] the starting point for sentencing for a breach of ASBO is custody. The Guidelines state:

> 'breach of an order is a criminal offence and is itself a serious matter. A court should not lapse into treating the breach of an ASBO as just another minor offence. It should be remembered that the order itself would normally have been a culmination of a course of persistent anit-social behaviour. An ASBO will not only be seen to be effective if breaches of it are taken seriously … Further breaches of a court order should be treated very seriously and may need to be referred to the Crown Court for more severe sentencing. The sentence should be both proportionate to the seriousness of the breach and importantly reflect the impact of the anti-social behaviour.'

This view obviously mirrors the Home Office Guidance on the issue. Whilst the entry point is custody, there is no doubt that the courts will be cautious of dramatically increasing the number of youths in custody, and it may well be that this Guideline is not given great weight in actual practice.

13.11 The court may request reports prior to sentencing in the usual way. However, it may also take them from a relevant applicant body. In this way, the court is told of the reasons why the ASBO was made originally, which will have an effect on the impact of the breach that has been proved. It is important for any applicant body to have close links with the CPS with regard to prosecutions of breaches (if not prosecuting itself), as the overall conduct of the defendant is only likely to be known to the applicant and not to the CPS representatives. One means of providing more information which has been instituted by some local authorities in the provision of a case summary to the CPS for each ASBO made, including both details of the proved schedule and those incidents outside the 6 months used to show necessity. This ensures that the sentencing court is appraised on the full background before reaching a decision. Further, if the breach has highlighted the need for an extension or variation of the original terms, it is worthwhile ensuring that the application for the same is made prior to any sentence hearing, so that both matters can be heard by the same tribunal. It will, in those circumstances, generally be appropriate for the CPS to allow the sentence hearing to be conducted by the solicitor or barrister whom the applicant body has instructed to deal with the variation or extension application.

---

[1] CDA 1998, s 1(11).
[2] 6th edition, implemented 1 January 2004. and reproduced in *Stone's Justices' Manual 2004* (Butterworths).

CHAPTER 14

ANTI-SOCIAL BEHAVIOUR ORDERS AND YOUNG PEOPLE

14.1 The introduction of ASBOs has provided an effective civil tool to deal with minors who act in an anti-social manner. ASBOs may be made against defendants as young as 10 years of age. There are, however, special considerations in respect of applications against young persons which will be explored further in this chapter.

Assessment of young people's needs and circumstances

14.2 The current Home Office Guidance calls for an assessment of a young person's needs and circumstances when applying for an ASBO.[1] An assessment is not strictly required by the Act, but is desirable and complies with other duties, e.g. under s 17 of the Children Act 1989. A young person is defined as a person between the ages of 10 and 17. The Guidance contains the following useful general remarks about assessments.

- The aim is twofold – to get information for the court *and* to ensure that the young person is provided with appropriate services.
- Assessments should not delay an application. Close liaison is therefore needed with the YOT or social services from the outset.
- Social services have a duty *in any event* to safeguard and promote the welfare of children in their area who may be 'in need'.[2]
- The assessment should be carried out in accordance with the guidance contained in the *Framework for the Assessment of Children In Need and their Families 2000*.[3]
- An initial assessment should be carried out within 7 working days. The Guidance does not specify when the 7 days commence, but, presumably, this is from the date of the initial referral.
- If the initial assessment identifies that a child is in need, a core assessment should be carried out within 35 working days.
- An assessment should deal with the child's needs and circumstances, the capacities of his or her parents and wider family, and any environmental factors.
- The assessment should run in parallel with the ASBO process.

14.3 The Guidance makes it clear that agencies have responsibilities to young people, irrespective of the ASBO process (e.g. social services, the local education authority or the health authority).

14.4 There is often a conflict of ideology between local authority agencies when ASBOs against young people are considered. Previous Home Office Guidance stated that the court hearing the application should satisfy itself that social services have been consulted and that the child's needs have been assessed before deciding whether an ASBO is appropriate. This was

---

[1] See current Home Office Guidance, reproduced in Appendix 3, p 208.
[2] Children Act 1989, s 17.
[3] Published by Department for Education and Employment.

interpreted by some as giving social services or the YOT a veto on the decision whether or not to proceed with an ASBO. The current Guidance makes it clear that no one agency has a veto over an applicant's decision to apply for an ASBO (see Chapter 3, dealing with consultation). It should be remembered that the guidance remains only that, and there is no requirement in the Act to conduct an assessment.

14.5 The defence may raise the lack of an assessment as proof that the underlying ASBO process has not been carried out properly. The point can be made that the court will not be able to make a judgment as to the necessity of an ASBO if the applicant has not carried out an assessment to see whether there are alternatives to an order (e.g. intensive social work input). Whilst the Home Office Guidance does not have the force of law, applicants are advised to be in a position to provide a good reason for not carrying out an assessment. There may not have been time to prepare a report or, perhaps, the child has recently been seen by the YOT or another agency, which has rendered a further assessment otiose. A matter sometimes raised by social workers is that the young person concerned is little different from many of the other children whom they see and that the imposition of an ASBO will stigmatise rather than reform. This is more often a personal perception of ASBOs, which also fails to consider the wider picture of the harm that the young person's behaviour causes to others, not least the other young persons in the area. However, the Home Office Guidance is clear:[1]

> '... there should be no confusion as to the purpose of the order, which is to protect the community. The welfare of a child is ... to be considered but ... is not the principal purpose of the order hearing.'

14.6 The issue of what weight the court should place on the welfare of the child has been raised in two cases. First, in *R (on the application of Kenny) v Leeds Magistrates' Court*; *R (on the application of M) v Secretary of State for Constitutional Affairs and another*,[2] as Kenny was aged 17 years and 360 days at the imposition of the without notice interim order, the defendant argued that, in considering whether it was just to impose an interim ASBO, the court must consider the interests of the child as a primary consideration. Mr Justice Owen, in agreeing, cited, with approval, the decision of Mr Justice Mumby,[3] where it was said that the Youth Court had to strike a fair balance between the competing interests of the particular child and the community but always having regard to the principle that the best interests of the child were a primary consideration. In relation to Kenny, the order was discharged for unrelated reasons but the judge failed to deal with the issue in relation to M (and most of the other defendants). It was not raised on appeal by M, but was raised as a test point by another defendant, A (aged 16), in *R (on the application of A) v Leeds Magistrates' Court and Leeds City Council*.[4] Whilst A's application for judicial review was refused on other grounds (see **12.9–12.12**), the judge, Mr Justice Stanley Burnton, expressly went on to consider the merits of the application. He concluded that, whilst the interests of the child were a primary consideration, they were not *the* primary consideration, and, further, that the interests of the public were themselves a primary consideration.[5] This is an important clarification of the bare principle which Mr Justice Owen stated. The judge, however, continued further to give more important guidance, saying:

> 'Secondly, it is by no means obvious that any of the prohibitions contained in the first order or the second order were contrary to the best interests of the claimant. This applies in particular to prohibitions 3, 5 to 7 and 9 and 10. At the hearing on 11 December 2003, Mr Message, not being able to

---

[1] See current Home Office Guidance, reproduced in Appendix 3, p 206.
[2] [2004] 1 All ER 1333.
[3] *R (on the application of the Howard League for Penal Reform v Secretary of State for the Home Dept* [2002] EWHC 2497 (Admin), [2002] All ER (D) 465 (Nov), at [67].
[4] [2004] EWHC 554 (Admin), (2004) *The Times*, 31 March.
[5] Ibid, at [49].

call the claimant, and not having a witness statement from him, could only make a submission in the most general terms that (as summarised in his note) "it was not just to make an order which restricted his liberty, freedom of movement and associations." There was thus nothing before the District Judge to show that any prejudice, except of the most general kind, was caused by the imposition of any of the prohibitions, including prohibitions 4 and 8.

If it is contended that the special interests of a child require either that there be no order, or an order in terms different from those proposed by the local authority, it is incumbent on a defendant to provide an explanation of his case and some relevant evidence. There will be cases where it is inappropriate to make any ASBO in respect of a child by reason of his age. That is not the present case: as I have stated, it is not contended that the evidence before the District Judge did not justify the making of an order against the Claimant, who was aged 16 and was allegedly participating in seriously anti-social behaviour. The phrase "the best interests of the child as a prime consideration" is not a magic talisman which, if not pronounced in a case concerning a child, will necessarily invalidate the order made.'[1]

14.7 The prohibitions expressly referred to were ones which related to matters which were already criminal offences, save for one which prevented the defendant's being present when controlled drugs were traded, sold or supplied, and another which prevented him from possessing or distributing drug supplier (dealer) cards. There was also an exclusion zone and a general term mirroring the terms of s 1(1).

14.8 The points which emerge from the above cases is that the balance of community and child in ASBO applications is an equal one and not weighted either way. In practical terms, however, as most interim terms should be confined to only those terms which are necessary pending a full hearing, the interests of the community should be higher, unless the restrictions sought of the defendant are so draconian that they fundamentally interfere with his or her life. Even if those restrictions are present, it will be the defendant's responsibility to show more than just general objection and restriction. It is submitted that the defendant will have to show that his or her welfare (as a child) would be detrimentally affected by the term. This could be shown, perhaps, if it prevented attendance at school, a job programme or other important place in his or her development. Other than for exclusion zones, it is hard to see how, in the light of the above judgment, interim orders preventing criminal offences could be contrary to a child's welfare more than the obvious prejudice in the imposition of the interim order. Finally, whilst this case involved interim orders, it is submitted that the basic principle must apply to the making of final orders as well.

14.9 The importance of a proper assessment, in appropriate circumstances, of a child's needs at a final hearing was underlined in the case of *R (on the application of AB and SB) v Nottingham City Council*.[2] This was an application for judicial review for alleged ongoing failure by the council to assess and provide for the applicants' needs. One of the applicants in this case was also the subject of an application for an ASBO, which had been adjourned pending the judicial review hearing. Part of the defence to the ASBO application was that an order should not be made because the local authority had failed to assess the child's needs or to consider other ways of dealing with the anti-social behaviour. Richards J underlined the importance of undertaking a systematic assessment of the child's needs, which he described as a three-stage process, including 'identification of needs, production of a care plan, and provision of identified services'. On the facts, it was held that there had been a failure properly to assess the child's needs. Richards J issued a warning to all applicant bodies:

'... on the general issue of assessment of need, I have to say that I am left with the impression that the defendant [Nottingham City Council] has concentrated unduly on the anti-social behaviour order

---

[1] [2004] EWHC 554 (Admin), (2004) *The Times*, 31 March, at [50]–[51].
[2] [2001] EWCA Admin 235, [2001] 3 FCR 350.

proceedings and insufficiently on the discharge of its duty, in particular under s 17 of the Children Act, to assess SB's needs and to make provision for them. No doubt the focus has been the result of SB's very serious behavioural problems, but those problems cannot excuse a failure to comply with the s 17 duty.'

14.10 This case pre-dates *Kenny* and *A* but is still valid and highlights the importance of an open-minded approach to cases of anti-social behaviour. It is unlikely, however, that failure to perform a s 17 assessment is sufficient to defeat an ASBO application. The Guidance has always stated that the court should be given all the relevant information about a child, and not that there has to be an assessment. Further, it is now clear that there is no claim which arises from a failure to make a s 17 assessment, as it is a 'target' duty and not an absolute one.[1] Finally, it would seem to us that if a court did not feel that it had sufficient information about a child to make an order which it otherwise would have considered (i.e. other elements of the test being proved), it is open to it to adjourn the proceedings in order for further information to be provided to it.

14.11 CDA 1998, s 37 states that the principal aim of the YOT is to prevent youth offending. If diversionary or other methods do not change a young person's behaviour, there may be little option left but to consider supporting an ASBO to fulfil this statutory function.

What form should the assessment take?

14.12 In Kirklees, the YOT carries out 'asset' assessments to fulfil the requirements of the Guidance. It is doubted if the core assessment, referred to in the Guidance, should be openly disclosed in ASBO application hearings, as they are open proceedings, which do not enjoy the same protection from publicity as other proceedings involving children (e.g. care proceedings). Core assessments are directed to the welfare of the child and are likely to contain sensitive information whose publication may harm the child and his or her immediate family (reporting restrictions could not be made to prevent details relating to the family being published). A better option may be to use a report based on the YOT's asset assessment, which can be written in a manner which more effectively provides the type of information that the court requires and can direct the appropriate authority to offer services which should be made available to the young person. For post-conviction ASBOs, if no asset assessment has been undertaken, the YOT representative in court can obtain information about the young person.

14.13 Many local authorities are now finding it difficult to resource all the assessments that ASBO applications now demand. Initial statistics relating to ASBOs showed the national proportion of orders made against young people to be 78%, although the Home Office's most recent information is that the figure has dropped to 50%. Nonetheless, it is likely that additional resources may be needed for busy social services departments and YOTs to meet the challenges and expectations laid down by the current Home Office Guidance. In particular, the time-scales envisaged would be beyond many departments. Agreements between divisional heads as to the appropriate protocols for referrals and allocation of resources will become more important as the number of applications against young persons increases.

Applications against children in the care of the local authority

14.14 Where a local authority has parental responsibility for a defendant who is either in its care or placed at home under the protection of a care order, there is an obvious conflict between

---

[1] See *R (on the application of G) v Barnet London Borough Council* [2003] 3 WLR 1194.

the potential need to apply for an ASBO and the local authority's duty to the child in its care. The procedure which a local authority should follow in such circumstances is not addressed in the Act nor in the Home Office Guidance, despite the issues raised by such applications. It has, however, recently been considered by the courts in R *(on the application of M) v Sheffield Magistrates' Court v Sheffield City Council*.[1] The defendant was made the subject of a care order at the age of 6 and placed in various care homes until he came to be living without statutory authority with his grandmother. The defendant had been convicted of numerous criminal offences and was alleged to be responsible for many other acts of anti-social behaviour in his community. The defendant's social worker recorded that the placement was not meeting the child's needs. Shortly after this was noted, the council's anti-social behaviour panel met and were told by the social worker that she believed he may have Attention Deficit Hyperactivity Disorder (ADHD) and his grandmother was take him for assessment. The local anti-social behaviour panel decided that the first limb of the test was satisfied (i.e. that he had acted in an anti-social manner), but adjourned the final decision to await a report from social services as to whether an order was necessary.

14.15 The panel sent the social worker a proforma report form which was duly completed. The social worker having answered the prescribed questions on the form added that she did not feel that an ASBO was likely to solve the child's problems and that he was making some progress. The panel subsequently met without the social worker present and decided that an order was necessary so as to protect other persons from the child's behaviour and that the application would be led by the housing department. There was no further contact with the social services, other than to serve proceedings on the social worker. This was despite the fact that the application was not made for a further 5 months and further ISSP conditions were imposed.

14.16 When the application came to be heard, the defendant's solicitor properly requested disclosure of the social services files. The solicitor attempted to contact the YOT team but was informed that he could not contact them as they were employed by the council, the applicant. The social worker (who had now changed) made it clear that he would only appear as a witness for his employer, the applicant, and at the interview with the defendant's solicitor was attended by the local authority solicitor who was prosecuting the ASBO.

14.17 The magistrates' court was asked to rule on a preliminary point as to whether the proceedings could continue given the conflict of interests and/or abuse of process. The district judge ruled that the local authority could continue with the application. As there was now insufficient time to hear the main application this was adjourned for 6 weeks. The applicant then for the first time applied for an interim order which the district judge duly granted. The defendant applied for judicial review of both decisions.

14.18 Mr Justice Newman held that the statutory purpose of the ASBO legislation was to protect the community and whilst making an order could be of benefit to a defendant this did not prevent a conflict of interest arising in these circumstances. He held that where a local authority discharged its duties in relation to a child in care it had to act so as to promote the welfare of the child in question and must consult with the child and give due consideration to the wishes and feelings of those consulted.[2] The effect of an ASBO was to render the defendant at risk of penal sanction and any parent, whether natural or statutory, would hesitate to place their child at risk of detention in custody. This therefore gave rise to a conflict of interests, which had caused prejudice to the defendant in this case. However, the judge considered that

---

[1] R *(on the application of M, a child) v Sheffield Magistrates' Court*, 27 July 2004, [2004] EWHC 1830 (Admin), per Mr Justice Newman at [57]. The case is unreported at the date of publication, but available at http://www.bailii.org/ew/cases/EWHC/Admin/2004/1830.html., and will be reported in *The Times Law Reports* in August/September 2004.

[2] Children Act 1989, s 22, particularly s 22(4).

the existence of a conflict did not preclude an application for an ASBO by a council against a child in its care.

14.19 The court stopped short of prescribing detailed measures and procedures to ensure that such conflict can be avoided. It did, however, attempt to identify the problem areas and define the relevant legal principles.

(a) *Consultation:* Mr Justice Newman held that the decision to apply for an ASBO was one within the meaning of s 22 (4) of the Children Act 1989 and therefore the 'wishes and feelings' of the child and the person with parental responsibility or other relevant person should have been sought. In this case that had not been done. The person who conducted such 'consultation' should be the social worker, who should provide a full report to the panel. The report should not be dictated by the panel but should be a report for the authority on behalf of the child. The information before this panel was deficient given the detailed information and assessments which social services had and were expected to be conducting (in relation to ADHD assessment).

(b) *Social Services Report:* the decision of the panel as to whether to continue with the application should have been made with the benefit of the report from social services but without their participation in that discussion. If the social worker participated then there was a risk to actual and perceived independence (from the child's view). If an application was to be made, then this should be communicated to all. Where there were exceptional circumstances a further report could be prepared.

(c) *Role of the solicitor:* the solicitor bringing the application should not attend meetings between the defendant's solicitor and the social worker. Further it should be rare for the social worker to need a solicitor in attendance. Once it has been decided to make an application there should be no contact on the issue between the ASBO team and the social services section unless the defendant's solicitor consents.

(d) *Role of the social worker:* the social worker should be available to assist the child at court and to be a witness if requested. Orders should not be made (save in exceptional circumstances) against children in care without the presence of someone from social services.

The judge further stated that if, after detailed consideration with the child and relevant persons, social services wished to support an ASBO application, different considerations may apply; however, the court was not in a position to deal with that possibility.

14.20 The judgment of Mr Justice Newman in this case provides welcome guidance as to the procedures to be adopted by local authorities in making applications against children in their care. The need to comply with s 22(4) is one which needs careful consideration and may not be possible if there is an urgent situation which requires a without notice interim order application or even where there is a group application where notice of a potential application is likely to lead to significant problems for residents. The requirement applies only so far as is reasonably practicable and is not an absolute duty. It is suggested, however, that if such situations arise in which it is not reasonably practicable it is important that very careful notes are taken by the social worker and the ASBO solicitors as to the steps taken and the reasons why the requirement was not complied with.

14.21 Where the social services support the making of an order it is important that their reasoning is properly recorded and the reasons explained to the child. Whilst left open by the court, it is submitted that it would still be preferable for the social services and the ASBO legal department not to contact each other after the decision has been made, save for making requests for updates etc, which should be sent to the defendant's solicitor as well. For those authorities which have a separate police team applying for ASBOs, the best course will always be for the application to be made by the police. This would allow the social services department to maintain actual and perceived independence.

Service of court forms

14.22 A copy of the summons should be served on any person with parental responsibility for the defendant. This is defined as a parent, which can include a social worker in the case of a 'looked after' child. A 'parent' has the same meaning as in s 3 of the Family Law Reform Act 1987. 'Guardian' is as defined in s 107 of the Children and Young Persons Act 1933. Both of these definitions are set out in full in the Guidance.[1]

Court procedure

14.23 The current Home Office Guidance makes the age of the defendant a specific factor for the court to consider in determining the duration of an ASBO. Further, it provides the following advice:

- Evidence is given on oath, save for those aged under 14, who should give unsworn testimony (s 98 of MCA 1980 and s 55(2) of the Youth Justice and Criminal Evidence Act 1999).
- If the young person is aged under 16, the parent or legal guardian *must* attend. It is not considered that the warrant and arrest powers of the court to compel attendance (ss 54–57 of MCA 1980) are available; therefore, the applicant must use best endeavours to secure the attendance of a natural parent or guardian if the defendant is not a 'looked after' child.
- The court will need a home circumstances report (the reason why is not given in the Guidance). The asset assessment referred to above should satisfy this.
- There are no automatic reporting restrictions, as ASBO applications are heard in the magistrates' court, and not in the Youth Court. Exceptions to the normal rules of the Youth Court have also been made since the Guidance was published. Publicity issues are dealt with in more detail in Chapter 9.

14.24 If an ASBO is made, it is advisable to serve a copy of the order on the child's parent or guardian. Additionally, the YOT should receive a copy of the order on the day on which it is made. They should arrange for the appropriate agency to ensure that the young person understands the seriousness of the ASBO, as well as considering appropriate support programmes and diversionary schemes to help prevent breaches of the order.

Which court?

14.25 The following courts have the power to impose ASBOs against young people:

- the magistrates' court, sitting in its civil capacity, hearing stand-alone applications;
- the Youth Court, making an order post-conviction;
- the county court. It is rare that a young person will be a party in his or her own right (e.g. a juvenile tenant in a possession proceedings case or an injunction sought against a minor to curb criminal activity). With the amendments brought by ASB Act 2003 (see **6.3–6.4**), it is

---

[1] See current Home Office Guidance, reproduced in Appendix 3, p 205.

likely that many more applications will be made in the county court against juveniles when possession proceedings are brought against their parents. This will not be in force, however, until 1 October 2004.

14.26 Steps can and should be taken to make the procedure less arduous for young persons. The Guidance states that 'the officer in charge of the application should contact the justices' clerk in advance of the hearing, to ensure that it will be conducted in a way that is suitable for the child or young person'.[1] Methods of achieving this include:

- the use of the Youth Court setting;
- the use of magistrates with Youth Court experience;
- regular breaks;
- the avoidance of jargon; and
- more informal court procedures (e.g. no robes on appeal, seated advocates).

Sentencing

14.27 Sentencing for breach is dealt with in Chapter 13. In summary, in the case of a young person, the maximum sentence for breach is:

- a 24-month detention and training order (with 12 months served in the community and 12 months in custody) for defendants between 12 and 17 years of age (note that if a detention and training order is to be imposed for 12–14-year-olds, they must also be persistent criminal offenders); and
- a community order for those aged 10 or 11 years.

14.28 Sentencing should be proportionate and reflect the impact of the anti-social conduct. Proportionality may lead to the consideration of a lighter sentence for the young defendant and makes age *per se* a mitigating factor.

Other available orders

14.29 Other orders are available in the CDA 1998 and elsewhere for tackling anti-social behaviour by youths. The following is a non-exhaustive list of other court options, more details of which can be found in Chapter 1:

- care orders;[2]
- supervision orders;[3]
- local child curfew schemes;[4]
- child safety orders;[5]
- parenting orders;[6]
- intensive surveillance and supervision programmes (ISSPs);
- criminal sentencing, including supervision orders, community penalties and reparation orders;
- individual support orders (see **14.31**).

---

[1] See current Home Office Guidance, reproduced in Appendix 3, p 208.
[2] Children Act 1989, s 33.
[3] Children and Young Persons Act 1969, s 12.
[4] CDA 1998, s 14.
[5] Ibid, s 11.
[6] Ibid, s 8.

14.30 Interventionist work also remains available, which can work instead of, or alongside, the more formal court remedies.

Individual support orders

14.31 On 1 May 2004 individual support orders (ISOs) were introduced.[1] Where the court makes an ASBO against a young person or child (i.e. a 10–17-year-old) it must consider whether the individual support conditions are fulfilled[2] and, if not, state this in open court, giving reasons.[3] Those conditions which need to be met are:[4]

(a) that an ISO is desirable in the interests of preventing repetition of the behaviour which led to the orders being made; and
(b) that there is not already such an order in place; and
(c) that the court has been notified by the Secretary of State that arrangements for the implementation of such orders are in place for the area where the child lives.

14.32 The obvious point to note therefore is that, whilst the legislation is in force, whether a particular court has the power to make an order depends on the individual area implementation dates. Many major cities do not have the arrangements in place at the time of publication, and applicants should check with their individual areas before hearings. The Home Office 'knowledgenetwork' website reproduces the Home Office Circular 25/2004 which notifies courts that ISOs are available.

14.33 Before making an ISO, the court shall obtain from a social worker or YOT worker any information which the court considers necessary to decide if the conditions are fulfilled or what requirements should be imposed in the ISO.[5] This requirement is likely to involve consideration of the additional strain on the social services and YOT officers, and it remains to be seen whether the present structure could cope with the additional workload of assessment and supervision of requirements imposed under this legislation.

14.34 If the conditions are met, the court *must* make an order which requires the defendant to comply with requirements in the order for not more than 6 months and to comply with directions given by the responsible officer with a view to the implementation of the order's requirements.[6] A responsible officer is defined as a social worker, personally nominated by a person appointed as chief education officer or member of a YOT.[7]

14.35 The requirements contained in an ISO should be those which are desirable to prevent repetition of the conduct which gave rise to the ASBO and may require the defendant:[8]

- to participate in activities specified in the ISO or as directed by the responsible officer at times as specified; and/or
- to attend at specified places at specified times and/or meet with specified persons; and/or
- tocomply with specified arrangements for education.

An ISO or directions given pursuant to it, however, cannot require a defendant to attend (the same place or others) on more than 2 days in any week (Sunday to Saturday).[9] Further, the requirements and directions given under them shall, as far as is practicable, avoid conflict with

---

[1] Criminal Justice Act 2003, s 322, inserting s 1AA into the CDA 1998.
[2] CDA 1998, s 1AA(1).
[3] Ibid, s 1AA(4).
[4] Ibid, s 1AA(3)(a)–(c).
[5] Ibid, s 1AA(9).
[6] Ibid, s 1AA(2)(a) and (b)
[7] Ibid, s 1AA(10).
[8] Ibid, s 1AA(6).
[9] Ibid, s 1AA(7).

the defendant's religious beliefs or school attendance.[1] Individual support orders are civil orders and are intended to help young people address the causes of their anti-social behaviour. An ISO could, for example, require a young person to attend counselling for substance abuse or anger management sessions which are overseen by the responsible officer.

14.36 Before the court makes an ISO, it must explain to the defendant in ordinary language the effects and requirements of the ISO and the consequences which may follow in the event of breach (see **1.61**) and that the court has the power to review the ISO on the application of either the defendant or the responsible officer.[2] Whilst an ISO can be varied or discharged on the defendant's or responsible officer's application,[3] it can also occur if the court varies the ASBO following which the ISO was made.[4]

Breach

14.37 Breach of the requirements of an ISO without a reasonable excuse is a criminal offence and can result in a fine of up to £250 for 10–13-year-olds and up to £1,000 for those aged 14 and over[5]. Any fine imposed on a person under 16 years of age must be paid by the parent of guardian.[6] For 16-17-year-olds, the court has a discretion as to whether to make the parent pay. This will, of course, mean that for children under 16 the emphasis will be placed on the parents to ensure the child's compliance with the terms of the ISO. Whilst a desire for parental control is laudable, it is difficult to see it being achieved by this means, although time will show whether it is successful or not. The Home Office has indicated, however, that it does not expect first breaches to be prosecuted.

Conclusion

14.38 The majority of ASBO applications are made against young people. Whilst it is clear that some young people's anti-social behaviour causes real misery for their community, some have questioned whether ASBOs are being correctly brought against this age group and why the number of applications against them is so high. What is clear is that, in appropriate cases, ASBOs against young persons have proved highly effective in deterring further anti-social behaviour. Provided that proper assessment of the young person's needs is made and the appropriateness of an application verified, ASBOs can and should be pursued against young persons.

---

[1] Ibid, s 1AA(8).
[2] CDA 1998, s 1AB(1), inserted by Criminal Justice Act 2003, s 322, in force from 1 May 2004: see SI 2004/829, art 3(1), (2)(b).
[3] Ibid, s 1AB(6).
[4] Ibid, s 1AB(7).
[5] Ibid, s 1AB(3).
[6] Powers of Criminal Courts (Sentencing) Act 2000, s 137(3).

CHAPTER 15

FUNDING

15.1 According to the very earliest Home Office statistics, the average cost of bringing an ASBO application was £4,800. The true cost now seems to have fallen to about £1,000 with greater familiarity and increased use of the legislation, although research is currently under way to ascertain a more accurate figure. Whilst the Government is committed to promoting ASBOs in the fight against anti-social behaviour, and has expressed concern that more applications are not made, it has not made any additional finances available.

The applicant

15.2 The most recent Home Office Guidance is surprisingly silent on the issue of who should fund ASBO applications, particularly in the light of the extensive commentary in the preceding two versions of the Guidance. Reference is made to buying in specialist legal advice in blocks, or pooling expertise and experience to obtain legal advice. However, no guidance is offered on the crucial question of who funds the applications. In practice, the various agencies have adopted a number of different methods to share the costs of investigation and bring the application, for example:

- The local authority agrees to fund all applications, with the police providing free assistance in the initial application. The police and the CPS are responsible for the funding of all breach proceedings.
- Police officers specially trained in anti-social behaviour issues (funded by the police or by corporate means) are detailed to work exclusively on ASBOs.
- The local authority agrees to fund all applications relating to behaviour occurring on or around council land (e.g. housing estates), with the police agreeing to fund all other applications.
- A corporate pot is created from contributions from the local authority, the community and the police.
- European funding is requested to provide specialist anti-social behaviour teams to address safety issues and re-integration work (e.g. Liverpool).
- Government funding (e.g. the Safer Communities Fund (used by Kirklees Metropolitan Council to obtain funding for its anti-social behaviour co-ordinator), the Communities Against Drugs Fund (used by Camden Borough Council to combat drugs) and other community regeneration schemes).
- A single local authority department funds all applications (e.g. in Manchester City Council all council-led ASBOs are funded by the housing department).
- City-wide anti-social behaviour teams take out ASBOs, including proceedings on behalf of clients (such as RSLs), who pay a charge for the service (e.g. Leeds City Council).
- Pooling legal resources and expertise amongst local authority legal teams (e.g. the scheme devised in Essex County Council).
- Accessing funds from local businesses to help fund ASBOs (e.g. Camden Borough Council, who obtained funds from Railtrack to obtain ASBOs in and around King's Cross Railway Station).

- RSLs fund applications for land that they manage or control, or contribute to a composite fund with other agencies to fund them.

15.3 Although it is hoped that a centralised consolidated system for the funding of applications will be established by the Government, for the moment, the Home Office's Anti-social Behaviour Unit may be able to provide information about available funding options. Current pledges include £75 million funding over the next 3 years. This will mean more funding available for every community safety partnership, and the funding of trailblazing schemes in some parts of the country to tackle issues such as street begging.

15.4 Each police authority is provided with a budget to spend on policing in its area. How that money is spent is a matter for that police force. A breakdown of local spending, sources and priorities is produced annually in the local police plan, which is available for inspection at local police stations. For the first time, tackling anti-social behaviour is a priority key performance indicator in the latest National Policing Plan. Local policing plans will undoubtedly be affected, with the result that tackling anti-social behaviour will be a higher priority to the police in terms of funding and resources.

The defendant

15.5 Funding issues will be of equal importance to a defendant, to ensure that he or she has access to appropriate advice and representation in court.

15.6 Details of available public funding are set out in the current Home Office Guidance.[1] Briefly, the available funding options are as follows:

- criminal public funding;
- advocacy assistance;
- representation order.

15.7 Advice, assistance and representation on behalf of legally assisted defendants in the magistrates' court must be undertaken by an approved solicitor from the Criminal Defence Service, under the terms of the General Criminal Contract. Funding under this scheme can take any of three forms:

- advice and assistance, namely general advice and letter writing, but does not include representation;
- advocacy and assistance, which allows limited representation, e.g. court duty solicitor advice or initial hearings; and
- full representation in the magistrates' court or Crown Court. Representation orders are only usually available where a defendant has been charged with a criminal offence.

15.8 Under the Criminal Defence Service (General) (No 2) Regulations 2001,[2] reg 3(2)(b), ASBO applications are deemed criminal proceedings. Applications for funding are made on prescribed forms and are available on the Legal Services Commission website. Advocacy assistance is 'self-granted' by the solicitor on completion of Form CDS 3. This is subject to an extendable financial limit of £1,500. Breach of an ASBO is a criminal offence, and a representation order may be obtained by the solicitor from the relevant court. Work done in respect of breach proceedings attracts its own standard fee. Appeals are also funded through self-granted advocacy assistance. The only difference on claiming payment is that Form CDS 6

---

[1] Current Home Office Guidance reproduced in Appendix 3, p 229.
[2] SI 2001/1437.

should be used with code 2H. Exceptionally, the Commission can grant a representation order but this will usually be refused. Advocacy assistance is available.

15.9 Under r 11.3 of the General Civil Contract (Solicitors) Specification, changes have now been introduced to allow practitioners with a housing franchise to represent tenants (and family members who live with them) or give them advocacy assistance in ASBO proceedings which are likely to lead to possession proceedings. Further details are also available from the Legal Services Commission website.

15.10 With the introduction of ASBOs in the county court, guidance should be issued on available public funding. Legal aid through firms certified by the Legal Services Commission will be the most likely source of funding. There is no equivalent of the duty solicitor scheme in the county court, but help and assistance can be available through local Citizens Advice Bureaux, charities such as Liberty, or organisations such as CHAS or Shelter, in appropriate cases. Many firms of solicitors also offer free initial consultations or even *pro bono* representation.

APPENDIX 1

LEGISLATION (as amended)

(A) CRIME AND DISORDER ACT 1998[1]

Part I
Prevention of Crime and Disorder

Chapter I
England and Wales

Crime and disorder: general

1[2] Anti-social behaviour orders

(1) An application for an order under this section may be made by a relevant authority if it appears to the authority that the following conditions are fulfilled with respect to any person aged 10 or over, namely—

(a) that the person has acted, since the commencement date, in an anti-social manner, that is to say, in a manner that caused or was likely to cause harassment, alarm or distress to one or more persons not of the same household as himself; and

[(b) that such an order is necessary to protect relevant persons from further anti-social acts by him.][3]

...[4]

[(1A) In this section and sections 1B and 1E 'relevant authority' means—

(a) the council for a local government area;

[(aa) in relation to England, a county council;][5]

---

[1] Act reference: 1998 c 37.
Royal Assent: 31 July 1998.
Long title: An Act to make provision for preventing crime and disorder; to create certain racially-aggravated offences; to abolish the rebuttable presumption that a child is doli incapax and to make provision as to the effect of a child's failure to give evidence at his trial; to abolish the death penalty for treason and piracy; to make changes to the criminal justice system; to make further provision for dealing with offenders; to make further provision with respect to remands and committals for trial and the release and recall of prisoners; to amend Chapter I of Part II of the Crime (Sentences) Act 1997 and to repeal Chapter I of Part III of the Crime and Punishment (Scotland) Act 1997; to make amendments designed to facilitate, or otherwise desirable in connection with, the consolidation of certain enactments; and for connected purposes.

[2] Commencement: 1 April 1999 (SI 1998/3263).

[3] Amendment: Paragraph substituted: Police Reform Act 2002, s 61(1), (2), with effect from 2 December 2002 (Police Reform Act 2002 (Commencement No 3) Order 2002, SI 2002/2750; Police Reform Act 2002, s 61(10)).

[4] Amendment: Words repealed: Police Reform Act 2002, ss 61(1), (3), 107(2), Sch 8, with effect from 2 December 2002 (Police Reform Act 2002 (Commencement No 3) Order 2002, SI 2002/2750; Police Reform Act 2002, s 61(10)).

[5] Amendment: Paragraph inserted: Anti-social Behaviour Act 2003, s 85(1), (2)(a), with effect from 20 January 2004 (Anti-social Behaviour Act 2003 (Commencement No 1 and Transitional Provisions) Order 2003, SI 2003/3300).

(b) the chief officer of police of any police force maintained for a police area;
(c) the chief constable of the British Transport Police Force; ...[1]
(d) any person registered under section 1 of the Housing Act 1996 as a social landlord who provides or manages any houses or hostel in a local government area[;
(e) a housing action trust established by order in pursuance of section 62 of the Housing Act 1988.][2]

(1B) In this section 'relevant persons' means—

(a) in relation to a relevant authority falling within paragraph (a) of subsection (1A), persons within the local government area of that council;

[(aa) in relation to England, a county council;][3]

(b) in relation to a relevant authority falling within paragraph (b) of that subsection, persons within the police area;

(c) in relation to a relevant authority falling within paragraph (c) of that subsection—

    (i) persons who are on or likely to be on policed premises in a local government area; or

    (ii) persons who are in the vicinity of or likely to be in the vicinity of such premises;

(d) in relation to a relevant authority falling within paragraph (d) [or (e)][4] of that subsection—

    (i) persons who are residing in or who are otherwise on or likely to be on premises provided or managed by that authority; or

    (ii) persons who are in the vicinity of or likely to be in the vicinity of such premises.][5]

(2) ...[6]

(3) Such an application shall be made by complaint to the magistrates' court whose commission area includes [the local government area or police area concerned][7].

(4) If, on such an application, it is proved that the conditions mentioned in subsection (1) above are fulfilled, the magistrates' court may make an order under this section (an 'anti-social behaviour order') which prohibits the defendant from doing anything described in the order.

(5) For the purpose of determining whether the condition mentioned in subsection (1)(a) above is fulfilled, the court shall disregard any act of the defendant which he shows was reasonable in the circumstances.

---

[1] Amendment: Word repealed: Anti-social Behaviour Act 2003, ss 85(1), (2)(b), 92, Sch 3, with effect from 20 January 2004 (Anti-social Behaviour Act 2003 (Commencement No 1 and Transitional Provisions) Order 2003, SI 2003/3300).

[2] Amendment: Paragraph and preceding word inserted: Anti-social Behaviour Act 2003, s 85(1), (2)(c), with effect from 20 January 2004 (Anti-social Behaviour Act 2003 (Commencement No 1 and Transitional Provisions) Order 2003, SI 2003/3300).

[3] Amendment: Paragraph inserted: Anti-social Behaviour Act 2003, s 85(1), (3)(a), with effect from 20 January 2004 (Anti-social Behaviour Act 2003 (Commencement No 1 and Transitional Provisions) Order 2003, SI 2003/3300).

[4] Amendment: Words inserted: Anti-social Behaviour Act 2003, s 85(1), (3)(b), with effect from 20 January 2004 (Anti-social Behaviour Act 2003 (Commencement No 1 and Transitional Provisions) Order 2003, SI 2003/3300).

[5] Amendment: Subsections inserted: Police Reform Act 2002, s 61(1), (4), with effect from 2 December 2002 (Police Reform Act 2002 (Commencement No 3) Order 2002, SI 2002/2750; Police Reform Act 2002, s 61(10)).

[6] Amendment: Subsection repealed: Police Reform Act 2002, s 61(1), (5), 107(2), Sch 8, with effect from 2 December 2002 (Police Reform Act 2002 (Commencement No 3) Order 2002, SI 2002/2750; Police Reform Act 2002, s 61(10)).

[7] Amendment: Words substituted: Police Reform Act 2002, s 61(1), (6), with effect from 2 December 2002 (Police Reform Act 2002 (Commencement No 3) Order 2002, SI 2002/2750; Police Reform Act 2002, s 61(10)).

[(6) The prohibitions that may be imposed by an anti-social behaviour order are those necessary for the purpose of protecting persons (whether relevant persons or persons elsewhere in England and Wales) from further anti-social acts by the defendant.][1]

(7) An anti-social behaviour order shall have effect for a period (not less than two years) specified in the order or until further order.

(8) Subject to subsection (9) below, the applicant or the defendant may apply by complaint to the court which made an anti-social behaviour order for it to be varied or discharged by a further order.

(9) Except with the consent of both parties, no anti-social behaviour order shall be discharged before the end of the period of two years beginning with the date of service of the order.

(10) If without reasonable excuse a person does anything which he is prohibited from doing by an anti-social behaviour order, he [is guilty of an offence and][2] liable—

(a) on summary conviction, to imprisonment for a term not exceeding six months or to a fine not exceeding the statutory maximum, or to both; or
(b) on conviction on indictment, to imprisonment for a term not exceeding five years or to a fine, or to both.

[(10A) The following may bring proceedings for an offence under subsection (10)—

(a) a council which is a relevant authority; or
(b) the council for the local government area in which a person in respect of whom an anti-social behaviour order has been made resides or appears to reside.

(10B) If proceedings for an offence under subsection (10) are brought in a youth court section 47(2) of the Children and Young Persons Act 1933 (c 12) has effect as if the persons entitled to be present at a sitting for the purposes of those proceedings include one person authorised to be present by a relevant authority.][3]

(11) Where a person is convicted of an offence under subsection (10) above, it shall not be open to the court by or before which he is so convicted to make an order under subsection (1)(b) (conditional discharge) of [section 12 of the Powers of Criminal Courts (Sentencing) Act 2000][4] in respect of the offence.

(12) In this section—

['British Transport Police Force' means the force of constables appointed under section 53 of the British Transport Commission Act 1949;][5]
'the commencement date' means the date of the commencement of this section;
'local government area' means—

(a) in relation to England, a district or London borough, the City of London, the Isle of Wight and the Isles of Scilly;

---

[1] Amendment: Subsection substituted: Police Reform Act 2002, s 61(1), (7), with effect from 2 December 2002 (Police Reform Act 2002 (Commencement No 3) Order 2002, SI 2002/2750; Police Reform Act 2002, s 61(10)).
[2] Amendment: Words substituted: Police Reform Act 2002, s 61(1), (8), with effect from 2 December 2002 (Police Reform Act 2002 (Commencement No 3) Order 2002, SI 2002/2750; Police Reform Act 2002, s 61(10)).
[3] Amendment: Subsections inserted: Anti-social Behaviour Act 2003, s 85(1), (4), subs (10A) with effect from 31 March 2004 (Anti-social Behaviour Act 2003 (Commencement No 2) Order 2004, SI 2004/690; subs (10B), with effect from 20 January 2004 (Anti-social Behaviour Act 2003 (Commencement No 1 and Transitional Provisions) Order 2003, SI 2003/3300).
[4] Amendment: Words substituted: Powers of Criminal Courts (Sentencing) Act 2000, s 165(1), Sch 9, para 192, with effect from 25 August 2000 (Powers of Criminal Courts (Sentencing) Act 2000, s 168(1)).
[5] Amendment: Definition inserted: Police Reform Act 2002, s 61(1), (9)(a), with effect from 2 December 2002 (Police Reform Act 2002 (Commencement No 3) Order 2002, SI 2002/2750; Police Reform Act 2002, s 61(10)).

(b) in relation to Wales, a county or county borough,

['policed premises' has the meaning given by section 53(3) of the British Transport Commission Act 1949][1].

[1A Power of Secretary of State to add to relevant authorities

The Secretary of State may by order provide that the chief officer of a body of constables maintained otherwise than by a police authority is, in such cases and circumstances as may be prescribed by the order, to be a relevant authority for the purposes of section 1 above.][2]

[1AA Individual support orders

(1) Where a court makes an anti-social behaviour order in respect of a defendant who is a child or young person when that order is made, it must consider whether the individual support conditions are fulfilled.

(2) If it is satisfied that those conditions are fulfilled, the court must make an order under this section ('an individual support order') which—

(a) requires the defendant to comply, for a period not exceeding six months, with such requirements as are specified in the order; and
(b) requires the defendant to comply with any directions given by the responsible officer with a view to the implementation of the requirements under paragraph (a) above.

(3) The individual support conditions are—

(a) that an individual support order would be desirable in the interests of preventing any repetition of the kind of behaviour which led to the making of the anti-social behaviour order;
(b) that the defendant is not already subject to an individual support order; and
(c) that the court has been notified by the Secretary of State that arrangements for implementing individual support orders are available in the area in which it appears to it that the defendant resides or will reside and the notice has not been withdrawn.

(4) If the court is not satisfied that the individual support conditions are fulfilled, it shall state in open court that it is not so satisfied and why it is not.

(5) The requirements that may be specified under subsection (2)(a) above are those that the court considers desirable in the interests of preventing any repetition of the kind of behaviour which led to the making of the anti-social behaviour order.

(6) Requirements included in an individual support order, or directions given under such an order by a responsible officer, may require the defendant to do all or any of the following things—

(a) to participate in activities specified in the requirements or directions at a time or times so specified;
(b) to present himself to a person or persons so specified at a place or places and at a time or times so specified;
(c) to comply with any arrangements for his education so specified.

---

[1] Amendment: Definition inserted: Police Reform Act 2002, s 61(1), (9)(b), with effect from 2 December 2002 (Police Reform Act 2002 (Commencement No 3) Order 2002, SI 2002/2750; Police Reform Act 2002, s 61(10)).

[2] Amendment: Section inserted: Police Reform Act 2002, s 62(1), with effect from 2 December 2002 (Police Reform Act 2002 (Commencement No 3) Order 2002, SI 2002/2750).

(7) But requirements included in, or directions given under, such an order may not require the defendant to attend (whether at the same place or at different places) on more than two days in any week; and 'week' here means a period of seven days beginning with a Sunday.

(8) Requirements included in, and directions given under, an individual support order shall, as far as practicable, be such as to avoid—

(a) any conflict with the defendant's religious beliefs; and
(b) any interference with the times, if any, at which he normally works or attends school or any other educational establishment.

(9) Before making an individual support order, the court shall obtain from a social worker of a local authority social services department or a member of a youth offending team any information which it considers necessary in order—

(a) to determine whether the individual support conditions are fulfilled, or
(b) to determine what requirements should be imposed by an individual support order if made,

and shall consider that information.

(10) In this section and section 1AB below 'responsible officer', in relation to an individual support order, means one of the following who is specified in the order, namely—

(a) a social worker of a local authority social services department;
(b) a person nominated by a person appointed as chief education officer under section 532 of the Education Act 1996 (c 56);
(c) a member of a youth offending team.][1]

[1AB Individual support orders: explanation, breach, amendment etc

(1) Before making an individual support order, the court shall explain to the defendant in ordinary language—

(a) the effect of the order and of the requirements proposed to be included in it;
(b) the consequences which may follow (under subsection (3) below) if he fails to comply with any of those requirements; and
(c) that the court has power (under subsection (6) below) to review the order on the application either of the defendant or of the responsible officer.

(2) The power of the Secretary of State under section 174(4) of the Criminal Justice Act 2003 includes power by order to—

(a) prescribe cases in which subsection (1) above does not apply; and
(b) prescribe cases in which the explanation referred to in that subsection may be made in the absence of the defendant, or may be provided in written form.

(3) If the person in respect of whom an individual support order is made fails without reasonable excuse to comply with any requirement included in the order, he is guilty of an offence and liable on summary conviction to a fine not exceeding—

(a) if he is aged 14 or over at the date of his conviction, £1,000;
(b) if he is aged under 14 then, £250.

(4) No referral order under section 16(2) or (3) of the Powers of Criminal Courts (Sentencing) Act 2000 (referral of young offenders to youth offender panels) may be made in respect of an offence under subsection (3) above.

---

[1] Amendment: Section inserted: Criminal Justice Act 2003, s 322, with effect from 1 May 2004 (Criminal Justice Act 2003 (Commencement No 3 and Transitional Provisions) Order 2004, SI 2004/829).

(5) If the anti-social behaviour order as a result of which an individual support order was made ceases to have effect, the individual support order (if it has not previously ceased to have effect) ceases to have effect when the anti-social behaviour order does.

(6) On an application made by complaint by—

(a) the person subject to an individual support order, or

(b) the responsible officer,

the court which made the individual support order may vary or discharge it by a further order.

(7) If the anti-social behaviour order as a result of which an individual support order was made is varied, the court varying the anti-social behaviour order may by a further order vary or discharge the individual support order.][1]

[1B Orders in county court proceedings

(1) This section applies to any proceedings in a county court ('the principal proceedings').

(2) If a relevant authority—

(a) is a party to the principal proceedings, and

(b) considers that a party to those proceedings is a person in relation to whom it would be reasonable for it to make an application under section 1,

it may make an application in those proceedings for an order under subsection (4).

(3) If a relevant authority—

(a) is not a party to the principal proceedings, and

(b) considers that a party to those proceedings is a person in relation to whom it would be reasonable for it to make an application under section 1,

it may make an application to be joined to those proceedings to enable it to apply for an order under subsection (4) and, if it is so joined, may apply for such an order.

[(3A) Subsection (3B) applies if a relevant authority is a party to the principal proceedings and considers—

(a) that a person who is not a party to the proceedings has acted in an anti-social manner, and

(b) that the person's anti-social acts are material in relation to the principal proceedings.

(3B) The relevant authority may—

(a) make an application for the person mentioned in subsection (3A)(a) to be joined to the principal proceedings to enable an order under subsection (4) to be made in relation to that person;

(b) if that person is so joined, apply for an order under subsection (4).

(3C) But a person must not be joined to proceedings in pursuance of subsection (3B) unless his anti-social acts are material in relation to the principal proceedings.][2]

---

[1] Amendment: Section inserted: Criminal Justice Act 2003, s 322, with effect from 1 May 2004 (Criminal Justice Act 2003 (Commencement No 3 and Transitional Provisions) Order 2004, SI 2004/829).

[2] Amendment: Subsections inserted: Anti-social Behaviour Act 2003, s 85(1), (5), with effect from 31 March 2004 in relation to persons aged 18 or over only (Anti-social Behaviour Act 2003 (Commencement No 2) Order 2004, SI 2004/690).

(4) If, on an application for an order under this subsection, it is proved that the conditions mentioned in section 1(1) are fulfilled as respects that other party, the court may make an order which prohibits him from doing anything described in the order.

(5) Subject to subsection (6), the *party to the principal proceedings* [person][1] against whom an order under this section has been made and the relevant authority on whose application that order was made may apply to the county court which made an order under this section for it to be varied or discharged by a further order.

(6) Except with the consent of the relevant authority and the person subject to the order, no order under this section shall be discharged before the end of the period of two years beginning with the date of service of the order.

(7) Subsections (5) to (7) and (10) to (12) of section 1 apply for the purposes of the making and effect of orders made under this section as they apply for the purposes of the making and effect of anti-social behaviour orders.][2]

[1C Orders on conviction in criminal proceedings

(1) This section applies where a person (the 'offender') is convicted of a relevant offence.

(2) If the court considers—

(a) that the offender has acted, at any time since the commencement date, in an anti-social manner, that is to say in a manner that caused or was likely to cause harassment, alarm or distress to one or more persons not of the same household as himself, and

(b) that an order under this section is necessary to protect persons in any place in England and Wales from further anti-social acts by him,

it may make an order which prohibits the offender from doing anything described in the order.

(3) The court may make an order under this section[—

(a) if the prosecutor asks it to do so, or

(b) if the court thinks it is appropriate to do so][3]

[(3A) For the purpose of deciding whether to make an order under this section the court may consider evidence led by the prosecution and the defence.

(3B) It is immaterial whether evidence led in pursuance of subsection (3A) would have been admissible in the proceedings in which the offender was convicted.][4]

(4) An order under this section shall not be made except—

(a) in addition to a sentence imposed in respect of the relevant offence; or

(b) in addition to an order discharging him conditionally.

(5) An order under this section takes effect on the day on which it is made, but the court may provide in any such order that such requirements of the order as it may specify shall,

---

[1] Amendment: Words in italics repealed and subsequent word in square brackets substituted: Anti-social Behaviour Act 2003, s 85(1), (6), with effect from 31 March 2004 in relation to persons aged 18 or over only (Anti-social Behaviour Act 2003 (Commencement No 2) Order 2004, SI 2004/690).

[2] Amendment: Section inserted: Police Reform Act 2002, s 63, with effect from 1 April 2003 (Police Reform Act 2002 (Commencement No 4) Order 2003, SI 2003/808).

[3] Amendment: Paragraphs substituted: Anti-social Behaviour Act 2003, s 86(1), with effect from 31 March 2004 (Anti-social Behaviour Act 2003 (Commencement No 2) Order 2004, SI 2004/690).

[4] Amendment: Subsections inserted: Anti-social Behaviour Act 2003, s 86(2), with effect from 31 March 2004 (Anti-social Behaviour Act 2003 (Commencement No 2) Order 2004, SI 2004/690).

during any period when the offender is detained in legal custody, be suspended until his release from that custody.

(6) An offender subject to an order under this section may apply to the court which made it for it to be varied or discharged.

(7) In the case of an order under this section made by a magistrates' court, the reference in subsection (6) to the court by which the order was made includes a reference to any magistrates' court acting for the same petty sessions area as that court.

(8) No application may be made under subsection (6) for the discharge of an order before the end of the period of two years beginning with the day on which the order takes effect.

(9) Subsections (7), (10) and (11) of section 1 apply for the purposes of the making and effect of orders made by virtue of this section as they apply for the purposes of the making and effect of anti-social behaviour orders.

[(9A) The council for the local government area in which a person in respect of whom an anti-social behaviour order has been made resides or appears to reside may bring proceedings under section 1(10) (as applied by subsection (9) above) for breach of an order under subsection (2) above.

(9B) Subsection (9C) applies in relation to proceedings in which an order under subsection (2) is made against a child or young person who is convicted of an offence.

(9C) In so far as the proceedings relate to the making of the order—

(a) section 49 of the Children and Young Persons Act 1933 (c 12) (restrictions on reports of proceedings in which children and young persons are concerned) does not apply in respect of the child or young person against whom the order is made;
(b) section 39 of that Act (power to prohibit publication of certain matter) does so apply.][1]

(10) In this section—

['child' and 'young person' have the same meaning as in the Children and Young Persons Act 1933 (c 12);][2]
'the commencement date' has the same meaning as in section 1 above;
'the court' in relation to an offender means—

(a) the court by or before which he is convicted of the relevant offence; or
(b) if he is committed to the Crown Court to be dealt with for that offence, the Crown Court; and

'relevant offence' means an offence committed after the coming into force of section 64 of the Police Reform Act 2002.][3]

[1D Interim orders

(1) The applications to which this section applies are—

(a) an application for an anti-social behaviour order; and
(b) an application for an order under section 1B.

---

[1] Amendment: Subsections inserted: Anti-social Behaviour Act 2003, s 86(3), subs (9A) with effect from 31 March 2004 (Anti-social Behaviour Act 2003 (Commencement No 2) Order 2004, SI 2004/690); subss (9B) and (9C) with effect from 20 January 2004 (Anti-social Behaviour Act 2003 (Commencement No 1 and Transitional Provisions) Order 2003, SI 2003/3300).

[2] Amendment: Definition inserted: Anti-social Behaviour Act 2003, s 86(4), with effect from 20 January 2004 (Anti-social Behaviour Act 2003 (Commencement No 1 and Transitional Provisions) Order 2003, SI 2003/3300).

[3] Amendment: Section inserted: Police Reform Act 2002, s 64, with effect from 2 December 2002 (Police Reform Act 2002 (Commencement No 3) Order 2002, SI 2002/2750).

(2) If, before determining an application to which this section applies, the court considers that it is just to make an order under this section pending the determination of that application ('the main application'), it may make such an order.

(3) An order under this section is an order which prohibits the defendant from doing anything described in the order.

(4) An order under this section—

(a) shall be for a fixed period;
(b) may be varied, renewed or discharged;
(c) shall, if it has not previously ceased to have effect, cease to have effect on the determination of the main application.

(5) Subsections (6), (8) and (10) to (12) of section 1 apply for the purposes of the making and effect of orders under this section as they apply for the purposes of the making and effect of anti-social behaviour orders.][1]

[1E Consultation requirements

(1) This section applies to—

(a) applications for an anti-social behaviour order; and
(b) applications for an order under section 1B.

(2) Before making an application to which this section applies, the council for a local government area shall consult the chief officer of police of the police force maintained for the police area within which that local government area lies.

(3) Before making an application to which this section applies, a chief officer of police shall consult the council for the local government area in which the person in relation to whom the application is to be made resides or appears to reside.

(4) Before making an application to which this section applies, a relevant authority other than a council for a local government area or a chief officer of police shall consult –

(a) the council for the local government area in which the person in relation to whom the application is to be made resides or appears to reside; and
(b) the chief officer of police of the police force maintained for the police area within which that local government area lies.][2]

[(5) Subsection (4)(a) does not apply if the relevant authority is a county council for a county in which there are no districts.][3]

2 ...[4]

2A ...[1]

---

[1] Amendment: Section inserted: Police Reform Act 2002, s 65(1), subss (1)(a), (2)–(5) with effect from 2 December 2002 (Police Reform Act 2002 (Commencement No 3) Order 2002, SI 2002/2750); subs (1)(b) with effect from 1 April 2003 (Police Reform Act 2002 (Commencement No 4) Order 2003, SI 2003/808).

[2] Amendment: Section inserted: Police Reform Act 2002, s 66, subss (1)(a), (2)–(4) with effect from 2 December 2002 (Police Reform Act 2002 (Commencement No 3) Order 2002, SI 2002/2750); subs (1)(b) with effect from 1 April 2003 (Police Reform Act 2002 (Commencement No 4) Order 2003, SI 2003/808).

[3] Amendment: Subsection inserted: Anti-social Behaviour Act 2003, s 85(1), (7), with effect from 20 January 2004 (Anti-social Behaviour Act 2003 (Commencement No 1 and Transitional Provisions) Order 2003, SI 2003/3300).

[4] Amendment: Section repealed: Sexual Offences Act 2003, ss 139, 140, Sch 6, para 38(1), (2), Sch 7, with effect from 1 May 2004 (Sexual Offences Act 2003 (Commencement) Order 2004, SI 2004/874).

2B ...[2]

3 ...[3]

4[4] Appeals against orders

(1) An appeal shall lie to the Crown Court against the making by a magistrates' court of an anti-social behaviour order[, an individual support order][5][, an order under section 1D above,][6] ...[7].

(2) On such an appeal the Crown Court—

(a) may make such orders as may be necessary to give effect to its determination of the appeal; and

(b) may also make such incidental or consequential orders as appear to it to be just.

(3) Any order of the Crown Court made on an appeal under this section (other than one directing that an application be re-heard by a magistrates' court) shall, for the purposes of section 1(8), [1AB(6)][8] ...[9], be treated as if it were an order of the magistrates' court from which the appeal was brought and not an order of the Crown Court.

Crime and disorder strategies

5[10] Authorities responsible for strategies

(1) Subject to the provisions of this section, the functions conferred by section 6 below shall be exercisable in relation to each local government area by the responsible authorities, that is to say—

(a) the council for the area and, where the area is a district and the council is not a unitary authority, the council for the county which includes the district; ...[11]
(b) every chief officer of police any part of whose police area lies within the area;
[(c) every police authority any part of whose police area so lies;
(d) every fire authority any part of whose area so lies;
(e) if the local government area is in England, every Primary Care Trust the whole or any part of whose area so lies; and

---

[1] Amendment: Section repealed: Sexual Offences Act 2003, ss 139, 140, Sch 6, para 38(1), (2), Sch 7, with effect from 1 May 2004 (Sexual Offences Act 2003 (Commencement) Order 2004, SI 2004/874).

[2] Amendment: Section repealed: Sexual Offences Act 2003, ss 139, 140, Sch 6, para 38(1), (2), Sch 7, with effect from 1 May 2004 (Sexual Offences Act 2003 (Commencement) Order 2004, SI 2004/874).

[3] Amendment: Section repealed: Sexual Offences Act 2003, ss 139, 140, Sch 6, para 38(1), (2), Sch 7, with effect from 1 May 2004 (Sexual Offences Act 2003 (Commencement) Order 2004, SI 2004/874).

[4] Commencement (in relation to sex offender orders): 1 December 1998 (SI 1998/2327); (for remaining purposes): 1 April 1999 (SI 1998/3263).

[5] Amendment: Words inserted: Criminal Justice Act 2003, s 323(1), (2)(a), with effect from 1 May 2004 (Criminal Justice Act 2003 (Commencement No 3 and Transitional Provisions) Order 2004, SI 2004/829).

[6] Amendment: Words inserted: Police Reform Act 2002, s 65(2), with effect from 2 December 2002 (Police Reform Act 2002 (Commencement No 3) Order 2002, SI 2002/2750).

[7] Amendment: Words repealed: Sexual Offences Act 2003, ss 139, 140, Sch 6, para 38(1), (3)(a), Sch 7, with effect from 1 May 2004 (Sexual Offences Act 2003 (Commencement) Order 2004, SI 2004/874).

[8] Amendment: Reference inserted: Criminal Justice Act 2003, s 323(1), (2)(b), with effect from 1 May 2004 (Criminal Justice Act 2003 (Commencement No 3 and Transitional Provisions) Order 2004, SI 2004/829).

[9] Amendment: Words repealed: Sexual Offences Act 2003, ss 139, 140, Sch 6, para 38(1), (3)(b), Sch 7, with effect from 1 May 2004 (Sexual Offences Act 2003 (Commencement) Order 2004, SI 2004/874).

[10] Commencement: 30 September 1998 (SI 1998/2327).

[11] Amendment: Word repealed: Police Reform Act 2002, s 107(2), Sch 8, with effect from 30 April 2004 (Police Reform Act 2002 (Commencement No 8) Order 2004, SI 2004/913).

(f) if the local government area is in Wales, every health authority the whole or any part of whose area so lies]¹.

[(1A) The Secretary of State may by order provide in relation to any two or more local government areas in England—

(a) that the functions conferred by sections 6 to 7 below are to be carried out in relation to those areas taken together as if they constituted only one area; and
(b) that the persons who for the purposes of this Chapter are to be taken to be responsible authorities in relation to the combined area are the persons who comprise every person who (apart from the order) would be a responsible authority in relation to any one or more of the areas included in the combined area.

(1B) The Secretary of State shall not make an order under subsection (1A) above unless—

(a) an application for the order has been made jointly by all the persons who would be the responsible authorities in relation to the combined area or the Secretary of State has first consulted those persons; and
(b) he considers it would be in the interests of reducing crime and disorder, or of combatting the misuse of drugs, to make the order.]²

(2) In exercising those functions, the responsible authorities shall act in co-operation with the following persons and bodies, namely—

[(b) every local probation board any part of whose area lies within the area;]³
(c) every person or body of a description which is for the time being prescribed by order of the Secretary of State under this subsection; [and
(d) where they are acting in relation to an area in Wales, every person or body which is of a description which is for the time being prescribed by an order under this subsection of the National Assembly for Wales;]⁴

and it shall be the duty of those persons and bodies to co-operate in the exercise by the responsible authorities of those functions.

(3) The responsible authorities shall also invite the participation in their exercise of those functions of at least one person or body of each description which is for the time being prescribed by order of the Secretary of State under this subsection [and, in the case of the responsible authorities for an area in Wales, of any person or body of a description for the time being prescribed by an order under this subsection of the National Assembly for Wales]⁵.

(4) In this section and sections 6 and 7 below 'local government area' means—

(a) in relation to England, each district or London borough, the City of London, the Isle of Wight and the Isles of Scilly;
(b) in relation to Wales, each county or county borough.

---

[1] Amendment: Paragraphs inserted: Police Reform Act 2002, s 97(1), (2), with effect from 30 April 2004 (Police Reform Act 2002 (Commencement No 8) Order 2004, SI 2004/913).

[2] Amendment: Subsections inserted in relation to England and prospectively inserted in relation to Wales: Police Reform Act 2002, s 97(1), (3), with effect from (in relation to England): 1 October 2002 (Police Reform Act 2002 (Commencement No 1) Order 2002, SI 2002/2306).

[3] Amendment: Paragraph substituted for paras (a), (b), as originally enacted: Police Reform Act 2002, s 97(1), (4)(a), with effect from 1 October 2002 (in relation to England) (Police Reform Act 2002 (Commencement No 1) Order 2002, SI 2002/2306); with effect from 1 April 2003 (in relation to Wales) (Police Reform Act 2002 (Commencement) (Wales) Order 2003, SI 2003/525).

[4] Amendment: Paragraph inserted: Police Reform Act 2002, s 97(1), (4)(b), with effect from 1 October 2002 (in relation to England) (Police Reform Act 2002 (Commencement No 1) Order 2002, SI 2002/2306); with effect from 1 April 2003 (in relation to Wales) (Police Reform Act 2002 (Commencement) (Wales) Order 2003, SI 2003/525).

[5] Amendment: Paragraph inserted: Police Reform Act 2002, s 97(1), (5), with effect from 1 April 2003 (in relation to Wales) (Police Reform Act 2002 (Commencement) (Wales) Order 2003, SI 2003/525); with effect from 23 February 2004 (in relation to England) (Police Reform Act 2002 (Commencement No 6) Order 2004, SI 2004/119).

[(5) In this section—

'fire authority' means—
- (a) any fire authority constituted by a combination scheme under the Fire Services Act 1947;
- (b) any metropolitan county fire and civil defence authority; or
- (c) the London Fire and Emergency Planning Authority; and

'police authority' means—
- (a) any police authority established under section 3 of the Police Act 1996; or
- (b) the Metropolitan Police Authority.][1]

6[2] Formulation and implementation of strategies

(1) The responsible authorities for a local government area shall, in accordance with the provisions of section 5 above and this section, formulate and implement, for each relevant period—

[(a) in the case of an area in England—

- (i) a strategy for the reduction of crime and disorder in the area; and
- (ii) a strategy for combating the misuse of drugs in the area;

and

(b) in the case of an area in Wales—

- (i) a strategy for the reduction of crime and disorder in the area; and
- (ii) a strategy for combating substance misuse in the area][3].

[(1A) In determining what matters to include or not to include in their strategy for combating substance misuse, the responsible authorities for an area in Wales shall have regard to any guidance issued for the purposes of this section by the National Assembly for Wales.][4]

(2) Before formulating a strategy, the responsible authorities shall—

[(a) carry out, taking due account of the knowledge and experience of persons in the area, a review—

- (i) in the case of an area in England, of the levels and patterns of crime and disorder in the area and of the level and patterns of the misuse of drugs in the area; and
- (ii) in the case of an area in Wales, of the levels and patterns of crime and disorder in the area and of the level and patterns of substance misuse in the area;][5]

(b) prepare an analysis of the results of that review;
(c) publish in the area a report of that analysis; and
(d) obtain the views on that report of persons or bodies in the area (including those of a

---

[1] Amendment: Subsection inserted: Police Reform Act 2002, s 97(1), (6), with effect from 1 April 2003 (in relation to local government areas in Wales) (Police Reform Act 2002 (Commencement) (Wales) Order 2003, SI 2003/525); 1 April 2003 (for remaining purposes) (Police Reform Act 2002 (Commencement No 4) Order 2004, SI 2003/808).

[2] Commencement: 30 September 1998 (SI 1998/2327).

[3] Amendment: Paragraphs substituted: Police Reform Act 2002, s 97(1), (7), with effect from 1 October 2002 (in relation to England) (Police Reform Act 2002 (Commencement No 1) Order 2002, SI 2002/2306); with effect from 1 April 2003 (in relation to Wales) (Police Reform Act 2002 (Commencement) (Wales) Order 2003, SI 2003/525).

[4] Amendment: Subsection inserted: Police Reform Act 2002, s 97(1), (8), from a date to be appointed, with effect from 1 April 2003 (in relation to Wales) (Police Reform Act 2002 (Commencement) (Wales) Order 2003, SI 2003/525); with effect from 23 February 2004 (in relation to England) (Police Reform Act 2002 (Commencement No 6) Order 2004, SI 2004/119).

[5] Amendment: Paragraph substituted: Police Reform Act 2002, s 97(1), (9), with effect from (in relation to England) 1 October 2002 (Police Reform Act 2002 (Commencement No 1) Order 2002, SI 2002/2306); with effect from 1 April 2003 (in relation to Wales) (Police Reform Act 2002 (Commencement) (Wales) Order 2003, SI 2003/525).

description prescribed by order under section 5(3) above), whether by holding public meetings or otherwise.

(3) In formulating a strategy, the responsible authorities shall have regard to the analysis prepared under subsection (2)(b) above and the views obtained under subsection (2)(d) above.

(4) A strategy shall include—

(a) objectives to be pursued by the responsible authorities, by co-operating persons or bodies or, under agreements with the responsible authorities, by other persons or bodies; and

(b) long-term and short-term performance targets for measuring the extent to which such objectives are achieved.

(5) After formulating a strategy, the responsible authorities shall publish in the area a document which includes details of—

(a) co-operating persons and bodies;
(b) the review carried out under subsection (2)(a) above;
(c) the report published under subsection (2)(c) above; and
(d) the strategy, including in particular—

   (i) the objectives mentioned in subsection (4)(a) above and, in each case, the authorities, persons or bodies by whom they are to be pursued; and
   (ii) the performance targets mentioned in subsection (4)(b) above.

(6) While implementing a strategy, the responsible authorities shall keep it under review with a view to monitoring its effectiveness and making any changes to it that appear necessary or expedient.

[(6A) Within one month of the end of each reporting period, the responsible authorities shall submit a report on the implementation of their strategies during that period—

(a) in the case of a report relating to the strategies for an area in England, to the Secretary of State; and

(b) in the case of a report relating to the strategies for an area in Wales, to the Secretary of State and to the National Assembly for Wales.][1]

(7) In this section—

'co-operating persons or bodies' means persons or bodies co-operating in the exercise of the responsible authorities' functions under this section;
'relevant period' means—

   (a) the period of three years beginning with such day as the Secretary of State may by order appoint; and
   (b) each subsequent period of three years.

['reporting period' means every period of one year which falls within a relevant period and which begins—

   (a) in the case of the first reporting period in the relevant period, with the day on which the relevant period begins; and
   (b) in any other case, with the day after the day on which the previous reporting period ends;

---

[1] Amendment: Subsection inserted: Police Reform Act 2002, s 97(1), (10), with effect from 1 October 2002 (in relation to England) (Police Reform Act 2002 (Commencement No 1) Order 2002, SI 2002/2306); with effect from 1 April 2003 (in relation to Wales) (Police Reform Act 2002 (Commencement) (Wales) Order 2003, SI 2003/525).

'substance misuse' includes the misuse of drugs or alcohol.]¹

[6A Powers of the Secretary of State and National Assembly for Wales

(1) The Secretary of State may, by order, require—

(a) the responsible authorities for local government areas to formulate any section 6 strategy of theirs for the reduction of crime and disorder so as to include, in particular, provision for the reduction of—

  (i) crime of a description specified in the order; or
  (ii) disorder of a description so specified.

(b) the responsible authorities for local government areas in England to prepare any section 6 strategy of theirs for combatting the misuse of drugs so as to include in it a strategy for combatting, in the area in question, such other forms of substance misuse as may be specified or described in the order.

(2) After formulating any section 6 strategy (whether in a case in which there has been an order under subsection or in any other case), the responsible authorities for a local government area shall send both—

(a) a copy of the strategy, and
(b) a copy of the document which they propose to publish under section 6(5),

to the Secretary of State.

(3) It shall be the duty of the responsible authorities, when preparing any document to be published under section 6(5), to have regard to any guidance issued by the Secretary of State as to the form and content of the documents to be so published.

(4) If the responsible authorities for a local government area propose to make any changes to a section 6 strategy of theirs, they shall send copies of the proposed changes to the Secretary of State.

(5) In subsections (2) to (4)—

(a) references to the Secretary of State, in relation to responsible authorities for local government areas in Wales shall have effect as references to the Secretary of State and the National Assembly for Wales; and

(b) accordingly, guidance issued for the purposes of subsection (3) in relation to local government areas in Wales must be issued by the Secretary of State and that Assembly acting jointly.

(6) In this section—

'responsible authorities' and 'local government area' have same meanings as in sections 5 and 6;

'section 6 strategy' means a strategy required to be formulated under section 6(1); and

'substance misuse' has the same meaning as in section 6.]²

---

[1] Amendment: Definitions inserted: Police Reform Act 2002, s 97(1), (11), with effect from 1 October 2002 (Police Reform Act 2002 (Commencement No 1) Order 2002, SI 2002/2306).

[2] Amendment: Section inserted: Police Reform Act 2002, s 98, with effect from (in relation to England): 1 October 2002 (Police Reform Act 2002 (Commencement No 1) Order 2002, SI 2002/2306); with effect from 1 April 2003 (in relation to Wales) (Police Reform Act 2002 (Commencement) (Wales) Order 2003, SI 2003/525).

7[1] Supplemental

(1) The responsible authorities for a local government area shall, whenever so required by the Secretary of State, submit to the Secretary of State a report on such matters connected with the exercise of their functions under section 6 above as may be specified in the requirement.

(2) A requirement under subsection (1) above may specify the form in which a report is to be given.

(3) The Secretary of State may arrange, or require the responsible authorities to arrange, for a report under subsection (1) above to be published in such manner as appears to him to be appropriate.

Youth crime and disorder

8[2] Parenting orders

(1) This section applies where, in any court proceedings—

(a) a child safety order is made in respect of a child;
(b) an anti-social behaviour order or sex offender order is made in respect of a child or young person;
(c) a child or young person is convicted of an offence; or
(d) a person is convicted of an offence under section 443 (failure to comply with school attendance order) or section 444 (failure to secure regular attendance at school of registered pupil) of the Education Act 1996.

(2) Subject to subsection (3) and section 9(1) below [and to section 19(5) of, and paragraph 13(5) of Schedule 1 to, the Powers of Criminal Courts (Sentencing) Act 2000][3], if in the proceedings the court is satisfied that the relevant condition is fulfilled, it may make a parenting order in respect of a person who is a parent or guardian of the child or young person or, as the case may be, the person convicted of the offence under section 443 or 444 ('the parent').

(3) A court shall not make a parenting order unless it has been notified by the Secretary of State that arrangements for implementing such orders are available in the area in which it appears to the court that the parent resides or will reside and the notice has not been withdrawn.

[(4) A parenting order is an order which requires the parent—

(a) to comply, for a period not exceeding twelve months, with such requirements as are specified in the order; and
(b) subject to subsection (5) below, to attend, for a concurrent period not exceeding three months, such counselling or guidance programme as may be specified in directions given by the responsible officer.

---

[1] Commencement: 30 September 1998: (SI 1998/2327).
[2] Commencement: 30 September 1998 (SI 1998/2327).
[3] Amendment: Words substituted: Powers of Criminal Courts (Sentencing) Act 2000, s 165(1), Sch 9, para 194, with effect from 25 August 2000 (Powers of Criminal Courts (Sentencing) Act 2000, ss 165(3), 168(1), Sch 11, Pt III, para 11(4)).

(5) A parenting order may, but need not, include such a requirement as is mentioned in subsection (4)(b) above in any case where a parenting order under this section or any other enactment has been made in respect of the parent on a previous occasion.][1]

(6) The relevant condition is that the parenting order would be desirable in the interests of preventing—

(a) in a case falling within paragraph (a) or (b) of subsection (1) above, any repetition of the kind of behaviour which led to the child safety order, anti-social behaviour order or sex offender order being made;

(b) in a case falling within paragraph (c) of that subsection, the commission of any further offence by the child or young person;

(c) in a case falling within paragraph (d) of that subsection, the commission of any further offence under section 443 or 444 of the Education Act 1996.

(7) The requirements that may be specified under subsection (4)(a) above are those which the court considers desirable in the interests of preventing any such repetition or, as the case may be, the commission of any such further offence.

[(7A) A counselling or guidance programme which a parent is required to attend by virtue of subsection (4)(b) above may be or include a residential course but only if the court is satisfied—

(a) that the attendance of the parent at a residential course is likely to be more effective than his attendance at a non-residential course in preventing any such repetition or, as the case may be, the commission of any such further offence, and

(b) that any interference with family life which is likely to result from the attendance of the parent at a residential course is proportionate in all the circumstances.][2]

(8) In this section and section 9 below 'responsible officer', in relation to a parenting order, means one of the following who is specified in the order, namely –

(a) [an officer of a local probation board][3];

(b) a social worker of a local authority social services department; and

[(bb) a person nominated by a person appointed as chief education officer under section 532 of the Education Act 1996;][4]

(c) a member of a youth offending team.

****

11[5] Child safety orders

(1) Subject to subsection (2) below, if a magistrates' court, on the application of a local authority, is satisfied that one or more of the conditions specified in subsection (3) below are fulfilled with respect to a child under the age of 10, it may make an order (a 'child safety order') which—

(a) places the child, for a period (not exceeding the permitted maximum) specified in the order, under the supervision of the responsible officer; and

---

[1] Amendment: Subsections substituted: Anti-social Behaviour Act 2003, s 18(1), (2), with effect from 27 February 2004 (Anti-social Behaviour Act 2003 (Commencement No 1 and Transitional Provisions) Order 2003, SI 2003/3300).

[2] Amendment: Subsection inserted: Anti-social Behaviour Act 2003, s 18(1), (3), with effect from 27 February 2004 (Anti-social Behaviour Act 2003 (Commencement No 1 and Transitional Provisions) Order 2003, SI 2003/3300).

[3] Amendment: Words substituted: Criminal Justice and Court Services Act 2000, s 74, Sch 7, Pt I, para 4(1)(a), (2), with effect from 1 April 2001 (Criminal Justice and Court Services Act 2000 (Commencement No 4) Order 2001, SI 2001/919).

[4] Amendment: Paragraph inserted: Criminal Justice and Court Services Act 2000, s 73, with effect from 1 April 2001 (Criminal Justice and Court Services Act 2000 (Commencement No 4) Order 2001, SI 2001/919).

[5] Commencement: 30 September 1998 (SI 1998/2327).

(b) requires the child to comply with such requirements as are so specified.

(2) A court shall not make a child safety order unless it has been notified by the Secretary of State that arrangements for implementing such orders are available in the area in which it appears that the child resides or will reside and the notice has not been withdrawn.

(3) The conditions are—

(a) that the child has committed an act which, if he had been aged 10 or over, would have constituted an offence;
(b) that a child safety order is necessary for the purpose of preventing the commission by the child of such an act as is mentioned in paragraph (a) above;
(c) that the child has contravened a ban imposed by a curfew notice; and
(d) that the child has acted in a manner that caused or was likely to cause harassment, alarm or distress to one or more persons not of the same household as himself.

(4) The maximum period permitted for the purposes of subsection (1)(a) above is three months or, where the court is satisfied that the circumstances of the case are exceptional, 12 months.

(5) The requirements that may be specified under subsection (1)(b) above are those which the court considers desirable in the interests of—

(a) securing that the child receives appropriate care, protection and support and is subject to proper control; or
(b) preventing any repetition of the kind of behaviour which led to the child safety order being made.

(6) Proceedings under this section or section 12 below shall be family proceedings for the purposes of the 1989 Act or section 65 of the Magistrates' Courts Act 1980 ('the 1980 Act'); and the standard of proof applicable to such proceedings shall be that applicable to civil proceedings.

(7) In this section 'local authority' has the same meaning as in the 1989 Act.

(8) In this section and section 12 below, 'responsible officer', in relation to a child safety order, means one of the following who is specified in the order, namely—

(a) a social worker of a local authority social services department; and
(b) a member of a youth offending team.

****

15[1] Contravention of curfew notices

(1) Subsections (2) and (3) below apply where a constable has reasonable cause to believe that a child is in contravention of a ban imposed by a curfew notice.

(2) The constable shall, as soon as practicable, inform the local authority for the area that the child has contravened the ban.

(3) The constable may remove the child to the child's place of residence unless he has reasonable cause to believe that the child would, if removed to that place, be likely to suffer significant harm.

(4) In subsection (1) of section 47 of the 1989 Act (local authority's duty to investigate)—

---

[1] Commencement: 30 September 1998 (SI 1998/2327).

(a) in paragraph (a), after sub-paragraph (ii) there shall be inserted the following sub-paragraph—

'(iii) has contravened a ban imposed by a curfew notice within the meaning of Chapter I of Part I of the Crime and Disorder Act 1998; or'; and

(b) at the end there shall be inserted the following paragraph—

'In the case of a child falling within paragraph (a)(iii) above, the enquiries shall be commenced as soon as practicable and, in any event, within 48 hours of the authority receiving the information.'

16[1] Removal of truants to designated premises etc

(1) This section applies where a local authority—

(a) designates premises in a police area ('designated premises') as premises to which children and young persons of compulsory school age may be removed under this section; and

(b) notifies the chief officer of police for that area of the designation.

(2) A police officer of or above the rank of superintendent may direct that the powers conferred on a constable by subsection (3) below—

(a) shall be exercisable as respects any area falling within the police area and specified in the direction; and

(b) shall be so exercisable during a period so specified;

and references in that subsection to a specified area and a specified period shall be construed accordingly.

(3) If a constable has reasonable cause to believe that a child or young person found by him in a public place in a specified area during a specified period—

(a) is of compulsory school age; and

(b) is absent from a school without lawful authority,

the constable may remove the child or young person to designated premises, or to the school from which he is so absent.

[(3A) The power of a police officer of or above the rank of superintendent under subsection (2) to specify any area falling within a police area shall be exercisable by such an officer who is a member of the British Transport Police as if the reference in that subsection to an area in the police area were a reference to—

(a) any area in or in the vicinity of any policed premises; or

(b) the whole or any part of any such premises;

and references in subsection (3) to the specified area shall have effect accordingly.][2]

(4) A child's or young person's absence from a school shall be taken to be without lawful authority unless it falls within subsection (3) (leave, sickness, unavoidable cause or day set apart for religious observance) of section 444 of the Education Act 1996.

---

[1] Commencement: 1 December 1998 (SI 1998/2327).

[2] Amendment: Subsection inserted: Police Reform Act 2002, s 75(1), with effect from 1 October 2002 (Police Reform Act 2002 (Commencement No 1) Order 2002, SI 2002/2306).

(5) In this section—

['British Transport Police' means the force of constables appointed under section 53 of the British Transport Commission Act 1949;][1]
'local authority' means—

    (a)   in relation to England, a county council, a district council whose district does not form part of an area that has a county council, a London borough council or the Common Council of the City of London;

    (b)   in relation to Wales, a county council or a county borough council;

['policed premises' has the meaning given by section 53(3) of the British Transport Commission Act 1949;][2]
'public place' has the same meaning as in section 14 above;
'school' has the same meaning as in the Education Act 1996.

Miscellaneous and supplemental

17[3] Duty to consider crime and disorder implications

(1) Without prejudice to any other obligation imposed on it, it shall be the duty of each authority to which this section applies to exercise its various functions with due regard to the likely effect of the exercise of those functions on, and the need to do all that it reasonably can to prevent, crime and disorder in its area.

(2) This section applies to a local authority, a joint authority, [the London Fire and Emergency Planning Authority,][4] [a fire authority constituted by a combination scheme under the Fire Services Act 1947,][5] a police authority, a National Park authority and the Broads Authority.

(3) In this section—

'local authority' means a local authority within the meaning given by section 270(1) of the Local Government Act 1972 or the Common Council of the City of London;
'joint authority' has the same meaning as in the Local Government Act 1985;
'National Park authority' means an authority established under section 63 of the Environment Act 1995.

****

---

[1] Amendment: Definition inserted: Police Reform Act 2002, s 75(2)(a), with effect from 1 October 2002 (Police Reform Act 2002 (Commencement No 1) Order 2002, SI 2002/2306).
[2] Amendment: Definition inserted: Police Reform Act 2002, s 75(2)(b), with effect from 1 October 2002 (Police Reform Act 2002 (Commencement No 1) Order 2002, SI 2002/2306).
[3] Commencement: 30 September 1998 (SI 1998/2327).
[4] Amendment: Words inserted: Greater London Authority Act 1999, s 328, Sch 29, Pt I, para 63, with effect from 3 July 2000 (Greater London Authority Act 1999 (Commencement No 5 and Appointment of Reconstitution Day) Order 2000, SI 2000/1094).
[5] Amendment: Words inserted: Police Reform Act 2002, s 97(1), (12), with effect from 1 April 2003 (Police Reform Act 2002 (Commencement No 4) Order 2003, SI 2003/808).

PART V
Miscellaneous and Supplemental

****

Supplemental

114[1] Orders and regulations

(1) Any power of a Minister of the Crown [or of the National Assembly for Wales][2] to make an order or regulations under this Act—

(a) is exercisable by statutory instrument; and
(b) includes power to make such transitional provision as appears to him necessary or expedient in connection with any provision made by the order or regulations.

(2) A statutory instrument containing an order under section [1A,][3] [5(1A), (2) or (3), 6A(1) or 10(6) above (other than one made by the National Assembly for Wales), or containing][4] regulations under paragraph 1 of Schedule 3 to this Act, shall be subject to annulment in pursuance of a resolution of either House of Parliament.

(3) No order under section [38(5) or 41(6)][5] above shall be made unless a draft of the order has been laid before and approved by a resolution of each House of Parliament.

115[6] Disclosure of information

(1) Any person who, apart from this subsection, would not have power to disclose information—

(a) to a relevant authority; or
(b) to a person acting on behalf of such an authority,

shall have power to do so in any case where the disclosure is necessary or expedient for the purposes of any provision of this Act.

(2) In subsection (1) above 'relevant authority' means—

(a) the chief officer of police for a police area in England and Wales;
(b) the chief constable of a police force maintained under the Police (Scotland) Act 1967;
(c) a police authority within the meaning given by section 101(1) of the Police Act 1996;
(d) a local authority, that is to say—

   (i) in relation to England, a county council, a district council, a London borough council[, a parish council][7] or the Common Council of the City of London;

---

[1] Commencement: 1 August 1998 (SI 1998/1883).
[2] Amendment: Words inserted: Police Reform Act 2002, s 97(1), (13)(a), with effect from 1 October 2002 (Police Reform Act 2002 (Commencement No 1) Order 2002, SI 2002/2306).
[3] Amendment: Reference inserted: Police Reform Act 2002, s 62(2), with effect from 2 December 2002 (Police Reform Act 2002 (Commencement No 3) Order 2002, SI 2002/2750).
[4] Amendment: Words substituted: Police Reform Act 2002, s 97(1), (13)(b), with effect from 1 October 2002 (Police Reform Act 2002 (Commencement No 1) Order 2002, SI 2002/2306).
[5] Amendment: Words substituted: Powers of Criminal Courts (Sentencing) Act 2000, s 165(1), Sch 9, para 199, with effect from 25 August 2000 (Powers of Criminal Courts (Sentencing) Act 2000, s 168(1)).
[6] Commencement: 30 September 1998 (SI 1998/2327).
[7] Amendment: Words inserted: Police Reform Act 2002, s 97(1), (14)(a), with effect from 1 October 2002 (Police Reform Act 2002 (Commencement No 1) Order 2002, SI 2002/2306).

(ii) in relation to Wales, a county council [, a county borough council or a community council]¹;

(iii) in relation to Scotland, a council constituted under section 2 of the Local Government etc (Scotland) Act 1994;

(e) a [local probation board]² in England and Wales;

[(ea) a Strategic Health Authority;]³

(f) a health authority;

[(g) a Primary Care Trust]⁴.

---

[1] Amendment: Words substituted: Police Reform Act 2002, s 97(1), (14)(b), with effect from 1 October 2002 (Police Reform Act 2002 (Commencement No 1) Order 2002, SI 2002/2306).

[2] Amendment: Words substituted: Criminal Justice and Court Services Act 2000, s 74, Sch 7, Pt II, paras 150, 151, with effect from 1 April 2001 (Criminal Justice and Court Services Act 2000 (Commencement No 4) Order 2001, SI 2001/919).

[3] Amendment: Paragraph inserted: National Health Service Reform and Health Care Professions Act 2002 (Supplementary, Consequential etc Provisions) Regulations 2002, SI 2002/2469, reg 4, Sch 1, Pt 1, para 25(1), (6), with effect from 1 October 2002.

[4] Amendment: Paragraph inserted: Health Act 1999 (Supplementary, Consequential etc Provisions) Order 2000, SI 2000/90, arts 2(1), 3(1), Sch 1, para 35(1), (7), with effect from 8 February 2000.

(B) CIVIL EVIDENCE ACT 1995

Admissibility of hearsay evidence

1[1] Admissibility of hearsay evidence

(1) In civil proceedings evidence shall not be excluded on the ground that it is hearsay.

(2) In this Act—

(a) 'hearsay' means a statement made otherwise than by a person while giving oral evidence in the proceedings which is tendered as evidence of the matters stated; and
(b) references to hearsay include hearsay of whatever degree.

(3) Nothing in this Act affects the admissibility of evidence admissible apart from this section.

(4) The provisions of sections 2 to 6 (safeguards and supplementary provisions relating to hearsay evidence) do not apply in relation to hearsay evidence admissible apart from this section, notwithstanding that it may also be admissible by virtue of this section.

Safeguards in relation to hearsay evidence

2[2] Notice of proposal to adduce hearsay evidence

(1) A party proposing to adduce hearsay evidence in civil proceedings shall, subject to the following provisions of this section, give to the other party or parties to the proceedings—

(a) such notice (if any) of that fact, and
(b) on request, such particulars of or relating to the evidence,

as is reasonable and practicable in the circumstances for the purpose of enabling him or them to deal with any matters arising from its being hearsay.

(2) Provision may be made by rules of court—

(a) specifying classes of proceedings or evidence in relation to which subsection (1) does not apply, and
(b) as to the manner in which (including the time within which) the duties imposed by that subsection are to be complied with in the cases where it does apply.

(3) Subsection (1) may also be excluded by agreement of the parties; and compliance with the duty to give notice may in any case be waived by the person to whom notice is required to be given.

(4) A failure to comply with subsection (1), or with rules under subsection (2)(b), does not affect the admissibility of the evidence but may be taken into account by the court—

(a) in considering the exercise of its powers with respect to the course of proceedings and costs, and
(b) as a matter adversely affecting the weight to be given to the evidence in accordance with section 4.

---

[1] Commencement: 31 January 1997 (SI 1996/3217).
[2] Commencement: 31 January 1997 (SI 1996/3217).

3[1] Power to call witness for cross-examination on hearsay statement

Rules of court may provide that where a party to civil proceedings adduces hearsay evidence of a statement made by a person and does not call that person as a witness, any other party to the proceedings may, with the leave of the court, call that person as a witness and cross-examine him on the statement as if he had been called by the first-mentioned party and as if the hearsay statement were his evidence in chief.

4[2] Considerations relevant to weighing of hearsay evidence

(1) In estimating the weight (if any) to be given to hearsay evidence in civil proceedings the court shall have regard to any circumstances from which any inference can reasonably be drawn as to the reliability or otherwise of the evidence.

(2) Regard may be had, in particular, to the following—

(a) whether it would have been reasonable and practicable for the party by whom the evidence was adduced to have produced the maker of the original statement as a witness;

(b) whether the original statement was made contemporaneously with the occurrence or existence of the matters stated;

(c) whether the evidence involves multiple hearsay;

(d) whether any person involved had any motive to conceal or misrepresent matters;

(e) whether the original statement was an edited account, or was made in collaboration with another or for a particular purpose;

(f) whether the circumstances in which the evidence is adduced as hearsay are such as to suggest an attempt to prevent proper evaluation of its weight.

Supplementary provisions as to hearsay evidence

5[3] Competence and credibility

(1) Hearsay evidence shall not be admitted in civil proceedings if or to the extent that it is shown to consist of, or to be proved by means of, a statement made by a person who at the time he made the statement was not competent as a witness.

For this purpose 'not competent as a witness' means suffering from such mental or physical infirmity, or lack of understanding, as would render a person incompetent as a witness in civil proceedings; but a child shall be treated as competent as a witness if he satisfies the requirements of section 96(2)(a) and (b) of the Children Act 1989 (conditions for reception of unsworn evidence of child).

(2) Where in civil proceedings hearsay evidence is adduced and the maker of the original statement, or of any statement relied upon to prove another statement, is not called as a witness—

(a) evidence which if he had been so called would be admissible for the purpose of attacking or supporting his credibility as a witness is admissible for that purpose in the proceedings; and

(b) evidence tending to prove that, whether before or after he made the statement, he made any other statement inconsistent with it is admissible for the purpose of showing that he had contradicted himself.

---

[1] Commencement: 31 January 1997 (SI 1996/3217).
[2] Commencement: 31 January 1997 (SI 1996/3217).
[3] Commencement: 31 January 1997 (SI 1996/3217).

Provided that evidence may not be given of any matter of which, if he had been called as a witness and had denied that matter in cross-examination, evidence could not have been adduced by the cross-examining party.

6[1] Previous statements of witnesses

(1) Subject as follows, the provisions of this Act as to hearsay evidence in civil proceedings apply equally (but with any necessary modifications) in relation to a previous statement made by a person called as a witness in the proceedings.

(2) A party who has called or intends to call a person as a witness in civil proceedings may not in those proceedings adduce evidence of a previous statement made by that person, except—

(a) with the leave of the court, or
(b) for the purpose of rebutting a suggestion that his evidence has been fabricated.

This shall not be construed as preventing a witness statement (that is, a written statement of oral evidence which a party to the proceedings intends to lead) from being adopted by a witness in giving evidence or treated as his evidence.

(3) Where in the case of civil proceedings section 3, 4 or 5 of the Criminal Procedure Act 1865 applies, which make provision as to—

(a) how far a witness may be discredited by the party producing him,
(b) the proof of contradictory statements made by a witness, and
(c) cross-examination as to previous statements in writing,

this Act does not authorise the adducing of evidence of a previous inconsistent or contradictory statement otherwise than in accordance with those sections.

This is without prejudice to any provision made by rules of court under section 3 above (power to call witness for cross-examination on hearsay statement).

(4) Nothing in this Act affects any of the rules of law as to the circumstances in which, where a person called as a witness in civil proceedings is cross-examined on a document used by him to refresh his memory, that document may be made evidence in the proceedings.

(5) Nothing in this section shall be construed as preventing a statement of any description referred to above from being admissible by virtue of section 1 as evidence of the matters stated.

7[2] Evidence formerly admissible at common law

(1) The common law rule effectively preserved by section 9(1) and (2)(a) of the Civil Evidence Act 1968 (admissibility of admissions adverse to a party) is superseded by the provisions of this Act.

(2) The common law rules effectively preserved by section 9(1) and (2)(b) to (d) of the Civil Evidence Act 1968, that is, any rule of law whereby in civil proceedings—

(a) published works dealing with matters of a public nature (for example, histories, scientific works, dictionaries and maps) are admissible as evidence of facts of a public nature stated in them,
(b) public documents (for example, public registers, and returns made under public authority with respect to matters of public interest) are admissible as evidence of facts stated in them, or

---

[1] Commencement: 31 January 1997 (SI 1996/3217).
[2] Commencement: 31 January 1997 (SI 1996/3217).

(c) records (for example, the records of certain courts, treaties, Crown grants, pardons and commissions) are admissible as evidence of facts stated in them,

shall continue to have effect.

(3) The common law rules effectively preserved by section 9(3) and (4) of the Civil Evidence Act 1968, that is, any rule of law whereby in civil proceedings—

(a) evidence of a person's reputation is admissible for the purpose of proving his good or bad character, or
(b) evidence of reputation or family tradition is admissible –

 (i) for the purpose of proving or disproving pedigree or the existence of a marriage, or
 (ii) for the purpose of proving or disproving the existence of any public or general right or of identifying any person or thing,

shall continue to have effect in so far as they authorise the court to treat such evidence as proving or disproving that matter.

Where any such rule applies, reputation or family tradition shall be treated for the purposes of this Act as a fact and not as a statement or multiplicity of statements about the matter in question.

(4) The words in which a rule of law mentioned in this section is described are intended only to identify the rule and shall not be construed as altering it in any way.

Other matters

8[1] Proof of statements contained in documents

(1) Where a statement contained in a document is admissible as evidence in civil proceedings, it may be proved—

(a) by the production of that document, or
(b) whether or not that document is still in existence, by the production of a copy of that document or of the material part of it,

authenticated in such manner as the court may approve.

(2) It is immaterial for this purpose how many removes there are between a copy and the original.

9[2] Proof of records of business or public authority

(1) A document which is shown to form part of the records of a business or public authority may be received in evidence in civil proceedings without further proof.

(2) A document shall be taken to form part of the records of a business or public authority if there is produced to the court a certificate to that effect signed by an officer of the business or authority to which the records belong.

For this purpose—

(a) a document purporting to be a certificate signed by an officer of a business or public authority shall be deemed to have been duly given by such an officer and signed by him; and
(b) a certificate shall be treated as signed by a person if it purports to bear a facsimile of his signature.

---

[1] Commencement: 31 January 1997 (SI 1996/3217).
[2] Commencement: 31 January 1997 (SI 1996/3217).

(3) The absence of an entry in the records of a business or public authority may be proved in civil proceedings by affidavit of an officer of the business or authority to which the records belong.

(4) In this section—

'records' means records in whatever form;
'business' includes any activity regularly carried on over a period of time, whether for profit or not, by any body (whether corporate or not) or by an individual;
'officer' includes any person occupying a responsible position in relation to the relevant activities of the business or public authority or in relation to its records; and
'public authority' includes any public or statutory undertaking, any government department and any person holding office under Her Majesty.

(5) The court may, having regard to the circumstances of the case, direct that all or any of the above provisions of this section do not apply in relation to a particular document or record, or description of documents or records.

10[1] *Admissibility and proof of Ogden Tables*

(1) The actuarial tables (together with explanatory notes) for use in personal injury and fatal accident cases issued from time to time by the Government Actuary's Department are admissible in evidence for the purpose of assessing, in an action for personal injury, the sum to be awarded as general damages for future pecuniary loss.

(2) They may be proved by the production of a copy published by Her Majesty's Stationery Office.

(3) For the purposes of this section—

(a) 'personal injury' includes any disease and any impairment of a person's physical or mental condition; and

(b) 'action for personal injury' includes an action brought by virtue of the Law Reform (Miscellaneous Provisions) Act 1934 or the Fatal Accidents Act 1976.[2]

General

11[3] Meaning of 'civil proceedings'

In this Act 'civil proceedings' means civil proceedings, before any tribunal, in relation to which the strict rules of evidence apply, whether as a matter of law or by agreement of the parties. References to 'the court' and 'rules of court' shall be construed accordingly.

12[4] Provisions as to rules of court

(1) Any power to make rules of court regulating the practice or procedure of the court in relation to civil proceedings includes power to make such provision as may be necessary or expedient for carrying into effect the provisions of this Act.

(2) Any rules of court made for the purposes of this Act as it applies in relation to proceedings in the High Court apply, except in so far as their operation is excluded by agreement, to arbitration proceedings to which this Act applies, subject to such modifications as may be appropriate.

---

[1] Commencement: Not yet in force.
[2] Prospective amendment: Section prospectively repealed in relation to Northern Ireland with savings by Civil Evidence (Northern Ireland) Order 1997, SI 1997/2983, art 13(2), Sch 2, from a date to be appointed.
[3] Commencement: 31 January 1997 (SI 1996/3217).
[4] Commencement: 31 January 1997 (SI 1996/3217).

Any question arising as to what modifications are appropriate shall be determined, in default of agreement, by the arbitrator or umpire, as the case may be.

13[1] Interpretation

In this Act—

'civil proceedings' has the meaning given by section 11 and 'court' and 'rules of court' shall be construed in accordance with that section;

'document' means anything in which information of any description is recorded, and 'copy', in relation to a document, means anything onto which information recorded in the document has been copied, by whatever means and whether directly or indirectly;

'hearsay' shall be construed in accordance with section 1(2);

'oral evidence' includes evidence which, by reason of a defect of speech or hearing, a person called as a witness gives in writing or by signs;

'the original statement', in relation to hearsay evidence, means the underlying statement (if any) by—

(a) in the case of evidence of fact, a person having personal knowledge of that fact, or

(b) in the case of evidence of opinion, the person whose opinion it is; and

'statement' means any representation of fact or opinion, however made.

14[2] Savings

(1) Nothing in this Act affects the exclusion of evidence on grounds other than that it is hearsay.

This applies whether the evidence falls to be excluded in pursuance of any enactment or rule of law, for failure to comply with rules of court or an order of the court, or otherwise.

(2) Nothing in this Act affects the proof of documents by means other than those specified in section 8 or 9.

(3) Nothing in this Act affects the operation of the following enactments –

(a) section 2 of the Documentary Evidence Act 1868 (mode of proving certain official documents);

(b) section 2 of the Documentary Evidence Act 1882 (documents printed under the superintendence of Stationery Office);

(c) section 1 of the Evidence (Colonial Statutes) Act 1907 (proof of statutes of certain legislatures);

(d) section 1 of the Evidence (Foreign, Dominion and Colonial Documents) Act 1933 (proof and effect of registers and official certificates of certain countries);

(e) section 5 of the Oaths and Evidence (Overseas Authorities and Countries) Act 1963 (provision in respect of public registers of other countries).

15[3] Consequential amendments and repeals

(1) The enactments specified in Schedule 1 are amended in accordance with that Schedule, the amendments being consequential on the provisions of this Act.

(2) The enactments specified in Schedule 2 are repealed to the extent specified.

---

[1] Commencement: 31 January 1997 (SI 1996/3217).
[2] Commencement: 31 January 1997 (SI 1996/3217).
[3] Commencement: 31 January 1997 (SI 1996/3217).

16[1] Short title, commencement and extent

(1) This Act may be cited as the Civil Evidence Act 1995.

(2) The provisions of this Act come into force on such day as the Lord Chancellor may appoint by order made by statutory instrument, and different days may be appointed for different provisions and for different purposes.

[(3) Subject to subsection (3A), the provisions of this Act shall not apply in relation to proceedings begun before commencement.]

[(3A) Transitional provisions for the application of the provisions of this Act to proceedings begun before commencement may be made by rules of court or practice directions.][2]

(4) This Act extends to England and Wales.

(5) *Section 10 (admissibility and proof of Ogden Tables) also extends to Northern Ireland.*

As it extends to Northern Ireland, the following shall be substituted for subsection (3)(b)—

> *'(b) "action for personal injury" includes an action brought by virtue of the Law Reform (Miscellaneous Provisions) (Northern Ireland) Act 1937 or the Fatal Accidents (Northern Ireland) Order 1977, SI 1977/1251.'*[3]

(6) The provisions of Schedules 1 and 2 (consequential amendments and repeals) have the same extent as the enactments respectively amended or repealed.

---

[1] Commencement: Subsections (1), (2), (4), (6): 31 January 1997 (SI 1996/3217). Subsection (5) not yet in force.

[2] Amendment: Subsection (3) substituted and subs (3A) inserted by Civil Procedure (Modification of Enactments) Order 1999, SI 1999/1217, arts 2, 4, with effect from 26 April 1999.

[3] Amendment: Subsection (5) prospectively repealed in relation to Northern Ireland with savings by Civil Evidence (Northern Ireland) Order 1997, SI 1997/2983, art 13(2), Sch 2, from a date to be appointed.

(C) MAGISTRATES' COURTS (HEARSAY EVIDENCE IN CIVIL PROCEEDINGS) RULES 1999, SI 1999/681

1[1] Citation and commencement

These Rules may be cited as the Magistrates' Courts (Hearsay Evidence in Civil Proceedings) Rules 1999 and shall come into force on 1st April 1999.

2[2] Application and interpretation

(1) In these Rules, the '1995 Act' means the Civil Evidence Act 1995.

(2) In these Rules—
'hearsay evidence' means evidence consisting of hearsay within the meaning of section 1(2) of the 1995 Act;
'hearsay notice' means a notice under section 2 of the 1995 Act.

(3) These Rules shall apply to hearsay evidence in civil proceedings in magistrates' courts.

3[3] Hearsay notices

(1) Subject to paragraphs (2) and (3), a party who desires to give hearsay evidence at the hearing must, not less than 21 days before the date fixed for the hearing, serve a hearsay notice on every other party and file a copy in the court by serving it on the [justices' chief executive].[4]

(2) Subject to paragraph (3), the court or the justices' clerk may make a direction substituting a different period of time for the service of the hearsay notice under paragraph (1) on the application of a party to the proceedings.

(3) The court may make a direction under paragraph (2) of its own motion.

(4) A hearsay notice must—

(a) state that it is a hearsay notice;
(b) identify the proceedings in which the hearsay evidence is to be given;
(c) state that the party proposes to adduce hearsay evidence;
(d) identify the hearsay evidence;
(e) identify the person who made the statement which is to be given in evidence; and
(f) state why that person will not be called to give oral evidence.

(5) A single hearsay notice may deal with the hearsay evidence of more than one witness.

4[5] Power to call witness for cross-examination on hearsay evidence

(1) Where a party tenders as hearsay evidence a statement made by a person but does not propose to call the person who made the statement to give evidence, the court may, on

---

[1] Commencement: 1 April 1999 (r 1).
[2] Commencement: 1 April 1999 (r 1).
[3] Commencement: 1 April 1999 (r 1).
[4] Amendment: In para (1), words substituted by Magistrates' Courts (Transfer of Justices' Clerks' Functions) (Miscellaneous Amendments) Rules 2001, SI 2001/615, r 2(xxxiv), Sch, para 141, with effect from 1 April 2001.
[5] Commencement: 1 April 1999 (r 1).

application, allow another party to call and cross-examine the person who made the statement on its contents.

(2) An application under paragraph (1) must—

(a) be served on the [justices' chief executive] with sufficient copies for all other parties;

(b) unless the court otherwise directs, be made not later than 7 days after service of the hearsay notice; and

(c) give reasons why the person who made the statement should be cross-examined on its contents.

[(3) On receipt of an application under paragraph (1)—

(a) the justices' clerk must—

 (i) unless the court otherwise directs, allow sufficient time for the applicant to comply with paragraph (4); and

 (ii) fix the date, time and place of the hearing; and

(b) the justices' chief executive must—

 (i) endorse the date, time and place of the hearing on the copies of the application filed by the applicant; and

 (ii) return the copies to the applicant forthwith.]

(4) Subject to paragraphs (5) and (6), on receipt of the copies from the [justices' chief executive] under paragraph (3)(c), the applicant must serve a copy on every other party giving not less than 3 days' notice of the hearing of the application.

(5) The court or the justices' clerk may give directions as to the manner in which service under paragraph (4) is to be effected and may, subject to the [justices' chief executive's][1] giving notice to the applicant, alter or dispense with the notice requirement under paragraph (4) if the court or the justices' clerk, as the case may be, considers it is in the interests of justice to do so.

(6) The court may hear an application under paragraph (1) ex parte if it considers it is in the interests of justice to do so.

(7) Subject to paragraphs (5) and (6), where an application under paragraph (1) is made, the applicant must file with the court a statement at or before the hearing of the application that service of a copy of the application has been effected on all other parties and the statement must indicate the manner, date, time and address at which the document was served.

(8) The court must notify all parties of its decision on an application under paragraph (1).

5[2] Credibility and previous inconsistent statements

(1) If—

(a) a party tenders as hearsay evidence a statement made by a person but does not call the person who made the statement to give oral evidence, and

(b) another party wishes to attack the credibility of the person who made the statement or allege that the person who made the statement made any other statement inconsistent with it,

that other party must notify the party tendering the hearsay evidence of his intention.

(2) Unless the court or the justices' clerk otherwise directs, a notice under paragraph (1) must be given not later than 7 days after service of the hearsay notice and, in addition to the

---

[1] Amendment: Words substituted in paras (2)(a), (4), words inserted in para (5), and para (3) substituted by Magistrates' Courts (Transfer of Justices' Clerks' Functions) (Miscellaneous Amendments) Rules 2001, SI 2001/615, r 2(xxxiv), Sch, paras 141–143, with effect from 1 April 2001.

[2] Commencement: 1 April 1999 (r 1).

requirements in paragraph (1), must be served on every other party and a copy filed in the court.

(3) If, on receipt of a notice under paragraph (1), the party referred to in paragraph (1)(a) calls the person who made the statement to be tendered as hearsay evidence to give oral evidence, he must, unless the court otherwise directs, notify the court and all other parties of his intention.

(4) Unless the court or the justices' clerk otherwise directs, a notice under paragraph (3) must be given not later than 7 days after the service of the notice under paragraph (1).

6[1] Service

(1) Where service of a document is required by these Rules it may be effected, unless the contrary is indicated—

(a) if the person to be served is not known by the person serving to be acting by solicitor—

    (i) by delivering it to him personally, or

    (ii) by delivering at, or by sending it by first-class post to, his residence or his last known residence, or

(b) if the person to be served is known by the person serving to be acting by solicitor—

    (i) by delivering the document at, or sending it by first-class post to, the solicitor's address for service,

    (ii) where the solicitor's address for service includes a numbered box at a document exchange, by leaving the document at that document exchange or at a document exchange which transmits documents on every business day to that document exchange, or

    (iii) by sending a legible copy of the document by facsimile transmission to the solicitor's office.

(2) In this rule, 'first-class post' means first-class post which has been pre-paid or in respect of which pre-payment is not required.

(3) A document shall, unless the contrary is proved, be deemed to have been served—

(a) in the case of service by first-class post, on the second business day after posting,

(b) in the case of service in accordance with paragraph (1)(b)(ii), on the second business day after the day on which it is left at the document exchange, and

(c) in the case of service in accordance with paragraph (1)(b)(iii), where it is transmitted on a business day before 4 pm, on that day and in any other case, on the next business day.

(4) In this rule, 'business day' means any day other than—

(a) a Saturday, Sunday, Christmas Day or Good Friday; or

(b) a bank holiday under the Banking and Financial Dealings Act 1971, in England and Wales.

7[2] Amendment to the Justices' Clerks Rules 1970

The Justices' Clerks Rules 1970 shall be amended by the insertion, after paragraph 18 of the Schedule, of the following paragraph—

---

[1] Commencement: 1 April 1999 (r 1).
[2] Commencement: 1 April 1999 (r 1).

'19

The giving, variation or revocation of directions in accordance with rules 3(2), 4(5), 5(2) and (4) of the Magistrates' Courts (Hearsay Evidence in Civil Proceedings) Rules 1999.'.

(D) MAGISTRATES' COURTS (ANTI-SOCIAL BEHAVIOUR ORDERS) RULES 2002, SI 2002/2784[1]

2[2] Citation, interpretation and commencement

(1) These Rules may be cited as the Magistrates' Courts (Anti-Social Behaviour Orders) Rules 2002 and shall come into force on 2nd December 2002.

(2) In these Rules any reference to a numbered section is a reference to the section so numbered in the Crime and Disorder Act 1998, any reference to a 'form' includes a form to like effect, and, unless otherwise stated, reference to a 'Schedule' is a reference to a Schedule hereto.

3[3] Transitional provisions

After these Rules come into force, rules 6 and 7 of, and Schedules 5 and 6 to the Magistrates' Courts (Sex Offender and Anti-Social Behaviour Orders) Rules 1998 shall (notwithstanding their revocation) continue to apply to proceedings commenced prior to the commencement of these Rules.

4[4] Forms

(1) An application for an anti-social behaviour order [may][5] be in the form set out in Schedule 1.

(2) ...[6]

(3) ...[7]

(4) ...[8]

(5) An application for an interim anti-social behaviour order made under section 1D [may][9] be in the form set out in Schedule 5.

(6) ...[10]

---

[1] Note: The numbering of these Rules is as per the Queen's Printer's copy. It is thought that this is a drafting error.
[2] Commencement: 2 December 2002 (r 2(1)).
[3] Commencement: 2 December 2002 (r 2(1)).
[4] Commencement: 2 December 2002 (r 2(1)).
[5] Amendment: Word substituted by Magistrates' Courts (Miscellaneous Amendments) Rules 2003, SI 2003/1236, rr 88, 89(1), with effect from 20 June 2003.
[6] Amendment: Paragraph revoked by Magistrates' Courts (Miscellaneous Amendments) Rules 2003, SI 2003/1236, rr 88, 89(2), with effect from 20 June 2003.
[7] Amendment: Paragraph revoked by Magistrates' Courts (Miscellaneous Amendments) Rules 2003, SI 2003/1236, rr 88, 89(2), with effect from 20 June 2003.
[8] Amendment: Paragraph revoked by Magistrates' Courts (Miscellaneous Amendments) Rules 2003, SI 2003/1236, rr 88, 89(2), with effect from 20 June 2003.
[9] Amendment: Word substituted by Magistrates' Courts (Miscellaneous Amendments) Rules 2003, SI 2003/1236, rr 88, 89(1), with effect from 20 June 2003.
[10] Amendment: Paragraph revoked by Magistrates' Courts (Miscellaneous Amendments) Rules 2003, SI 2003/1236, rr 88, 89(2), with effect from 20 June 2003.

5[1] Interim orders

(1) An application for an interim order under section 1D, may, with leave of the justices' clerk, be made without notice being given to the defendant.

(2) The justices' clerk shall only grant leave under paragraph (1) of this rule if he is satisfied that it is necessary for the application to be made without notice being given to the defendant.

(3) If an application made under paragraph (2) is granted, then the interim order and the application for an anti-social behaviour order under section 1 (together with a summons giving a date for the defendant to attend court) shall be served on the defendant in person as soon as practicable after the making of the interim order.

(4) An interim order which is made at the hearing of an application without notice shall not take effect until it has been served on the defendant.

(5) If such an interim order made without notice is not served on the defendant within seven days of being made, then it shall cease to have effect.

(6) An interim order shall cease to have effect if the application for an anti-social behaviour order is withdrawn.

(7) Where the court refuses to make an interim order without notice being given to the defendant it may direct that the application be made on notice.

(8) If an interim order is made without notice being given to the defendant, and the defendant subsequently applies to the court for the order to be discharged or varied, his application shall not be dismissed without the opportunity for him to make oral representations to the court.

6[2] Application for variation or discharge

(1) This rule applies to the making of an application for the variation or discharge of an order made under section 1, 1C or, subject to rule 5(8) above, 1D.

(2) An application to which this rule applies shall be made in writing to the magistrates' court which made the order, or in the case of an application under section 1C to any magistrates' court in the same petty sessions area, and shall specify the reason why the applicant for variation or discharge believes the court should vary or discharge the order, as the case may be.

(3) Subject to rule 5(8) above, where the court considers that there are no grounds upon which it might conclude that the order should be varied or discharged, as the case may be, it may determine the application without hearing representations from the applicant for variation or discharge or from any other person.

(4) Where the court considers that there are grounds upon which it might conclude that the order should be varied or discharged, as the case may be, the justices' chief executive shall, unless the application is withdrawn, issue a summons giving not less than 14 days' notice in writing of the date, time and place appointed for the hearing.

(5) The justices' chief executive shall send with the summons under paragraph 4 above a copy of the application for variation or discharge of the anti-social behaviour order.

---

[1] Commencement: 2 December 2002 (r 2(1)).
[2] Commencement: 2 December 2002 (r 2(1)).

7[1]   Service

(1) Subject to rule 5(3), any summons, or copy of an order or application required to be sent under these Rules to the defendant shall be either given to him in person or sent by post to the last known address, and, if so given or sent, shall be deemed to have been received by him unless he proves otherwise.

(2) Any summons, copy of an order or application required to be sent to the defendant under these Rules shall also be sent by the justices' chief executive to the applicant authority, and to any relevant authority whom the applicant is required by section 1E to have consulted before making the application and, where appropriate, shall invite them to make observations and advise them of their right to be heard at the hearing.

8[2]   Delegation by justices' clerk

(1) In this rule, 'employed as a clerk of the court' has the same meaning as in rule 2(1) of the Justices' Clerks (Qualifications of Assistants) Rules 1979.

(2) Anything authorised to be done by, to or before a justices' clerk under these Rules, may be done instead by, to or before a person employed as a clerk of the court where that person is appointed by the magistrates' courts committee to assist him and where that person has been specifically authorised by the justices' clerk for that purpose.

(3) Any authorisation by the justices' clerk under paragraph (2) shall be recorded in writing at the time the authority is given or as soon as practicable thereafter.

---

[1] Commencement: 2 December 2002 (r 2(1)).
[2] Commencement: 2 December 2002 (r 2(1)).

Schedule 1[1]

Form

Rule 4(1)

Application for Anti-Social Behaviour Order (Crime and Disorder Act 1998, s 1(1))

Magistrates' Court

(Code)

Date:

Defendant:

Address:

Applicant Authority:

Relevant authorities consulted:

And it is alleged

(a) that the defendant has acted on

[dates(s)] at [place(s)] in an anti-social manner, that is to say, in a manner that caused or was likely to cause harassment, alarm or distress to one or more persons not of the same household as himself; and

(b) that an anti-social behaviour order is necessary to protect relevant persons from further anti-social acts by him, and accordingly application is made for an anti-social behaviour order containing the following prohibition(s):—

Short description of acts:

The complaint of:

Name of Applicant Authority:

Address of Applicant Authority:

who [upon oath] states that the defendant was responsible for the acts of which particulars are given above, in respect of which this complaint is made.

Taken [and sworn] before me

Justice of the Peace

[By order of the clerk of the court]

Schedule 2

...[2]

---

[1] Commencement: 2 December 2002 (r 2(1)).
[2] Amendment: Schedule revoked by Magistrates' Courts (Miscellaneous Amendments) Rules 2003, SI 2003/1236, rr 88, 89(3), with effect from 20 June 2003.

Appendix 1(D) – Magistrates' Courts (Anti-Social Behaviour Orders) Rules 2002

Schedule 3

...[1]

Schedule 4

...[2]

Schedule 5[3]

Form

Rule 4(5)

Application for an Interim Order
(Crime and Disorder Act 1998, s 1D)

Magistrates' Court

    (Code)

Date: _____

Defendant: _____

Address: _____

_____

Applicant Authority: _____

Relevant Authorities Consulted: _____

_____

_____

Reasons for applying for an interim order: _____

Do you wish this application to be heard: ☐ without notice being given to the defendant

    ☐ with notice being given to the defendant

If you wish the application to be heard without notice state reasons:

_____

_____

The complaint of: _____

Address of Applicant Authority: _____

Who [upon oath] states that the information given above is correct.

Taken [and sworn] before me.

    Justice of the Peace

    [By order of the clerk of the court]

---

[1] Amendment: Schedule revoked by Magistrates' Courts (Miscellaneous Amendments) Rules 2003, SI 2003/1236, rr 88, 89(3), with effect from 20 June 2003.
[2] Amendment: Schedule revoked by Magistrates' Courts (Miscellaneous Amendments) Rules 2003, SI 2003/1236, rr 88, 89(3), with effect from 20 June 2003.
[3] Commencement: 2 December 2002 (r 2(1)).

NOTE: This application must be accompanied by an application for an anti-social behaviour order (Crime and Disorder Act 1998, s 1).

Schedule 6

...[1]

---

[1] Amendment: Schedule revoked by Magistrates' Courts (Miscellaneous Amendments) Rules 2003, SI 2003/1236, rr 88, 89(3), with effect from 20 June 2003.

(E) CIVIL PROCEDURE RULES, SI 1998/3132, PARTS 19, 25, AND 65, WITH SUPPLEMENTING PRACTICE DIRECTIONS

[PART 19
PARTIES AND GROUP LITIGATION][1]

[19.1 Parties – general

Any number of claimants or defendants may be joined as parties to a claim.][2]

[I Addition and Substitution of Parties

19.2 Change of parties – general

(1) This rule applies where a party is to be added or substituted except where the case falls within rule 19.5 (special provisions about changing parties after the end of a relevant limitation period).

(2) The court may order a person to be added as a new party if –

(a) it is desirable to add the new party so that can resolve all the matters in dispute in the proceedings; or

(b) there is an issue involving the new party and an existing party which is connected to the matters in dispute in the proceedings, and it is desirable to add the new party so that the court can resolve that issue.

(3) The court may order any person to cease to be a party if it is not desirable for that person to be a party to the proceedings.

(4) The court may order a new party to be substituted for an existing one if –

(a) the existing party's interest or liability has passed to the new party; and

(b) it is desirable to substitute the new party so that can resolve the matters in dispute in the proceedings.][3]

****

[19.4 Procedure for adding and substituting parties

(1) The court's permission is required to remove, add or substitute a party, unless the claim form has not been served.

(2) An application for permission under paragraph (1) may be made by –

(a) an existing party; or
(b) a person who wishes to become a party.

---

[1] Amendment: Title substituted: Civil Procedure (Amendment) Rules 2000, SI 2000/221, with effect from 2 May 2000.

[2] Amendment: Rule inserted: Civil Procedure (Amendment) Rules 2000, SI 2000/221, with effect from 2 May 2000.

[3] Amendment: Rule inserted: Civil Procedure (Amendment) Rules 2000, SI 2000/221, with effect from 2 May 2000.

(3) An application for an order under rule 19.2(4) (substitution of a new party where existing party's interest or liability has passed) –

(a) may be made without notice; and
(b) must be supported by evidence.

(4) Nobody may be added or substituted as a claimant unless –

(a) he has given his consent in writing; and
(b) that consent has been filed with the court.

(5) An order for the removal, addition or substitution of a party must be served on –

(a) all parties to the proceedings; and
(b) any other person affected by the order.

(6) When the court makes an order for the removal, addition or substitution of a party, it may give consequential directions about –

(a) filing and serving the claim form on any new defendant;
(b) serving relevant documents on the new party; and
(c) the management of the proceedings.][1]

****

Practice Direction – Addition and Substitution of Parties[2]
This Practice Direction supplements CPR Part 19

Changes of Parties

GENERAL

1.1 Parties may be removed, added or substituted in existing proceedings either on the court's own initiative or on the application of either an existing party or a person who wishes to become a party.

1.2 The application may be dealt with without a hearing where all the existing parties and the proposed new party are in agreement.

1.3 The application to add or substitute a new party should be supported by evidence setting out the proposed new party's interest in or connection with the claim.

1.4 The application notice should be filed in accordance with rule 23.3 and, unless the application is made under [rule 19.2(4)][3], be served in accordance with rule 23.4.

1.5 An order giving permission to amend will, unless the court orders otherwise, be drawn up. It will be served by the court unless the parties wish to serve it or the court orders them to do so.

---

[1] Amendment: Rule inserted: Civil Procedure (Amendment) Rules 2000, SI 2000/221, with effect from 2 May 2000.
[2] Commencement: 26 April 1999 (issued January 1999).
[3] Amendment: Rule reference substituted: Supplement 15 (issued 31 May 2000), with effect from 14 June 2000.

ADDITION OR SUBSTITUTION OF CLAIMANT

2.1 Where an application is made to the court to add or to substitute a new party to the proceedings as claimant, the party applying must file:

(1) the application notice,
(2) the proposed amended claim form and particulars of claim, and
(3) the signed, written consent of the new to be so added or substituted.

2.2 Where the court makes an order adding or substituting a party as claimant but the signed, written consent of the new claimant has not been filed:

(1) the order, and
(2) the addition or substitution of the new party as claimant,

will not take effect until the signed, written consent of the new claimant is filed.

2.3 Where the court has made an order adding or substituting a new claimant, the court may direct:

(1) a copy of the order to be served on every party to the proceedings and any other person affected by the order,
(2) copies of the statements of case and of documents referred to in any statement of case to be served on the new party,
(3) the party who made the application to file within 14 days an amended claim form and particulars of claim.

ADDITION OR SUBSTITUTION OF DEFENDANT

3.1 The Civil Procedure Rules apply to a new defendant who has been added or substituted as they apply to any other defendant (see in particular the provisions of Parts 9, 10, 11 and 15).

3.2 Where the court has made an order adding or substituting a defendant whether on its own initiative or on an application, the court may direct:

(1) the claimant to file with the court within 14 days (or as ordered) an amended claim form and particulars of claim for the court file,
(2) a copy of the order to be served on all parties to the proceedings and any other person affected by it,
(3) the amended claim form and particulars of claim, forms for admitting, defending and acknowledging the claim and copies of the statements of case and any other documents referred to in any statement of case to be served on the new defendant,
(4) unless the court orders otherwise, the amended claim form and particulars of claim to be served on any other defendants.

3.3 A new defendant does not become a party to the proceedings until the amended claim form has been served on him[1].

****

---

[1] *Kettleman v Hansel Properties Ltd* [1987] AC 189, HL.

[PART 25
INTERIM REMEDIES AND SECURITY FOR COSTS][1]

[I Interim remedies][2]

25.1[3] Orders for interim remedies

(1) The court may grant the following interim remedies –

(a) an interim injunction;
(b) an interim declaration;
(c) an order –
  (i) for the detention, custody or preservation of relevant property;
  (ii) for the inspection of relevant property;
  (iii) for the taking of a sample of relevant property;
  (iv) for the carrying out of an experiment on or with relevant property;
  (v) for the sale of relevant property which is of a perishable nature or which for any other good reason it is desirable to sell quickly; and
  (vi) for the payment of income from relevant property until a claim is decided;
(d) an order authorising a person to enter any land or building in the possession of a party to the proceedings for the purposes of carrying out an order under sub-paragraph (c);
(e) an order under section 4 of the Torts (Interference with Goods) Act 1977 to deliver up goods;
(f) an order (referred to as a 'freezing injunction') –
  (i) restraining a party from removing from the jurisdiction assets located there; or
  (ii) restraining a party from dealing with any assets whether located within the jurisdiction or not;
(g) an order directing a party to provide information about the location of relevant property or assets or to provide information about relevant property or assets which are or may be the subject of an application for a freezing injunction;
(h) an order (referred to as a 'search order') under section 7 of the Civil Procedure Act 1997 (order requiring a party to admit another party to premises for the purpose of preserving evidence etc);
(i) an order under section 33 of the Supreme Court Act 1981 or section 52 of the County Courts Act 1984 (order for disclosure of documents or inspection of property before a claim has been made);
(j) an order under section 34 of the Supreme Court Act 1981 or section 53 of the County Courts Act 1984 (order in certain proceedings for disclosure of documents or inspection of property against a non-party);
(k) an order (referred to as an order for interim payment) under rule 25.6 for payment by a defendant on account of any damages, debt or other sum (except costs) which the court may hold the defendant liable to pay;
(l) an order for a specified fund to be paid into court or otherwise secured, where there is a dispute over a party's right to the fund;
(m) an order permitting a party seeking to recover personal property to pay money into court pending the outcome of the proceedings and directing that, if he does so, the

---

[1] Title substituted: Civil Procedure (Amendment) Rules 2000, SI 2000/221, with effect from 2 May 2000.
[2] Amendment: Heading inserted: Civil Procedure (Amendment) Rules 2000, SI 2000/221, with effect from 2 May 2000.
[3] Commencement: 26 April 1999.

property shall be given up to him; ...[1]
(n) an order directing a party to prepare and file accounts relating to the dispute[;
(o) an order directing any account to be taken or inquiry to be made by the court][2].

(Rule 34.2 provides for the court to issue a witness summons requiring a witness to produce documents to the court at the hearing or on such date as the court may direct)

(2) In paragraph (1)(c) and (g), 'relevant property' means property (including land) which is the subject of a claim or as to which any question may arise on a claim.

(3) The fact that a particular kind of interim remedy is not listed in paragraph (1) does not affect any power that the court may have to grant that remedy.

(4) The court may grant an interim remedy whether or not there has been a claim for a final remedy of that kind.

25.2[3] Time when an order for an interim remedy may be made

(1) An order for an interim remedy may be made at any time, including –

(a) before proceedings are started; and
(b) after judgment has been given.

(Rule 7.2 provides that proceedings are started when the court issues a claim form)

(2) However –

(a) paragraph (1) is subject to any rule, practice direction or other enactment which provides otherwise;
(b) the court may grant an interim remedy before a claim has been made only if –
  (i) the matter is urgent; or
  (ii) it is otherwise desirable to do so in the interests of justice; and
(c) unless the court otherwise orders, a defendant may not apply for any of the orders listed in rule 25.1(1) before he has filed either an acknowledgment of service or a defence.

(Part 10 provides for filing an acknowledgment of service and Part 15 for filing a defence)

(3) Where the court grants an interim remedy before a claim has been commenced, it may give directions requiring a claim to be commenced.

(4) In particular, the court need not direct that a claim be commenced where the application is made under section 33 of the Supreme Court Act 1981 or section 52 of the County Courts Act 1984 (order for disclosure, inspection etc before commencement of a claim).

25.3[4] How to apply for an interim remedy

(1) The court may grant an interim remedy on an application made without notice if it appears to the court that there are good reasons for not giving notice.

(2) An application for an interim remedy must be supported by evidence, unless orders otherwise.

(3) If the applicant makes an application without giving notice, the evidence in support of the application must state the reasons why notice has not been given.

(Part 3 lists general powers of the court)

---

[1] Amendment: Word deleted: Civil Procedure (Amendment) Rules 2002, SI 2002/2058, with effect from 2 December 2002.
[2] Amendment: Sub-paragraph inserted: Civil Procedure (Amendment) Rules 2002, SI 2002/2058, with effect from 2 December 2002.
[3] Commencement: 26 April 1999.
[4] Commencement: 26 April 1999.

(Part 23 contains general rules about making an application)

****

Practice Direction – Interim Injunctions[1]
This Practice Direction supplements Part 25

JURISDICTION

1.1 High Court judges and any other judge duly authorised may grant 'search orders'[2] and 'freezing injunctions'[3].

1.2 In a case in the High Court, masters and district judges have the power to grant injunctions:

(1) by consent,
(2) in connection with charging orders and appointments of receivers,
(3) in aid of execution of judgments.

1.3 In any other case any judge who has jurisdiction to conduct the trial of the action has the power to grant an injunction in that action.

1.4 A master or district judge has the power to vary or discharge an injunction granted by any judge with the consent of all the parties.

MAKING AN APPLICATION

2.1 The application notice must state:

(1) the order sought, and
(2) the date, time and place of the hearing.

2.2 The application notice and evidence in support must be served as soon as practicable after issue and in any event not less than 3 days before the court is due to hear the application[4].

2.3 Where the court is to serve, sufficient copies of the application notice and evidence in support for the court and for each respondent should be filed for issue and service.

2.4 Whenever possible a draft of the order sought should be filed with the application notice and a disk containing the draft should also be available to [in a format compatible with the word processing software used by the court][5]. This will enable the court officer to arrange for any amendments to be incorporated and for the speedy preparation and sealing of the order.
…[6]

---

[1] Commencement: 26 April 1999 (issued January 1999).
[2] Rule 25.1(1)(h).
[3] Rule 25.1(1)(f).
[4] Rule 23.7(1) and (2) and see rule 23.7(4) (short service).
[5] Amendment: Words inserted: Supplement 26 (issued 28 January 2002), with effect from 25 March 2002.
[6] Amendment: Words deleted: Supplement 26 (issued 28 January 2002), with effect from 25 March 2002.

EVIDENCE

3.1 Applications for search orders and freezing injunctions must be supported by affidavit evidence.

3.2 Applications for other interim injunctions must be supported by evidence set out in either:

(1) a witness statement, or
(2) a statement of case provided that it is verified by a statement of truth[1], or
(3) the application provided that it is verified by a statement of truth,

unless the court, an Act, a rule or a practice direction requires evidence by affidavit.

3.3 The evidence must set out the facts on which the applicant relies for the claim being made against the respondent, including all material facts of which the court should be made aware.

3.4 Where an application is made without notice to the respondent, the evidence must also set out why notice was not given.

(See Part 32 and the practice direction that supplements it for information about evidence)

URGENT APPLICATIONS AND APPLICATIONS WITHOUT NOTICE

4.1 These fall into two categories:

(1) applications where a claim form has already been issued, and
(2) applications where a claim form has not yet been issued,

and, in both cases, where notice of the application has not been given to the respondent.

4.2 These applications are normally dealt with at a court hearing but cases of extreme urgency may be dealt with by telephone.

4.3 Applications dealt with at a court hearing after issue of a claim form:

(1) the application notice, evidence in support and a draft order (as in 2.4 above) should be with filed two hours before the hearing wherever possible,
(2) if an application is made before the application notice has been issued, a draft order (as in 2.4 above) should be provided at the hearing, and the application notice and evidence in support must be filed with the court on the same or next working day or as ordered by the court, and
(3) except in cases where secrecy is essential, the applicant should take steps to notify the respondent informally of the application.

4.4 Applications made before the issue of a claim form:

(1) in addition to the provisions set out at 4.3 above, unless the court orders otherwise, either the applicant must undertake to the court to issue a claim form immediately or the court will give directions for the commencement of the claim[2],
(2) where possible the claim form should be served with the order for the injunction,
(3) an order made before the issue of a claim form should state in the title after the names of the applicant and respondent 'the Claimant and Defendant in an Intended Action'.

4.5 Applications made by telephone:

(1) where it is not possible to arrange a hearing, application can be made between 10.00 am

---

[1] See Part 22.
[2] Rule 25.2(3).

and 5.00 pm weekdays by telephoning the Royal Courts of Justice on [020 7947 6000][1] and asking to be put in contact with a High Court judge of the appropriate Division available to deal with an emergency application in a High Court matter. [The appropriate district registry may also be contacted by telephone.][2] In county court proceedings, the appropriate county court should be contacted,

(2) where an application is made outside those hours the applicant should either –
   (a) telephone the Royal Courts of Justice on [020 7947 6000][3] where he will be put in contact with the clerk to the appropriate Duty Judge in the High Court (or the appropriate area circuit judge where known), or
   (b) the Urgent Court Business Officer of the appropriate circuit who will contact the local Duty Judge,
(3) where the facility is available it is likely that the judge will require a draft order to be faxed to him,
(4) the application notice and evidence in support must be filed with the court on the same or next working day or as ordered, together with two copies of the order for sealing,
(5) injunctions will be heard by telephone only where the applicant is acting by counsel or solicitors.

****

[PART 65
PROCEEDINGS RELATING TO ANTI-SOCIAL BEHAVIOUR AND HARASSMENT][4]

[65.1 Scope of this Part

This Part contains rules –

(a) in Section I, about injunctions under the Housing Act 1996;
(b) in Section II, about applications by local authorities under section 91(3) of the Anti-social Behaviour Act 2003 for a power of arrest to be attached to an injunction;
(c) in Section III, about claims for demotion orders under the Housing Act 1985 and Housing Act 1988 and proceedings relating to demoted tenancies;
(d) in Section IV, about anti-social behaviour orders under the Crime and Disorder Act 1998;
(e) in Section V, about claims under section 3 of the Protection from Harassment Act 1997.][5]

****

II Applications by Local Authorities for Power of Arrest to be Attached to Injunction

[65.8 Scope of this Section and interpretation

(1) This Section applies to applications by local authorities under section 91(3) of the Anti-social Behaviour Act 2003 for a power of arrest to be attached to an injunction.

---

[1] Amendment: Telephone number substituted: Supplement 27 (issued 8 March 2002), with effect from 25 March 2002.
[2] Amendment: Words inserted: Supplement 2 (issued 1 April 1999), with effect from 26 April 1999.
[3] Amendment: Telephone number substituted: Supplement 27 (issued 8 March 2002), with effect from 25 March 2002.
[4] Amendment: Part inserted: Civil Procedure (Amendment) Rules 2004, SI 2004/1306, with effect from 30 June 2004.
[5] Amendment: Rule inserted: Civil Procedure (Amendment) Rules 2004, SI 2004/1306, with effect from 30 June 2004.

(Section 91 of the 2003 Act applies to proceedings in which a local authority is a party by virtue of section 222 of the Local Government Act 1972 (power of local authority to bring, defend or appear in proceedings for the promotion or protection of the interests of inhabitants in their area)

(2) In this Section 'the 2003 Act' means the Anti-social Behaviour Act 2003.][1]

[65.9 Applications under section 91(3) of the 2003 Act for a power of arrest to be attached to any provision of an injunction

(1) An application under section 91(3) of the 2003 Act for a power of arrest to be attached to any provision of an injunction must be made in the proceedings seeking the injunction by –

(a) the claim form;
(b) the acknowledgment of service;
(c) the defence or counterclaim in a Part 7 claim; or
(d) application under Part 23.

(2) Every application must be supported by written evidence.

(3) Every application made on notice must be served personally, together with a copy of the written evidence, by the local authority on the person against whom the injunction is sought not less than 2 days before the hearing.

(Attention is drawn to rule 25.3(3) – applications without notice)][2]

[65.10 Injunction containing provisions to which a power of arrest is attached

(1) Where a power of arrest is attached to a provision of an injunction on the application of a local authority under section 91(3) of the 2003 Act, the following rules in Section I of this Part shall apply –

(a) rule 65.4; and
(b) paragraphs (1), (2), (4) and (5) of rule 65.6.

(2) CCR Order 29, rule 1 shall apply where an application is made in a county court to commit a person for breach of an injunction.][3]

****

*IV Anti-Social Behaviour Orders under the
Crime and Disorder Act 1998*

[65.21 Scope of this Section and interpretation

(1) This Section applies to applications in proceedings in a county court under sub-sections (2), (3) or (3B) of section 1B of the Crime and Disorder Act 1998 by a relevant authority, and to applications for interim orders under section 1D of that Act.

(2) In this Section –

---

[1] Amendment: Rule inserted: Civil Procedure (Amendment) Rules 2004, SI 2004/1306, with effect from 30 June 2004.
[2] Amendment: Rule inserted: Civil Procedure (Amendment) Rules 2004, SI 2004/1306, with effect from 30 June 2004.
[3] Amendment: Rule inserted: Civil Procedure (Amendment) Rules 2004, SI 2004/1306, with effect from 30 June 2004.

(a) 'the 1998 Act' means the Crime and Disorder Act 1998;
(b) 'relevant authority' has the same meaning as in section 1(1A) of the 1998 Act; and
(c) 'the principal proceedings' means any proceedings in a county court.][1]

[65.22 Application where the relevant authority is a party in principal proceedings

(1) Subject to paragraph (2) –

(a) where the relevant authority is the claimant in the principal proceedings, an application under section 1B(2) of the 1998 Act for an order under section 1B(4) of the 1998 Act must be made in the claim form; and

(b) where the relevant authority is a defendant in the principal proceedings, an application for an order must be made by application notice which must be filed with the defence.

(2) Where the relevant authority becomes aware of the circumstances that lead it to apply for an order after its claim is issued or its defence filed, the application must be made by application notice as soon as possible thereafter.

(3) Where the application is made by application notice, it should normally be made on notice to the person against whom the order is sought.][2]

[65.23 Application by a relevant authority to join a person to the principal proceedings

(1) An application under section 1B(3B) of the 1998 Act by a relevant authority which is a party to the principal proceedings to join a person to the principal proceedings must be made –

(a) in accordance with Section I of Part 19;
(b) in the same application notice as the application for an order under section 1B(4) of the 1998 Act against the person; and
(c) as soon as possible after the relevant authority considers that the criteria in section 1B(3A) of the 1998 Act are met.

(2) The application notice must contain –

(a) the relevant authority's reasons for claiming that the person's anti-social acts are material in relation to the principal proceedings; and
(b) details of the anti-social acts alleged.

(3) The application should normally be made on notice to the person against whom the order is sought.][3]

[65.24 Application where the relevant authority is not party in principal proceedings

(1) Where the relevant authority is not a party to the principal proceedings –

(a) an application under section 1B(3) of the 1998 Act to be made a party must be made in accordance with Section I of Part 19; and

---

[1] Amendment: Rule inserted: Civil Procedure (Amendment) Rules 2004, SI 2004/1306, with effect from 30 June 2004.
[2] Amendment: Rule inserted: Civil Procedure (Amendment) Rules 2004, SI 2004/1306, with effect from 30 June 2004.
[3] Amendment: Rule inserted: Civil Procedure (Amendment) Rules 2004, SI 2004/1306, with effect from 30 June 2004.

(b) the application to be made a party and the application for an order under section 1B(4) of the 1998 Act must be made in the same application notice.

(2) The applications –

(a) must be made as soon as possible after the authority becomes aware of the principal proceedings; and

(b) should normally be made on notice to the person against whom the order is sought.][1]

[65.25 Evidence

An application for an order under section 1B(4) of the 1998 Act must be accompanied by written evidence, which must include evidence that section 1E of the 1998 Act has been complied with.][2]

[65.26 Application for an interim order

(1) An application for an interim order under section 1D of the 1998 Act must be made in accordance with Part 25.

(2) The application should normally be made –

(a) in the claim form or application notice seeking the order; and

(b) on notice to the person against whom the order is sought.][3]

****

Practice Direction – Anti-Social Behaviour and Harassment[4]
This Practice Direction supplements Part 65

****

SECTION IV – ANTI-SOCIAL BEHAVIOUR ORDERS UNDER THE CRIME AND DISORDER ACT 1998

Service of an order under sections 1B(4) or 1D of the 1998 Act

13.1 An order under section 1B(4) or an interim order under section 1D of the 1998 Act must be served personally on the defendant.

****

---

[1] Amendment: Rule inserted: Civil Procedure (Amendment) Rules 2004, SI 2004/1306, with effect from 30 June 2004.

[2] Amendment: Rule inserted: Civil Procedure (Amendment) Rules 2004, SI 2004/1306, with effect from 30 June 2004.

[3] Amendment: Rule inserted: Civil Procedure (Amendment) Rules 2004, SI 2004/1306, with effect from 30 June 2004.

[4] Commencement: 30 June 2004: Supplement 35 (issued 28 May 2004).

APPENDIX 2

PRECEDENTS

(A) DRAFT ASBO APPLICATION

SCHEDULE 1
FORM
Application for Anti-Social Behaviour Order
Crime and Disorder Act 1998, Section 1(1)

In the .... Magistrates' Court

[*address of the court*] [*court code*]

Date ....

Defendant: Fred Anti-Social dob 7th June 1989

[*defendant's address*]

Local government area in respect of which application is made: .... Council

Relevant authorities consulted: .... Police/ .... council etc.

And it is alleged:

(a) That the Defendant has acted on the dates and at the places listed in the schedule below in an anti-social manner, that is to say, in a manner that has caused or is likely to cause harassment, alarm or distress to one or more persons not of the same household as himself; and

(b) That an anti-social behaviour order is necessary to protect relevant persons from further anti-social acts by him,

The Applicant applies for an order that:

Fred Anti-social must not

1. Engage in conduct which causes or is likely to cause alarm, distress or harassment to others or inciting or encouraging others to do so within the .... Council area;

2. Engage in behaviour which is or is likely to be threatening, abusive or insulting to others, or encouraging or inciting others to do so within the .... Council area;

3. Buy, attempt to buy or to possess fireworks;

4. Have any contact with, and/or attempt to communicate with Mr and Mrs White;

5. Enter or attempt to enter Careful Secondary School or its grounds without the express written permission of the headmaster or deputy headmaster at the time;

6. Enter or attempt or enter and/or remain in any place within the area bordered in green as marked on the attached map.

Schedule/Short description of Acts

Date	Details
21 May 2003	Was verbally abusive to Mrs Black calling her a 'bitch'
5 June 2003	Threatened Mr White and said 'I'll punch you and your son's going to get a punch'
6 July 2003	Shouted abuse repeatedly at Mrs Pink
10 Aug 2003	Left the classroom without permission, disrupted other lessons by banging on windows and doors and being verbally abusive. Climbed onto the roof and caused damage to the roof and then absconded.
13 Aug 2003	Re-entered the Careful Secondary School having been excluded from the same. Whilst there, was abusive to staff and threatened them.
19 Aug 2003	Re-entered the Careful Secondary School and was verbally abusive banging on objects to disrupt other classes and threw apples at staff
1 Sept 2003	Punched another child in the face without provocation at school
2 Sept 2003	Assaulted a pupil and repeated this although removed by staff. Was abusive to staff and damaged 2 cars when leaving
12 Sept 2003	Verbally abused and/or was part of a group that verbally abused Mr Black and fired fireworks at his house and later told Mr Black that he was going to chin him.
13 Sept 2003	Made an obscene gesture and shouted 'Oi Wanker' at Mr Green
13 Sept 2003	Made an obscene finger gesture to Mrs White
31 Oct 2003	Assaulted a fellow pupil at Careful Secondary School. When challenged was extremely violent threatening people and threw bricks at the school and staff
30 Nov 2003	Shouted abuse and threw an egg at Mr and Mrs White's home

Further the Applicant alleges that the Defendant has been responsible in the last 6 months for a number of incidents of anti-social behaviour including abusive and threatening behaviour to members of the public, details of which are contained within the attached statements of witnesses, police officers and housing officers who provide details of complaints.

The applicant will also rely on the Defendant's criminal convictions and incidents of anti-social behaviour prior to the above incidents in support of the application. Evidence of the same will be served with the evidence of the above incidents.

The complaint of: ....

Applying body

[*Address of applying body*]

Who [upon oath] states that the Defendant was responsible for the acts of which the particulars are given above, in respect of which this complaint is made.

Taken before me, ...

Justice of the Peace/Justices' Clerk

(B) DRAFT ASBO

Anti-social Behaviour Order Crime and Disorder Act 1998, Section 1(1)

In the .... Magistrates' Court

[*Court address*] [*court code*]

Date ....

Defendant: **Fred Anti-Social** dob 7th June 1989

[*Defendant's address*]

Local government area in
respect of which application is made: .... Council

Relevant authorities consulted: .... Police/ .... Council

The .... Magistrates' Court having found:

(a) that Fred Anti-Social has acted on the dates and at the places listed in the schedule below/attached in an anti-social manner, that is to say, in a manner that has caused or is likely to cause harassment, alarm or distress to one or more persons not of the same household as himself; and

(b) that an anti-social behaviour order is necessary to protect relevant persons from further anti-social acts by him.

Fred Anti-Social is prohibited from [*delete as appropriate from sample terms below*]:

1 Acting in a manner which causes or is likely to cause nuisance, harassment, alarm or distress to any person.

2 Using or threatening violence towards any person

3 Acting in a manner, or using language, which is or is likely to be threatening, racially abusive, or racially insulting to any person.

4 Entering or attempting to enter the area marked and outlined in red on the attached map save:
   (a) to and from his place of residence and then only by means of the route marked blue on the attached map
   (b) for the purposes attending pre-arranged doctors or dentists appointments within the area and then by and returning by the most direct route [or marked route if appropriate]
   (c) when in the company of or under the direction of the probation service or youth offending team workers

5 Painting, drawing, spraying, writing, or otherwise putting graffiti on any surface not belonging to you, except with the express permission of the owner of the surface.

6 Throwing objects (including stones) in a public place.

7 Causing, or attempting to cause, any damage to property not belonging to you.

8 Having contact with, in public, whether by being in a group with, talking to or otherwise associating with [*insert names*].

9 Entering, or attempting to enter any motor vehicle without the permission of the owner

10   Being in possession of alcohol in open bottles, cans, cups or containers in a public place.

11   Being in possession of any solvent, for example glue, thinner, petrol, butane gas, etc, in a public place.

12   Being present when someone else starts or tries to start a fire in a public place except when at an event organised by the council or other public body

13   Being in possession of any solvent, for example glue, thinner, petrol, butane gas etc. in a public place.

14   Being in the company of any persons who you know to be in possession of any solvent for example glue, thinner, petrol, butane gas, etc, in a public place.

15   Being in possession of a drug or substance prescribed as controlled by the Misuse of Drugs Act 1971.

16   Being present when controlled drugs (as defined by the Misuse of Drugs Act 1971) or substances are to your knowledge traded, sold, supplied (commercial or otherwise) or otherwise distributed in any place to which the public have access

17   Wearing clothing within the …….. area, whether a balaclava, hood, mask, scarf or other item of clothing so as to hide your facial features or identity

18   Possessing or using a '2-way' radio, walkie-talkie, open band radio, police radio or radio scanner

19   Encouraging or inciting others to carry out any of the prohibited acts on your behalf

20   Being in possession of any bladed instrument or weapon in a public place

21   Lighting or being present at a fire which has been set on land to which the public has access at any time save for organised events for the celebration of Bonfire Night between 1 November and 8 November inclusive

22   Driving any mechanically propelled vehicle unless in accordance with a valid driving licence and valid MOT certificate and insurance policy relating to that vehicle

23   Contacting, whether directly or indirectly [*insert names of witnesses*]

24   Being away from his home between the hours of 22:00 and 8:00 the next morning unless accompanied by one or both parents, social worker, youth team worker or person authorised as a carer by social services

25   Acting in a manner which causes or is likely to cause nuisance, harassment, alarm or distress to any person.

26   Using or threatening violence towards any person

THIS ORDER SHALL REMAIN IN FORCE UNTIL ………………………………………………………

IF WITHOUT REASONABLE EXCUSE, YOU DO ANYTHING WHICH YOU MUST NOT DO BY REASON OF THIS ORDER YOU WILL BE LIABLE ON CONVICTION TO IMPRISONMENT FOR A TERM NOT EXCEEDING 5 YEARS (2 years if a minor) OR TO A FINE OR BOTH

……………………………………………………………

Justice of the Peace/ District Judge (Magistrates' Courts)

(C) APPLICATION FOR INTERIM ANTI-SOCIAL BEHAVIOUR ORDER

SCHEDULE 5 FORM

Application for INTERIM Order
Crime and Disorder Act 1998, Section 1D

In the .... Magistrates' Court

[*Court address*] [*Court code*]

Date ....

Defendant: Name: .... dob ....

              Defendant's address...................................

Local government area in
respect of which application is made: .... Council

Relevant authorities consulted: ....

Reasons for applying for an interim order:

> The Defendant has been responsible for anti-social behaviour in the area which has been of a serious nature. Many witnesses are too intimidated by fear of reprisals if they give evidence. His conduct has caused severe distress to several of the witnesses, one of whom is seriously ill and it is feared that if the application is delayed for any reason, eg pending criminal charges, then the witnesses will be at severe risk of intimidation. Further the Defendant has conducted such a large number of acts of anti-social behaviour despite being served with an intention to seek an order that it is feared that the behaviour will not cease unless an interim order is granted. The Defendant's response to being challenged is to be aggressive and to commit further acts. There is an urgent need for an interim order to prevent further acts pending the hearing of the full application.

Do you wish this application to be heard: [ ] without notice being given to the Defendant

                                             [ ] with notice being given to the Defendant

If you wish the application to be heard without notice state reasons:

> The order has been made without notice because the defendant's acts of anti-social behaviour are serious and escalating and there is a significant risk that he will further intimidate witnesses if he is given notice of the intention to apply for an interim order. There is therefore an urgent need to obtain protection for the community and witnesses.

Reasons for applying without notice

> SAMPLE REASONS: This interim order is required to be made initially without notice as the Defendant has committed and continues to commit acts against the main witnesses which include physical threats and verbal abusive and intimidation. If the Defendant is given notice of this hearing there is a real likelihood that he will commit acts of anti-social behaviour particularly against the witnesses before any hearing of the application for an interim order could take place. Therefore there is an urgent need for an interim order without notice.

The complaint of: ....

[*name and address of applying body*]

Who [upon oath] states that the Defendant was responsible for the acts of which the particulars are given above, in respect of which this complaint is made.

Taken [and sworn] before me, ...

Justice of the Peace/Justices' Clerk/District Judge (Magistrates' Court)

(D) INTERIM ANTI-SOCIAL BEHAVIOUR ORDER

**............. Magistrates' Courts Service
Interim Order
(Crime and Disorder Act 1998, s 1D)
.... Magistrates' Court [*CODE*]**

Date:

Defendant: FRED ANTI-SOCIAL (Date of Birth: 2/10/83)

Address:

On the complaint of:

Applicant Authority:

Address of the Applicant:

Authority:

The court makes an Interim Anti-Social Behaviour Order against the defendant.

Reasons for making this order are:
The Defendant is alleged to have conducted a number of acts of anti-social behaviour and it is feared that this behaviour will not cease prior to the full hearing of this matter unless an interim order is granted.

And the court found that it is just to make this order pending the determination of the application for an anti-social behaviour order, which application is attached to this order.

This order has been made with notice.

The court orders that **FRED ANTI-SOCIAL** is prohibited from:

1. Acting in a manner which causes or is likely to cause nuisance, harassment, alarm or distress to any person in the area of ……............;
2. Abusing, insulting, harassing or threatening any person in the area of …….........;
3. Using or threatening violence towards any person in the area of ………........ ;
4. Causing criminal damage in the area of …….........;
5. Not to enter the area marked in green on the attached map as the exclusion zone;
6. Encouraging or inciting others to carry out any of the prohibited acts on your behalf.

Address of the Applicant Authority:

This order will end on

The court also orders all parties to attend at .... Magistrates' Court, …………..

On [*insert date if pre-trial review date or further consideration of interim order*]

Or [*use if main application date is fixed*]

A hearing will take place in respect of the main application on …………. Magistrates' Court on …………….. at ………… am/pm

....
District Judge (Magistrates' Courts)/Justice of the Peace

NOTE: If, without reasonable excuse, the defendant does anything which she is prohibited from doing by this order, he shall be liable on conviction to a term of imprisonment not exceeding five years (two if a minor) or to a fine or to both.

About this Order
This is an interim anti-social behaviour order. The court has made this order because it considers it just to do so pending the determination of an application for an anti-social behaviour order against you. The court believes that you have acted in an anti-social manner, and that this order is necessary to protect people from further anti-social acts by you. Anti-social behaviour is behaviour which caused or was likely to cause harassment, alarm or distress to people outside of your household.

If, without reasonable excuse, you do anything which is prohibited by this order you will be guilty of an offence, for which you could be punished by a term of imprisonment or by a fine or by both.

The order will end on the date specified unless a further order is made.

You may apply to the court to end or to vary this order. You should consult a solicitor or the court office to find out how to do this.

You must attend court for the next hearing date, which is specified in the summons accompanying this order.

(E) ORDERS ON CONVICTION

I CROWN COURT POST-CONVICTION ORDER

Order on Conviction
(Crime and Disorder Act 1998, s 1C)

.... Crown Court
[*Code*]

1   On the .... [date] Crown Court sitting at .... convicted

Name: .... [the defendant] of

Address: ....

                 ....

Date of Birth: ....of

Offence(s)   .... [relevant offence(s)]

and imposed the following sentence/conditional discharge ....

2   The court found that

(i)   the defendant had acted in an anti-social manner which caused or was likely to cause harassment, alarm or distress to one or more persons not of the same household as himself

....
....
.... [details of behaviour]

and that

(ii) an order was necessary to protect persons in England and Wales from further anti-social acts by him.

3   It is ordered that the defendant .... [name] is prohibited from:

....
....

[Where appropriate, the court must specify whether any of the requirements of the order are suspended until the defendant's release from custody]

....
....

Until [ ] [further order].

The Judge

NOTE: If without reasonable excuse the defendant does anything which he is prohibited from doing by this order, he shall be liable on conviction to a term of imprisonment not exceeding five years or to a fine or to both.

II SUGGESTED PRECEDENT FOR POST-CONVICTION ORDER IN THE MAGISTRATES' COURT

Order on Conviction (Crime and Disorder Act 1998, s 1C)

Magistrates' Court / Youth Court [*Court Code*]

1. On the _____

[date] the Magistrates' Court / Youth Court sitting at _____

convicted

Name: _____ [defendant]

Address: _____

Date of Birth: _____

of

Offence(s) _____

[relevant offence(s)]

and imposed the following sentence/conditional discharge _____

2. The court found that:

(i) the defendant had acted in the following anti-social manner, which caused or was likely to cause harassment, alarm or distress to one or more persons not of the same household as himself,

_____

[details of behaviour] (see attached schedule)

and that

(ii) an order was necessary to protect persons in England and Wales from further anti-social acts by him.

3. It is ordered that the defendant _____

[name] is prohibited from:

_____

[Where appropriate, the court must specify whether any of the requirements of the order are suspended until the defendant's release from custody]

_____

Until [   ]/[further order]

Justice of the Peace/District Judge (Magistrates' Courts)

NOTE: If without reasonable excuse the defendant does anything which he is prohibited from doing by this order, he shall be liable on conviction to a term of imprisonment not exceeding five years (two years if a minor) or to a fine or to both.

(F) COUNTY COURT ANTI-SOCIAL BEHAVIOUR ORDER (FORM N113)

Anti-social behaviour
(Order under section 1B(4) of
the Crime and Disorder Act 1998)

In the	
	County Court
Claim No.	
Claimant	
Applicant	
Defendant	

(SEAL)

On   20   , District Judge
sitting at

considered the application of the [claimant] [applicant] [defendant] and found that
the [claimant] [defendant] has acted in an anti-social manner that caused or was likely to cause
harassment, alarm or distress to one or more persons not of the same household as [himself] [herself]; **and**
that this order is necessary to protect persons from further anti-social acts by the [claimant] [defendant]
and the court ordered that the [claimant] [defendant] is forbidden from:-

until [   ] [further order]

[The [claimant] [applicant] [or] [defendant] may apply to the court for this order to be varied or discharged.
Unless both parties consent, this order may not be discharged within two years of the order being served.]

To

You **must** obey this order. If, without reasonable excuse, you do anything which you are forbidden from doing
by this order, you will be liable on conviction to a term of imprisonment not exceeding five years or to a
fine or to both.

[Notice of further hearing [(see also note overleaf)]
The court will re-consider the application and whether the order should continue at a further hearing
at

on   the   day of   20   at   o'clock

If you do not attend at the time shown the court may make an order in your absence.]

N113 Anti-social behaviour (Order under s1B(4) of the Crime and Disorder Act 1998) (04.03)

Anti social behaviour order - Record of hearing   Claim No.

On   the   day of   20

Before District Judge

The court was sitting at

The   [claimant]   [applicant]

was   ☐ represented by counsel
       ☐ represented by a solicitor
       ☐ in person

The   [claimant]   [defendant]

was   ☐ represented by counsel
       ☐ represented by a solicitor
       ☐ in person
       ☐ not given notice of this hearing

or

       ☐ did not appear having been given notice of this hearing

The court read the statements of
       ☐ the claimant
       ☐ the applicant
       ☐ the defendant

[And of]

[The court heard spoken evidence on oath from]

Signed_____ Dated_____

[**Note:** This order was made without notice being given to you. You may apply for it to be set aside, varied or stayed. If you wish to apply, do not delay. You must make your application to the court within 7 days of the date you received it. You may make your application by writing to the court or asking the court for a Form N244 Application Notice. You will have to pay a fee to make your application unless you qualify for fee exemption or remission]

(G) ANTI-SOCIAL BEHAVIOUR ORDER SPECIMEN COURT SERVICE LEVEL AGREEMENT

BETWEEN

WEST YORKSHIRE MAGISTRATES' COURTS SERVICE

AND

CITY OF BRADFORD METROPOLITAN DISTRICT COUNCIL
CALDERDALE METROPOLITAN DISTRICT COUNCIL
KIRKLEES METROPOLITAN DISTRICT COUNCIL
LEEDS CITY COUNCIL
CITY OF WAKEFIELD METROPOLITAN DISTRICT COUNCIL
WEST YORKSHIRE POLICE
BRITISH TRANSPORT POLICE
WEST YORKSHIRE CROWN PROSECUTION SERVICE

Introduction

This document seeks to set down the agreed minimum standard required to deal with Anti-Social Behaviour Orders.

This agreement will be subject to annual review each September, commencing in September 2004.

1 Listing – Timings and purpose

Application for hearing <u>without notice</u> to defendant (s 1D Crime and Disorder Act 1998 and r 5 The Magistrates' Courts (ASBO) Rules 2002 + schedules – hereinafter described as the 'Rules' and 'Schedules').

This application (forms in Schedules 1 and 5) will be considered by a delegated legal adviser (currently District Legal Directors and Legal Managers) within 4 hours of notice to the court.

This may be considered by telephone call or attendance at court, with forms being faxed or e-mailed to the legal adviser dealing with the application.

The applicant must supply adequate information to demonstrate that such a hearing is 'necessary'.

Necessary' = protection would be likely to be frustrated if notice were given, or would be likely to result in increased/repeated anti-social acts, including harassment/interference of witnesses.

Estimated time – 15 to 20 minutes.

Hearing without notice for interim order

Application to be heard as soon as reasonably practicable and in any event within 24 hours (excluding weekends/bank holidays).

The applicant must demonstrate that it is 'just' to make an interim order.

'Just' = application for the full order is properly made and there is sufficient evidence of an urgent need to protect the community (p 19 'Guide to ASBOs – Home Office Communication Directorate' – November 2002 – hereinafter described as the 'Guidance').

An interim order (form in schedule 6) will be granted to expire 'on a fixed date or earlier order'. The interim order may be renewed (s 1D (4) CDA 1998).

Estimated time – 30 minutes.

Inter partes hearing, including interim order application

If the application is made following a hearing without notice, it will be listed within 7 days.

If the application is made following a hearing with notice, it will be listed within 14 days.

If a full order is not agreed, an interim order will be considered at the first hearing provided that there is service of the summons, if it is 'just' to make the order (see above).

An effective pre-trial review will also be conducted with all witness availability dates produced to the court and appropriate directions including exchange of evidence normally within 4 weeks of the pre-trial review.

Estimated time – 30 minutes.

Contested hearing

A final date for a contested hearing will be fixed within 12 weeks of the pre-trial review.

Any subsequent variation of direction or order to be listed in open court following notification to all parties.

Every attempt will be made to avoid adjournment or delay.

Ancillary order made in criminal proceedings

The court will be alert to the criteria for making an ASBO on the day of sentencing for the offence(s) before the court, based upon the information disclosed to the defendant prior to the hearing. Adjournments will not be made purely to explore/consider facts or circumstances relating to a potential ASBO.

The court will ensure that notification is passed to the Community Safety Department of the relevant local authority/police force if a case is adjourned to consider the substantive sentence and an ASBO is actively under consideration, so that additional factors may be presented to the court by the police and/or local authority on the next date. The case will not be further adjourned thereafter for the purpose of making an ASBO, unless there are exceptional reasons for doing so.

The terms of the order will be compiled by the court using the form in Schedule 4.

2 Summons procedure (Guide to ASBOs – Home Office Communication Directorate = 'Guidance', p 35)

The lead individual in charge of the case will arrange for a summons form to be completed, with a copy retained on the application file, and for the defendant to be served with the following:

- Summons (Form in Schedule 2, Magistrates' Courts (ASBO) Rules 2002 – 'Rules').
- Application (Form in Schedule 1, 'Rules': Form in Schedule 5, Rules – interim application) – to include any evidence of 'likely' wide geographical spread of behaviour ('Guidance').
- Interim order if made without notice (Form in Schedule 6, 'Rules') – subject to service within 7 days, otherwise it will cease to have effect.
- Documentary evidence of statutory consultation in the form of a certificate of consultation.
- Guidance on how the defendant may obtain legal advice and representation.
- Notice of intention to proceed in the absence of the defendant and any notice of hearsay evidence.
- Details of evidence in support of the application as agreed with the applicant agency's solicitor.
- A warning to the defendant that it is an offence to pervert the course of justice, and that witness intimidation is liable to lead to prosecution.
- Notice as to claims for investigative and legal costs (where required by the applicant).

3 Service of summons ('Guidance' p 36)

Wherever possible the lead officer will ensure that service of the summons is made on the defendant in person. If personal service is not possible, the summons will be served by first class post as soon as possible to the last known address, normally allowing at least 7 days notice before the hearing.

Where a child or a young person is concerned, a person with parental responsibility must also receive a copy of the summons.

4 Warrants

If the defendant fails to attend and if the magistrates require his/her attendance, a warrant normally backed for bail to a fixed hearing date will be issued to a fixed date.

The court accepts that the applicant's advocate can substantiate the complaint on oath for the purpose of applying for the warrant.

5 Case Presentation and Evidence

The parties will follow the procedure laid down in the Civil Evidence Act 1995 and Magistrates' Courts (Hearsay Evidence in Civil Proceedings) Rules 1999 for presenting evidence as this is accepted as good practice for these applications.

Witness statements containing a statement of truth, having been served on the defendant in advance of the hearing, will be accepted as evidence in chief. Oral evidence given by the witness should be limited to amplification or clarification of issues in the statement, or new events that have happened subsequent to the making of the statement.

The order of evidence and speeches will follow Rule 14 Magistrates' Courts Rules 1981. This will allow, with the leave of the court, a second submission to be made by either party on both law and fact.

6 Youths

Youths who are defendants in applications will be dealt with in the adult court.

Good practice dictates and subject to availability the court will provide a more informal court setting for the case. Where possible the court will use magistrates with youth court experience.

In respect of defendants under 16, a parent or guardian is required to attend and they should be served with a copy of the summons. If it is deemed impractical for the parent/guardian to attend, an appropriate adult will be sought through the Youth Offending Team.

In respect of defendants aged between 16–17, it is at the court discretion whether to proceed in the absence of a parent or guardian. It is however good practice that the parent or guardian is served with a copy of the summons.

A copy of any order made will also be served upon the parent/guardian.

Representations will be sought regarding whether an order should be made under s 39 Children and Young Persons Act 1933 to prohibit publication of details of the child or young person.

7 The Order

The applicant will deliver to court a draft order (Forms in Schedule 3/Schedule 6, 'Rules') in paper format and also on either e-mail to the legal adviser dealing with the case, prior to the hearing, or on disc, together with any ancillary documents which are necessary, eg a map highlighting the exclusion area.

The court legal adviser will endeavour to serve a signed copy of any order made on the defendant who attends court before he/she leaves the court building and otherwise by first class post to the last known address, and will endorse the copy as to service. *Orders in absence will be served personally by the applicant.*

A formula to create a unique police reference number, and a current list of police notification points is attached to the protocol in appendices 1 and 2.

The number will be compiled and allocated upon service of an order made without notice (as it will only take effect upon service within 7 days of making the order), and upon making an order with notification.

Following allocation of the number and service, the applicant or nominee will send a copy of the order to the police notification point and community safety department within 24 hours. The court will send a copy of an ancillary criminal order to the community safety department for number allocation and notification.

Any cancellation/discharge/variation of an order will be notified immediately by fax to the community safety department by the court and to PNC by the community safety department, together with reasons.

A list of community safety department contact details is attached at appendix 2. An order without notice will be served personally by the applicant.

Each magistrates' court will hold a file of current Anti-Social Behaviour Orders made by that court, together with reasons, and certified copies will be provided upon request to the police and CPS for the purpose of breach action if necessary.

It is not necessary for the Crown Prosecution Service to have given prior approval to the order, though consultation in unusual or exceptional cases may be desirable before the proceedings are commenced.

8 Applications for variation/discharge (r 6 MC (ASBO) 2002)

Application will be made in writing together with the reasons for the application and a time estimate for a full hearing.

Where the court considers that there are grounds upon which it might conclude that the order should be varied or discharged, the court will issue and send a summons with a copy of the application, giving not less than 14 days' notice to the parties.

The case will be listed as soon as practicable, taking account of all the circumstances.

9 Breach

As for a criminal offence, the police will be responsible for the investigation.

The Crown Prosecution Service will be responsible for prosecution.

The youth offending team will be consulted by the police/CPS before the matter is brought to court if the defendant is under 18 years and youth breaches will be dealt with in the youth court.

Upon conviction the court will consider any reports submitted by the police, local authority or any other applicant agency (p 21 HOG).

'Rules' = The Magistrates' Courts (Anti-Social Behaviour Orders) Rules 2002.

'Schedules' = as attached to the Rules.

'Guidance' = 'Guide to ASBOs – Home Office Communication Directorate' – November 2002. Obtainable from: Tel: 0870 241 4680.

APPENDIX 1

PROCEDURE AFTER ORDER IS MADE

Order made on application

1   Creation and notation of police unique reference number for each order by Legal Services Lawyer.

West Yorkshire code/ASBO/local court reference and consecutive number/year.

- West Yorkshire = 13HQ
- Local court references. Leeds = LS. Bradford = BD. Keighley = KY. KS = Kirklees. WF = Wakefield. CD = Calderdale

Example 13HQ/ASBO/LS256/03

1 Black ink or type required please.

2 After endorsing the reference number, and serving the order (ie it is effective), please fax to Police National Computer Bureau on **01924 293644**.

Order made on criminal conviction

1   Order to be served in court by the legal adviser and fax copy endorsed as to service to Community Safety Division (details in Appendix 2).
2   Community Safety Division to allocate unique reference number and notify court for court file records.

(H) HEARSAY NOTICE

IN AN APPLICATION FOR AN ANTI-SOCIAL BEHAVIOUR ORDER
PURSUANT TO SECTION 1(1) OF THE CRIME AND DISORDER ACT 1998
AND Magistrates' Courts (Hearsay Evidence in Civil Proceedings) Rules 1999

BETWEEN

	[applicant authority]	Applicant
	and	
	V. ANTI-SOCIAL	Defendant

NOTICE OF INTENTION
TO RELY ON
HEARSAY EVIDENCE

1. The Complainant intends to rely on hearsay evidence at trial and that evidence is contained in the witness statements of Mr Blue dated 3rd January 2003 which has already been served but is also attached to this notice.

2. Mr Blue is a Tenancy Enforcement Officer who has been provided with information that has been relayed to him by other housing officers and by witnesses to incidents who are have either moved away and cannot be contacted or are too frightened due to fear of reprisals by the Defendant. Those witnesses who names are known and were content for their identity to be disclosed are given in the statement. The remaining witnesses names are either not known to the applicant or the witnesses were too afraid to have their names disclosed. The statement indicates in each case the source of the evidence and whether as above the identity of the giver is known and/or can be disclosed.

3 The Applicant seeks rely on the above evidence in its application for an anti-social behaviour order against the Defendant.

Signed .... Dated ....

APPENDIX 3

A GUIDE TO ANTI-SOCIAL BEHAVIOUR ORDERS AND ACCEPTABLE BEHAVIOUR ORDERS

Contents

Foreword	184
Taking a strategic approach	185
Why ASBOs and ABCs?	186
The relationship between ASBOs and ABCs	187
ANTI-SOCIAL BEHAVIOUR ORDERS	
1. Anti-Social Behaviour Orders: the basics	
What are anti-social behaviour orders?	188
Legal definition of anti-social behaviour for the purpose of obtaining an order	188
Standard of proof	189
Types of behaviour for which ASBOs have been used	189
Who can an order be made against?	190
Who can apply for an order?	191
Which courts can make ASBOs?	192
Where is an ASBO valid?	193
Can interim orders be made?	194
Orders against children and young people	195
Breach of an order	195
2. Managing the application process	
Partnership working	196
Statutory consultation requirements	198
Collection of evidence	199
Time limits	200
Use of hearsay and professional witness evidence	200
Witness development and support	201
Information sharing	203
The terms of the order (the prohibitions)	204
Duration of an order	205
Summons procedure	205
Disclosure	205
Court procedures	206
Court procedures for juveniles	207
Good practice – managing procedures and timescales	210
Immediate post-order procedure	210
3. After the order is made	
Police National Computer (PNC)	211
Appeals	211
Breaches	212
Variation and discharge of an order	214
Monitoring and recording	214

Promoting awareness of orders	215
ACCEPTABLE BEHAVIOUR CONTRACTS	
What are acceptable behaviour contracts?	215
Types of behaviour ABCs have been used for	216
Multi-agency working	217
Publicity	218
Identifying individuals for ABCs	218
The ABC meeting	219
Drawing up the contract	220
Monitoring	221
Dealing with breaches	221
APPENDICES	
A. Summary of legislation governing ASBOs	222
B. Anti-social behaviour orders and orders on conviction – step by step	225
C. Relevant court judgements	229
D. Public funding for defendants	229
E. The process of obtaining and monitoring an ABC – Islington Anti-Social Behaviour Team	230
F. An example of an acceptable behaviour contract	231
G. Conducting an ABC meeting – Islington Anti-Social Behaviour Team	232
H. ABC Good Practice Tips – Circle 33 Housing Group	236

FOREWORD BY THE RT HON JOHN DENHAM MP, MINISTER OF STATE FOR CRIME REDUCTION, POLICING AND COMMUNITY SAFETY AT THE HOME OFFICE

Of the problems which most affect neighbourhoods up and down the country, antisocial behaviour – covering as it does a whole complex of thoughtless, inconsiderate or malicious activity – has perhaps the greatest potential to blight the quality of community life. Every week I hear of aggressive or loutish behaviour which can cause something close to despair among people who are forced to put up with it. Anti-social behaviour is never victimless, and too often the victims are the elderly, the minorities, the poor, and the vulnerable.

But as a society we can fight back. And you, the practitioners to whom this guidance is primarily addressed, are the people who can lead that fight back. Recognising the extent and urgency of the problem is the first step; working in partnership with each other, bringing to bear a co-ordinated and strategic approach to the problem, is the next; and using the full range of instruments available to you is the third. And this guidance note is intended to help you to make the most effective possible use of two of the most important of the weapons in your armoury – the antisocial behaviour order or ASBO, and the acceptable behaviour contract or ABC.

This Government brought in the ASBO in the Crime and Disorder Act 1998. It represented a completely new approach to the problem, bringing the flexibility of civil law procedures to bear on perpetrators while ensuring that the strength of the criminal law was brought into play in case of breach. Although they have had a comparatively short life, they have already had a real impact in reducing anti-social behaviour and protecting individuals and communities. But the procedures have not been trouble-free. Too often, the process of applying for an ASBO has been protracted and expensive, while the remedy available has not always proved adequate. We have listened to practitioners, and brought forward a major package of changes in the Police Reform Act 2002. This guidance sets out to explain exactly what those changes are and how they can help.

But the guidance goes much wider than that. It completely overhauls the guidance produced when ASBOs first came out, offering you a single point of reference for all the questions which arise most frequently when an ASBO is being contemplated or applied for. Supplementary information will also be made available on the Crime Reduction website.

And the guidance also, for the first time, offers practitioners a ready source of information and guidance on acceptable behaviour contracts. I cannot praise too highly the professionals in local authorities and police forces, in Islington and elsewhere, who came up with the concept of the acceptable behaviour contract and made it work. It is hard to think of a better example of local initiative bringing practical results in the whole field of social policy. This guidance is written in the belief that ASBOs and ABCs are not competing alternatives: the circumstances of the case will determine which is the right intervention – and you, the professional, are the right person to make that decision.

All of this is of course undermined without the effective enforcement of ASBO breaches by the court. Those who continue to bring fear, distress and misery to local communities should not go unpunished. Sentences should reflect the seriousness of the crime and do so in a consistent manner. Without this communities are denied the justice to which they are entitled and ASBOs are deprived of their powerful deterrent effect.

Tackling anti-social behaviour effectively is one of the greatest challenges facing our communities and those whose job it is to protect them. I hope that this guidance will prove itself to be of real help in that task.

John Denham

Taking a strategic approach

The crime and disorder reduction partnership lies at the heart of the Government's approach to the reduction of both crime and anti-social behaviour (much of which is of course criminal in nature). All crime and disorder reduction partnerships have been strongly recommended to appoint an anti-social behaviour co-ordinator, and over 90% of them have now done so. All partnerships, too, are required to draw up strategies for the reduction of anti-social behaviour in their areas, and the anti-social behaviour co-ordinators are in the best position to ensure that those strategies genuinely reflect the needs of the community served by the partnerships.

Anti-social behaviour has a wide legal definition – to paraphrase the Crime and Disorder Act 1998, it is behaviour which causes or is likely to cause harassment, alarm or distress to one or more people who are not in the same household as the perpetrator. Among the forms it can take are:

- graffiti – which can on its own make even the tidiest urban spaces look squalid
- abusive and intimidating language, too often directed at minorities
- excessive noise, particularly late at night
- fouling the street with litter
- drunken behaviour in the streets, and the mess it creates
- dealing drugs, with all the problems to which it gives rise.

All these are issues which concern everyone in the community. They cannot be written off as generational issues – they impact on the quality of life of young and old alike. And they require a response which puts partnership into action.

Just as the problems of anti-social behaviour are multifarious, the solution too must operate equally effectively on many levels. While an energetic and constructive police response is essential, it must be supplemented by engagement from a wide variety of partners. To take only the most obvious, schools need to have effective policies in place against truancy and bullying. Local authorities and registered social landlords need to take responsibility for acting against anti-social behaviour by their tenants, and against their tenants. Social services need to ensure that they are taking the welfare of the community fully into account when making their decisions. And, just as important, all of these bodies need to be sharing information with each other to the fullest possible extent in order to act fairly and decisively against the problems of anti-social behaviour.

ASBOs and ABCs can only work properly when they are based on this approach of partnership in action. As the guidance which follows will make clear, they are powerful instruments, and they will be at their most effective when all the agencies confronted by an individual's anti-social behaviour collaborate to make the best possible use of them.

Why ASBOs and ABCs?

ASBOs and ABCs are both comparatively recent developments designed to put a stop to anti-social behaviour by the individuals on whom they are imposed. But they work in very different ways, and these differences will inform the judgement of professionals on which of them may be the best option in any particular case.

The most obvious difference is that the ASBO is a statutory creation, and carries legal force; the ABC is an informal procedure, though not, as will be made clear, without legal significance. Both types of intervention are aimed at stopping the problem behaviour, rather than punishing the offender. Because the ABC is a voluntary contract, it has greater flexibility, while the ASBO, because of its more formal status, offers advantages in terms of enforcement.

ASBOs were introduced by Section 1 of the Crime and Disorder Act 1998 and first used in 1999. Home Office research published in 2002[1] found that the orders had delivered real improvement in the quality of life to communities around the country; its use of civil law procedures and the wide powers granted to courts to impose conditions once satisfied that an ASBO was necessary were widely welcomed. But the research also made clear that these new procedures had brought new problems with them, and these problems were part of the explanation for the fact that in some parts of the country ASBOs were being very little used by practitioners.

Once identified, the Government acted quickly to address these difficulties. The Police Reform Act 2002 contains five important changes, four of which are now (November 2002) being implemented. Courts may decide that an ASBO will be valid throughout the country; it will be possible to apply for interim ASBOs; registered social landlords and the British Transport Police will be able to apply for ASBOs; and it will be possible for a court to impose an order at the same time as passing sentence for a criminal conviction. From spring 2003 the fifth change, enabling county courts to impose orders under certain circumstances, will also be in force.

This guidance, which supersedes the guides to ASBOs produced by the Home Office in 1999 and 2000,[2] explains these changes and aims to provide all the information with practitioners are likely to need in making the most effective possible use of these orders.

Acceptable behaviour contracts are voluntary agreements made between people involved in anti-social behaviour and the local police, the housing department, the registered social landlord, or the perpetrator's school. They are flexible in terms of content and format. Initially

---

[1] Home Office Research Study 236, 'A Review of anti-social behaviour orders' by Dr Siobhan Campbell, published April 2002.
[2] Home Office, 'Anti-Social Behaviour Orders: Guidance', published March 1999; Home Office, 'Anti-Social Behaviour Orders: Guidance on drawing up Local ASBO Protocols', published June 2000.

introduced in the London Borough of Islington to deal with problems on estates being caused by young people aged between 10 and 17, they are now used with adults as well as young people, and in a wide variety of circumstances. They have proved effective as a means of encouraging young adults, children, and importantly, parents to take responsibility for unacceptable behaviour. They are being used to improve the quality of life for local people by tackling behaviour such as harassment, graffiti, criminal damage and verbal abuse.

This guidance on ASBOs and ABCs draws on the experience of police services, local authorities, youth offending teams, and other organisations. It is intended for use by practitioners – people with a professional responsibility for tackling anti-social behaviour, whether they represent local authorities, the police, youth offending teams, registered social landlords, prosecutors, the judiciary, or any other agency which seeks to tackle the problem of anti-social behaviour.

The relationship between ASBOs and ABCs

It is important that all concerned should understand that ASBOs and ABCs are in no sense competing for business. Both are potentially extremely powerful tools for dealing with cases of anti-social behaviour, and it will be very much a matter for the individual practitioner to decide which of them it might be appropriate to go for in any particular case. It is particularly important to dispel any impression that anti-social behaviour orders should be regarded as measures of last resort, only to be tried when other interventions such as acceptable behaviour contracts have already failed.

Where an ABC is selected as the best option, it is recommended that it should contain a statement that the continuation of unacceptable behaviour may lead to an application for an ASBO. Where a contract is broken, that should be used as evidence in the application for an ASBO. It may also be possible to use the evidence of anti-social behaviour which was originally collected for the ABC in any subsequent ASBO application.

Anti-social behaviour that can be tackled by ASBOs and ABCs includes:

- Harassment of residents or passers by
- Verbal abuse
- Criminal damage
- Vandalism
- Noise nuisance
- Writing graffiti
- Engaging in threatening behaviour in large groups
- Racial abuse
- Smoking or drinking alcohol while under age
- Substance misuse
- Joyriding
- Begging
- Prostitution
- Kerb-crawling
- Throwing missiles
- Assault
- Vehicle crime.

The terms of each order or contract should be tailored to the circumstances of the individual case.

ANTI-SOCIAL BEHAVIOUR ORDERS

1. Anti-social behaviour orders: the basics

What are anti-social behaviour orders?

Anti-social behaviour orders (ASBOs) were introduced by section 1 of the Crime and Disorder Act 1998 in England and Wales and have been available since April 1999. The powers to impose ASBOs were strengthened and extended by the Police Reform Act 2002, which introduced orders made on conviction in criminal proceedings, orders in county court proceedings and interim orders. Orders can now also extend across any defined part of England and Wales.

ASBOs are civil orders that exist to protect the public from behaviour that causes or is likely to cause harassment, alarm or distress. An order contains conditions prohibiting the offender from specific anti-social acts or entering defined areas and is effective for a minimum of two years. The orders are not criminal penalties and are not intended to punish the offender. An order should not be viewed as an option of last resort.

Stand-alone applications for ASBOs are made to the magistrates' court acting in its civil capacity. The order can be applied for during related proceedings in the county court; and requested (without the need for a formal application) if a defendant is convicted of an offence in the criminal courts. It remains a civil order irrespective of the issuing court.

ASBOs are community-based orders that involve local people not only in the collection of evidence but also in helping to enforce breaches. By their nature they encourage local communities to become actively involved in reporting crime and disorder and contributing actively to building and protecting the community.

The civil status of ASBOs has implications for the type of court proceedings at which applications are heard. The civil nature of the order means that hearsay and professional witness evidence can be heard. This is an extremely important feature of ASBOs because those subjected to the anti-social behaviour or those reporting the behaviour can be protected (see [p 201]).

Legal definition of anti-social behaviour for the purpose of obtaining an order

Under the terms of the Crime and Disorder Act 1998 the agency applying for the order must show that:

- the defendant behaved in an anti-social manner *and*
- an order is necessary for the protection of persons from further anti-social behaviour by the defendant.

This is sometimes referred to as the 'two stage test'.

Section 1(1) of the Act defines acting in an 'anti-social manner' as 'a manner that caused or was likely to cause harassment, alarm or distress to one or more persons not of the same household' as the perpetrator. The definition is intentionally wide-ranging to allow for the orders to be used in a variety of circumstances.

The expression 'likely to cause' has the effect that someone other than a victim of the anti-social behaviour can give evidence of its occurrence. This is intended specifically to validate the use of professionals as witnesses where those targeted by the behaviour feel unable to come forward, for example, for fear of reprisals or intimidation.

Standard of Proof

The House of Lords confirmed in the case of *McCann*[1] that ASBOs were civil orders and set out the law on the standard of proof as follows:

> 'they [magistrates] must in all cases under section 1 apply the criminal standard ... it will be sufficient for the magistrates, when applying section 1(1)(a) to be sure that the defendant has acted in an anti-social manner, that is to say in a manner which caused or was likely to cause harassment, alarm, or distress to one or more persons not of the same household as himself.' (Lord Steyn, paragraph 37)

This means that the criminal standard of proof applies to the past acts of anti-social behaviour alleged against the defendant.

However, Lord Steyn went on to explain,

> 'The inquiry under section 1(1)(b), namely that such an order is necessary to protect persons from further anti-social acts by him, does not involve a standard of proof: it is an exercise of judgement or evaluation.'

It should be noted that it is the effect or likely effect of the behaviour on other people that determines whether the behaviour is anti-social. The agency applying for the order does not have to prove an *intention* on the part of the defendant to cause harassment, alarm or distress.

The Court will, however, disregard any behaviour shown to be reasonable in the circumstances under section 1(5) of the 1998 Act.

Types of behaviour for which ASBOs have been used

The most common behaviour tackled by ASBOs is general loutish and unruly conduct such as verbal abuse, harassment, assault, graffiti and excessive noise. ASBOs have also been used to combat racial harassment, drunk and disorderly behaviour, throwing missiles, vehicle crime and prostitution. Many other problems, for instance the use of air guns, would also lend themselves to this approach.

The wide range of anti-social behaviour that can be tackled by ASBOs and the ability to tailor the terms of the order to each specific case illustrates their flexibility.

Protecting hospital staff and patients – Cumbria Constabulary

Issue Two men persistently caused problems in the Accident and Emergency Department in Carlisle. Sometimes they came in with a genuine complaint (usually an injury, drug overdose or alcohol related problem), sometimes not. They were disruptive and abusive to patients and staff, caused a nuisance, used threatening behaviour and obstructed the proper treatment of the other patients.

Approach Timely case conferences where held with agencies relevant to the case – in this instance the probation service and social services. The issues explored included what had been done previously to address the behaviour and what new action should be taken. All participants supported the ASBO applications; the probation service saw the orders as an incentive to get the individuals into treatment. Evidence was collected by police community beat managers.

---

[1] House of Lords, *Clingham (formerly C (a minor)) v Royal Borough of Kensington and Chelsea* (on Appeal from a Divisional Court of the Queen's Bench Division); *Regina v Crown Court at Manchester Ex p McCann* (FC) and Others (FC), October 2002.

Outcome The ASBOs clearly defined the limits of acceptable behaviour. Prior to the orders being made the A&E department put up with a high level of nuisance before calling the police. Once the orders were in place staff felt able to call the police immediately if either of the men became abusive or disruptive. The police enforced breaches of the order, which have resulted in a range of sentences including custody. There was an 83% reduction in the number of incidents attended and an 81% reduction in arrests during the period of the order for one of the offenders. ASBOs are seen as having teeth and the threat of an order has resulted in a reduction of anti-social behaviour amongst several other individuals.

Lessons learned Case conferences put on record everyone's involvement and their accountability. Two-year orders were used but the anti-social behaviour by one of the men escalated when it expired. Carlisle police are preparing a new application for this man and are considering five-year orders for new cases. In addition, a planned programme of reviews will be introduced so that all parties are updated on progress. ABCs will also be considered for new cases.

Contact Sgt Andy Baines, Community Safety, Carlisle Police, North Cumbria Area Police Headquarters, 01228 528191

Who can an order be made against?

An order can be made against anyone aged 10 years or more who has acted in an anti-social manner and where an order is needed to protect person(s) from further anti-social acts.

The orders are tenure-neutral and can be used against offenders living in any type of housing (not just social housing). ASBOs can be used to combat anti-social behaviour in a wide range of situations and settings. They are highly relevant to misconduct in public spaces such as parks, shopping centres, transport hubs; but are by no means confined to such areas.

Where groups of people are engaged in anti-social behaviour a case needs to be made against each individual against whom an order is sought. However, the cases can be heard together by the court. Agencies have found that targeting ringleaders with orders is an effective deterrent to other members of the group.

Targeting Ringleaders – West Mercia Police

Issue A group of youths hanging around a village engaged in abusing drink and drugs, racially motivated incidents and causing damage

Approach Four ASBOs were obtained on the ringleaders, which prohibited them from:
- loitering in particular areas,
- entering named shops, and
- using threatening, abusive or racist language.

The police engaged the community in the process. The local beat manager and local councillor arranged a meeting with local people where they were able to voice their concerns. The police anti-social behaviour representative set out the plan to tackle the problems and explained what support and assistance was needed from the community for gathering evidence.

The ASBOs were used in parallel with other measures. These included:
- Targeting shop keepers selling alcohol to under 18s
- Tackling the local drugs problems by preventing incoming phone calls to local telephone boxes which were being used to arrange drug deals

> - Working with the local bus company to make it more difficult for the troublemakers to get to their usual meeting place. Alternative arrangements were made for other users of the bus service
> - Following up on the behaviour after the ASBO has been made
> - Meeting with the community again to review progress
> - Prosecuting for breach
>
> **Outcome** Local police measured 24 reports of disorder in the month before the order, and five in the month after. There was no evidence of displacement of the problem to other areas. Following the success of the ASBOs local councillors took ownership of the situation and the community committed itself to helping with local initiatives to deter anti-social behaviour.
>
> **Contact** Sgt Singh, West Mercia Police, Clive Road, Monkmoor, Shrewsbury, SY2 5RW 01743 232888

When investigating complaints about anti-social behaviour, it is vital that agencies satisfy themselves that complaints are well founded. In particular, they should consider the possibility that complaints may have been motivated by discrimination, perhaps on racist grounds, or to further a pre-existing grudge.

Failing to act against instances of anti-social behaviour can lead to an escalation of the problem by increasing fear of crime or leading those subjected to the anti-social behaviour to retaliate.

Who can apply for an order?

Agencies able to apply for orders are defined as 'relevant authorities' in the legislation (section 1(1A) of the Crime and Disorder Act 1998). These are:

- Local authorities
- Police forces (including the British Transport Police)
- Registered Social Landlords as defined by section 1 of the Housing Act 1996

Under section 1(12) of the 1998 Act the local authority is the district council or unitary authority. This is defined as the council for the local government area, which in relation to England means a district or London borough, the City of London, the Isle of Wight and the Isles of Scilly; and in relation to Wales, a county or county borough.

Local authorities and the police may apply for an order where they consider it necessary to protect persons in their area ('relevant persons') irrespective of where the original anti-social behaviour took place. An order can be sought which provides protection not just to the relevant persons but also, where necessary, to any persons in England and Wales.

The British Transport Police (BTP) and registered social landlords (RSLs) are empowered to apply for orders by changes introduced under the Police Reform Act 2002. This enables these agencies to deal with their particular problems of anti-social behaviour in a more effective and timely manner. RSLs may apply for orders against non-residents as well as residents and should consider doing so where the anti-social behaviour of non-residents is affecting the quality of life for residents.

Applications from the BTP or RSLs must concern anti-social behaviour related to the premises for which they are responsible by persons who are on or in the vicinity of such premises or likely to be either on or in the vicinity of such premises.

The British Transport Police and registered social landlords are required to consult both the local authority and local police force when applying for an order.

Neither agency is compelled to use the power. The police or local authority may still apply for ASBOs on their behalf. Under section 17 of the 1998 Act, the police and local authorities have a joint responsibility to develop and implement strategies for tackling anti-social behaviour and disorder in the local area. This responsibility is not changed in any way by allowing registered social landlords and the British Transport Police to apply for orders.

Which courts can make ASBOs?

- Magistrates' courts (acting in their civil capacity)
- County courts (where the principal proceedings involve anti-social behaviour by those who are party to the proceedings)
- Magistrates' courts (on conviction in criminal proceedings)
- The Crown Court (on conviction in criminal proceedings)
- Youth courts (on conviction in criminal proceedings)

Improving communication with the Courts – Coventry CDRP

Issue The need to improve understanding amongst the local judiciary of (1) the impact of anti-social behaviour on the community, (2) the potential benefits of ASBOs as a tool to protect the local community, and (3) the work that is put into an ASBO application and prosecuting breaches.

Approach The ASB co-ordinator and the court clerk arranged a seminar on ASBOs for lay magistrates and clerks in the area. Speakers included representatives from the police, a registered social landlord, the local authority and the Home Office. The local authority also produced a ten-minute video comprising of professional witness footage of ASB in the local area, which graphically illustrated the behaviour to which communities are being subjected.

Outcome The event was attended by over 70 magistrates, many of whom had been unclear about the problem of anti-social behaviour and the purpose of ASBOs. The event increased awareness of local issues as well as the powers available under the ASBO legislation. It has also raised awareness of the partnership approach used by local agencies, particularly the ongoing efforts of the local police, local authority and registered social landlords.

Lessons learned The video has been used as part of a series of training sessions for the police and neighbourhood wardens and there are plans to use it for community safety officers.

Contact Andrea Poole, andrea.poole@coventry.gov.uk, 02476 832580

Orders made in county court proceedings (section 1B of the Crime and Disorder Act 1998)

The person who is the subject of an application made in the county court must also be party to the 'principal proceedings' (such as an eviction). Where the relevant authority is not a party to the principal proceedings, an application to be made a party and the application for an ASBO should be made as soon as possible after the authority becomes aware of the principal proceedings. The county court will be able to grant orders where the principal proceedings involve evidence of anti-social behaviour.

Enabling the county courts to make ASBOs may remove the need for a separate legal process in the magistrates' court and enables the public to be protected from anti-social behaviour more quickly.

An order made in county court proceedings might, for example, be useful to prevent an individual who is evicted from their accommodation for harassing their neighbours and/or others in the area from returning to the same area to continue the harassment.

An application could also be made in the county court for an order made where, for example, a private landlord was seeking a possession order and a relevant authority successfully applied to be joined to the proceedings.

The county court will be able to make ASBOs on the application of any relevant authority.

Orders made on conviction in criminal proceedings

Criminal courts – the magistrate's court, the Crown Court and the youth court – will be able to make orders against an individual who has been convicted of a criminal offence.

The order on conviction is considered and made by the court after the verdict during a civil hearing. It is not part of the sentence the offender receives for the criminal offence. It can only be made in addition to a sentence or a conditional discharge. The order will be granted on the basis of the evidence presented to the court during the criminal proceedings and any additional evidence provided to the court after the verdict.

The court may make an order on conviction on its own initiative and an application for an order is not required. Alternatively, the order can be requested by the police or local authority, who may make representations to the court in support of the request.

The order on conviction is a civil order and has the same effect as an ASBO made on application – it contains prohibitions rather than penalties and is made in civil proceedings. It is similar to the football banning order on conviction in that it is a civil order made following a criminal procedure.[1]

If the offender is detained in custody the court may make provision for the order on conviction to become effective on his or her release.

Where is an ASBO valid?

Before the changes introduced by the Police Reform Act 2002, the conditions an ASBO could impose applied only in the local government area in which the behaviour occurred and adjoining areas. An order can now extend across any defined area within, or indeed the whole of, England or Wales.[2]

The power to make an order over a wide area is for use where there is reason to believe that the person concerned may move or has already moved. It goes some way to addressing the problem of offenders moving to other areas and continuing the behaviour.

---

[1] Section 1C(2) of the Crime and Disorder Act 1998 states that the court may make an order which prohibits the offender from doing anything described in the order. Section 14A of the Football Spectators Act 1989 places a duty on the court to impose a Football Banning Order if a person is convicted of a relevant offence or to state in open court why such an order has not been made.

[2] The geographical area over which an order may cover is defined by section 1(6) for ASBOs and orders made in county court proceedings; and section 1C(2)(b) for orders made on conviction in criminal proceedings.

An order covering a wider area could address problems such as ticket touting at different train stations, anti-social behaviour on trains and help deal with the minority of the travelling community who persistently engage in anti-social behaviour around the country.

Any evidence of the itinerant nature of the defendant's lifestyle; evidence that the individual may move to another area; or wide geographical spread of offending behaviour should be submitted with the application file. The applicant does not have to prove that anti-social behaviour will occur elsewhere, just show that it is likely to. The more serious the behaviour, the more likely that the court will grant a geographically wide order.

Can interim orders be made?

Interim orders are available under section 1D of the Crime and Disorder Act 1998 (as amended by section 65 of the Police Reform Act 2002) in both the magistrates' court and the county court. This is an order made at an initial court hearing held in advance of the full hearing. This temporary order can impose the same prohibitions and has the same penalties for breach as ASBOs.

The interim order can, with leave of the justices' clerk, be made *ex parte* (without notice of proceedings being given to the defendant).

The benefit of the interim order is that it enables the courts to order an immediate stop to anti-social behaviour and thereby to protect the public more quickly. It reduces the scope for witness intimidation by making it unlawful for the offender to continue the behaviour whilst the ASBO application is being processed. It also removes any incentive for delaying the proceedings on the part of the perpetrator. The interim order will send a clear message to the community that swift action against anti-social behaviour is possible.

The orders can be made at the outset of proceedings for an application for an ASBO if the court considers that it is *just* to make such an order. The applicant authority should request an interim order at the same time as submitting an application for a full order.

When considering whether to make an interim order the court will be aware that it may not be possible at the time of the interim order application to compile all the evidence which would prove that a full ASBO is necessary. Rather the court will determine the application for the interim order on the question of whether the application for the full order has been properly made and where there is sufficient evidence of an urgent need to protect the community.

Applications for interim orders will be appropriate, for example, in cases where the applicant feels that persons need to be protected from the threat of further antisocial acts which might occur before the main application can be determined.

Where an interim order is granted *ex parte* (without notice of proceedings to the defendant) it is expected that the court will usually arrange an early return date. An individual who is subject to an interim order will have the opportunity to respond to the case at the hearing for the full order. The defendant is also able apply to the court for the interim order to be varied or discharged. In this instance the matter will be dealt with at a hearing dealing specifically with the interim matter.

The interim order:

- Will be for a fixed period
- Can be varied or discharged on application by the defendant
- Will cease to have effect if the application for the ASBO or county court order is withdrawn or refused

- May extend over any defined area of England and Wales
- Has the same breach penalties as for a full order.

Interim Orders made in the Magistrates' Court (acting in its civil capacity)

An application for an *ex parte* interim order is subject to leave being given by the justice's clerk or court clerk. If agreement is given, a hearing may go ahead without notice being given to the defendant.

If the order is granted it should be served personally on the defendant together with the application for a full order and a summons giving a date for the defendant to attend court. The order will not take effect until it is served.

The court procedures and forms to be used when applying for or making an interim order are set out in the Magistrates' Courts (Anti-Social Behaviour Orders) Rules 2002, which will be available on introduction.

Interim Orders made in the county courts

A relevant authority may apply for an interim order in the county court once it is party to the 'principal proceedings'. The application for an interim order should be made early in the proceedings.

The procedure for making applications for orders in the County Court will be set out in the Practice Direction of the updated Civil Procedure Rules.[1]

Orders against children and young people

Under the Crime and Disorder Act 1998 applications for ASBOs against juveniles can be heard in the magistrates' court. Applications for orders are not heard in the youth court as a matter of course because of the civil status of the orders, although youth courts may as indicated above make orders where appropriate on conviction. Automatic reporting restrictions would apply (under Section 39 of the Children and Young Persons Act 1933) to orders made on conviction in the youth court, but there are *no automatic reporting restrictions* in the magistrates' courts against juveniles.

A court making an ASBO does have the power to impose restrictions to protect the identity of a person under 18. But the imposition of reporting restrictions may restrict the effectiveness of the order if the effectiveness of the ASBO will largely depend on the wider community knowing the details.

Under the 1998 Act as amended applications for ASBOs against juveniles can also be heard in the county court. But such applications will happen only rarely where, for example, a juvenile is a tenant in possession proceedings.

Breach of an order

Breach of an order is a criminal offence; criminal procedures and penalties apply. The standard of proof required is the criminal standard. Guilt must be established beyond reasonable doubt. Breach proceedings are heard in the magistrates' court and may be referred to the Crown Court. Such proceedings are the same irrespective of whether the order is a full

---

[1] Available in January 2003; the order in county court proceedings is available from 1 April 2003.

or interim order made on application to the magistrates' court or the county court, or an order on conviction in criminal proceedings.

The maximum penalty for breach of an order is five years imprisonment for an adult offender.

The maximum sentence for breach by juvenile is a detention and training order, which has a maximum term of 24 months – 12 months of which is custodial and 12 months is in the community. The DTO is available for 12–17-year-olds (although a 12–14 year old must be a persistent (criminal) offender to be given a DTO). A 10–11-year-old can be given a community order for breach of ASBO.

The sentence given should be proportionate and reflect the *impact* of the anti-social behaviour. Proceedings should be swift and not fractured by unnecessary adjournments either during the proceedings or before sentencing.

When the offender has been found guilty of breaching an order, and before sentencing, the court may take reports from the local authority or police and any applicant agency. The court should also consider the original reasons for the making of the order.

2. Managing the application process

This section focuses on the main issues involved in applying for an order. For an ASBO to be effective the process of evidence gathering and applying to the courts should be as swift as possible.

Groups of organisations and partnerships such as crime and disorder reduction partnerships may wish to consider buying specialist legal advice in blocks or pool expertise and experience. This is likely to be more cost-effective than buying in legal advice on a case by case basis.

Partnership working

A fully co-ordinated approach is essential if anti-social behaviour is to be tackled. Effective defence of communities depends on all agencies – including housing organisations, social services, education authorities and youth services – accepting that promoting safe and orderly neighbourhoods is a priority and working together to agree a response to unacceptable behaviour.

Taking Ownership

It is vital that a specified individual within the lead agency takes on a lead role with responsibility for the ownership, direction and management of the case. This will help to ensure that there is no confusion about who is expected to make sure that the necessary actions are taken on the right timescale.

The lead individual should manage and co-ordinate the involvement of other agencies so that they add value by contributing their own specialist knowledge and expertise.

A multi-agency approach should be adopted so that all agencies that could hold information on the individual in question are involved in the process at an early stage. Such agencies include the probation service, social services, health services, the youth offending team and voluntary organisations, all of which may have come into contact with the individual or members of their family.

Crime and disorder reduction partnerships should consider adopting the 'orders group' structure developed by Coventry CDRP.

- The orders group has delegated authority from the CDRP to establish and manage protocols and processes for implementing ASBOs (including information sharing).
- The orders group should comprise the local authority ASB co-ordinator and designated representatives from the police, education, social services, youth offending team, probation, RSLs, health, Crown Prosecution Service and the Courts. Other agencies should engage as is appropriate to the local area or particular case.
- Members of the orders group are senior officers with delegated decision making authority from their respective agencies. Each is responsible for the communication of the relevant protocols and partnership arrangements within their organisations.

A comprehensive protocol for the consideration of potential ASBOs and the pursuit of applications, where appropriate, should be committed to by the relevant partner agencies.[1] A lead officer should be identified to oversee each case.

- The protocol should also enable communication with agencies not directly represented on the main orders group or the CDRP (e.g. other RSLs or the fire service).
- A case conference approach should be established whereby potential ASBO cases are considered by the agencies who are able to contribute to the case and have information about the individual in question. The case conference could be held by the orders group where established, but is perhaps more likely to involve staff from agencies who are directly concerned with the case in question. It should be attended by the person with lead responsibility for the case.
- The role of the lead officer is to manage the case. This will include instructing solicitors, witness liaison and support, co-ordinating service of summonses, communicating developments to partners and ensuring that appropriate monitoring arrangements are in place to facilitate enforcement of orders granted.
- Case management meetings should be action oriented and outcome focused, the primary objective being to identify and implement appropriate measures to protect communities from anti-social acts. This may be an ASBO or another form of intervention as appropriate.
- Any agency should be able to request a case management meeting.
- Case management meetings should be held within two weeks of the identification of a case.
- In the majority of instances a single meeting should be sufficient to establish the action plan, inclusive of monitoring and review arrangements and a publicity strategy, where relevant.
- The action points of each case management meeting should be recorded by the lead officer.
- Where the case involves a young person, case management meetings should routinely include representatives from education, social services and the youth offending team. An assessment of the young person should be undertaken as soon as it is deemed appropriate. This may happen in parallel with the application.

The arrangements established by the CDRP should seek to combine robust procedures that comply with relevant legislative requirements (for example, for information sharing) with flexible operation – a pragmatic approach that avoids prescription and enables the agency most suitable in an individual case to fulfil the lead officer role.

---

[1] The protocol is available on the Crime Reduction Website.

The protocol and operational arrangements should be subject to review and change by the orders group, or where no orders group exists by the main CDRP, to promote effectiveness.

Other considerations

Local authorities have a duty under the NHS and Community Care Act 1990 to assess any person who may be in need of community care services. If there is any evidence to suggest that the person against whom the order is being sought may be suffering from drug, alcohol, or mental health problems, the necessary support should be provided by social services or other support agencies. Such support should run parallel with the collection of evidence and application for an order, where an application for an order is deemed necessary.

Partnership working – Thames Valley Police and Oxford City Council

Issue A lack of information amongst agencies about ASBOs and the working practices of different partners.

Approach Oxford City Council police liaison officer and the Crime and Nuisance Action Team (CANAcT) provide training to other agencies and local authority teams. The objective is to bring all teams to a level where they are able to identify cases of anti-social behaviour in their day-to-day work and understand how to tackle it. Each team is taught how to initiate an investigation and make a referral to CANAcT. Agencies and witnesses use incident diaries produced by CANAcT to gather evidence. CANAcT then take over the investigation and deal with the case. CANAcT also have a service level agreement with registered social landlords in the Oxford City Council area to deal with their anti-social behaviour problems. Each case is studied either by the legal department of the police or the local authority, depending on which agency is leading the investigation.

Outcome Improved partnership working amongst agencies working to reduce anti-social behaviour. A variety of tools are considered in resolving problems and a mixture of criminal and civil remedies have been used. CANAcT is dealing with cases on a daily basis on behalf of registered social landlords.

Contact PC Jim Abram, police liaison officer, 01865 252502

Statutory consultation requirements

Section 1E of the Crime and Disorder Act 1998 (as amended by section 66 of the Police Reform Act 2002) sets out the consultation requirements for agencies applying for orders. These are that:

- The police and local authorities must consult each other
- Registered social landlords and the British Transport Police must consult both the local authority and police force for the area.

Consultation takes place with the agency whose area includes the address where the subject of the order resides or appears to reside. Each district or borough council and police division/basic command unit should have a nominated contact.

Consultation is required to inform the appropriate agency or agencies of the intended application for the order and to check whether they have any relevant information. Where the partnership working arrangements recommended in earlier paragraphs are in force, they will normally satisfy (and exceed) the statutory requirement for consultation.

The statutory requirement for consultation does not mean that the agencies must agree to an application being made but rather they are told of the intended application and given the opportunity to comment. This should ensure at the very minimum that actions taken by each agency regarding the same individual do not conflict.

While no agency has a veto over another agency's application for an ASBO, the expectation is that any reservations or alternative proposals should be discussed carefully, against the background of the overriding need to bring the anti-social behaviour to a speedy end. Again, the case conference procedure is designed to ensure that this happens.

A signed document of consultation is all that is required by the court. This should *not* indicate whether the party consulted was or was not in agreement. This is not required by the legislation. Supporting statements or reports from partner agencies should be provided separately.

The changes introduced by the 2002 Act reduce bureaucracy by removing the need for applying agencies to consult with every local authority and police service whose areas are included in the order.

In addition to the consultation requirements set out above, it may be helpful for police forces to contact the British Transport Police as they may hold information on the anti-social behaviour of the subject. The availability of this information may assist the evidence gathering process for an ASBO. The British Transport Police hold a national database of offenders committing summary offences (these include railway specific summary offences as well as those included in Home Office counting rules). Home Office police forces can request a search on a particular offender, in writing, from the Force Crime Registrar, British Transport Police, Force Headquarters, 15 Tavistock Place, London WC1H 9SJ.

Collection of evidence

When applying for an order the lead agency will be required to gather evidence to prove its case beyond reasonable doubt. This evidence can include hearsay evidence.

The evidence in support of an ASBO application should prove:

(1) That the defendant acted in a specific way on specific dates and at specific places *and*
(2) That these acts caused or were likely to cause harassment, alarm or distress to one or more persons not in the same household as the defendant.

The court then needs to evaluate whether an order is necessary to protect persons from further anti-social acts by the defendant. This is not a test to which a standard of proof will be applied. Instead it is an assessment of future risk. The applicant can present evidence or argument to assist the court in making this evaluation.

Witness evidence need not prove that they were alarmed or distressed themselves, but only that the behaviour they witnessed was likely to produce such an effect on others. As hearsay evidence is allowed it may be given by 'professional witnesses' – officers of public agencies whose job it is to prevent anti-social behaviour.

Experience has shown that elaborate court files are not normally required or advantageous. Where the anti-social behaviour has been persistent, agencies should focus on a few well-documented cases. A large volume of evidence and/or a large number of witnesses creates its own problems. There is more material for the defence to contest and timetabling issues may increase delays in the process. Agencies applying for orders should strike a balance and focus on what is most relevant and necessary to provide sufficient evidence for the court to arrive at a clear understanding of the matter.

Evidence may include:

Breach of an acceptable behaviour contract
Witness statements of officers who attended incidents
Witness statements of people affected by the behaviour
Evidence of complaints recorded by police, housing providers or other agencies
Statements from professional witnesses, for example council officials, health visitors or truancy officers
Video or CCTV evidence (effective where resolution is high and high quality still images can be used)
Supporting statements or reports from other agencies, for example probation reports
Previous successful civil proceedings which are relevant, such as an eviction order for similar behaviour
Previous relevant convictions
Copies of custody records of previous arrests relevant to the application
Information from witness diaries.

Time limits

Magistrates' courts (acting in their civil capacity)

Under Section 127 of the Magistrates' Court Act 1980 a complaint must be made within six months from the time when the matter of the complaint (the behaviour) arose. One incidence of serious anti-social behaviour may be sufficient for an order to be made. Earlier incidents may be used as background information to support a case and show a pattern of behaviour.

As long as the complaint is made within the six-month timeframe, a summons may be served outside this time period; although delay is not encouraged.

Use of hearsay and professional witness evidence

Hearsay and professional witness evidence allows for the identities of those too fearful to give evidence to be protected. This is especially vital as cases often involve anti-social behaviour in residential areas by local people where those targeted by the behaviour feel unable to come forward for fear of reprisals.

Hearsay evidence cannot be excluded (at the request of defence lawyers) simply on the grounds that it is hearsay.

Order on conviction in criminal proceedings

Evidence of anti-social behaviour which occurs at any time after the commencement of section 1[1] may be taken into account when the court considers whether or not to grant an order on conviction under section 1C.

The House of Lords judgement in the *McCann* case confirmed that hearsay evidence is admissible. Lord Steyn stated that:[2]

> 'Having concluded that the proceedings in question are civil under domestic law and article 6, it follows that the machinery of the Civil Evidence Act 1995 and the Magistrates' Courts (Hearsay Evidence in Civil Proceedings) Rules 1999 allow the introduction of such evidence under the first part of section 1.

---

[1] Section 1 of the Crime and Disorder Act 1998 commenced on 1 April 1999.
[2] Taken from paragraphs 35, 36 and 37 of *Clingham (formerly C (a minor)) v Royal Borough of Kensington and Chelsea (on Appeal from a Divisional Court of the Queen's Bench Division); Regina v Crown Court at Manchester Ex p McCann* (FC) and Others (FC).

... use of the Civil Evidence Act 1995 and the Rules in cases under the first part of section 1 are not in any way incompatible with the Human Rights Act 1998

'... hearsay evidence will often be of crucial importance. For my part, hearsay evidence depending on its logical probativeness is quite capable of satisfying the requirements of section 1(1).'

It is a matter for the judge or magistrate to decide what weight they attach to hearsay evidence.

Hearsay allows a police officer to provide a statement on behalf of a witness or witnesses who remain anonymous. Hearsay evidence must be relevant to the matters to be proved. It could include details such as dates, places, times, specific descriptions of actions, who was present and who said what.

Hearsay can include evidence from the person taking the statement. The person giving the hearsay evidence may attest to the observable conditions of the witness, for example that the witness appeared upset, and may give evidence based on their own judgement of the situation.

Where an applicant intends to rely on hearsay evidence in the county court, they must act in accordance with Part 33 of the Civil Procedure Rules.

Professional witnesses

Professional witnesses can be called to give their opinions as to matters within their expertise and can give evidence on their assessments of the respondent or his/her behaviour. Examples of witnesses who may be called as professional witnesses include council officials, health visitors, station staff, teachers, doctors and police officers.

Care should be taken to ensure that a professional witness does not inadvertently enable the vulnerable or intimidated witnesses to be identified, for example from their home address.

Witness development and support

The principal purpose of the ASBO is to protect those who directly experience antisocial behaviour. The protection provided should where necessary include those who are personally targeted by perpetrators, other witnesses who see this happen and the wider local community. It follows that engaging, developing and supporting these individuals and groups of people must be a primary concern of any agency managing a case and seeking to use ASBOs. Without the initial complaint of the witness the agency will have no detailed knowledge of the problem. Without their continuing development and engagement there will be no evidence on which to build a case.

Local strategies to promote the use of orders should have the interests of the witnesses and the community at their centre.

The welfare and safety of residents whose complaints form the basis of any action must at every stage of the process be the first consideration. The use of hearsay evidence and professional witnesses is one way of achieving this (see above).

While professional witnesses have a duty to engage, lay witnesses can only be expected to do so if they can see a point in doing it; if the agency is credible and authoritative; if the case work is visibly focused on the interests of the witnesses; if the order protects them and stops the anti-social behaviour quickly and effectively; if the case manager offers them well informed, practical personal support throughout the period of evidence collection, court proceedings and afterwards, as necessary.

The experience of the witnesses must be given value and significance by case managers. The witnesses' status and importance in case development must be made clear. They should be provided, as appropriate, with:

- a simple method of capturing information – diaries, video/audio recording facilities, translation services
- information on services and procedures – about the way witness support services will work, service access points, telephone numbers, name of the case manager working on their case
- an active and respected role in developing the case – the case strategy should reflect their needs, particularly for reassurance about their safety, and they should have control over any information they provide, including agreeing the form in which it will be provided to the defence
- protection for themselves and their family – security for door and window access, emergency contact equipment, panic alarms and mobile phones may all be appropriate in particularly serious cases
- regular contact from the case manager including telephone contact as agreed with the witness (daily, weekly etc.)
- support for any court appearance – a briefing on court procedures and what they should expect, the presence with them in court of the case-manager, transport to and from court (if necessary) and a secure space separate from perpetrators in which they can wait to be called
- support after a court appearance – speedy delivery of information, copies of any orders which have been made and an explanation of the implications of the court decision.

Each key witness should also be engaged in a face-to-face meeting including those who do not wish to give a statement or attend court.

Agencies should publicise positive results – one way this can be done is through leaflet drops (these can be cost-effective when targeted appropriately).

Improving protection of witnesses in court – Manchester City Council Nuisance Strategy Group

Issue Witnesses felt anxious about giving evidence. Their concerns included the prospect of appearing in court, coming face to face with defendants and being threatened by defendants at the court building as well as uncertainties about waiting room and refreshment facilities available.

Approach Manchester City Council negotiated the following arrangements with local courts for anti-social behaviour cases:

- Access to a quiet room for witnesses
- A video link for juvenile witnesses
- A video link for perpetrators in prison where it would be expensive to bring them back for an ASBO or injunction hearing (this also has the benefit of being less stressful for the witnesses)
- Police presence where appropriate.

In addition, the council provides practical information and support to witnesses. They are made aware of what to expect, including court layout, where they and the defendant(s) will be sitting and how people will be dressed. Practical support includes transport to and from the court, being met by a council officer when they arrive and information about refreshment and bathroom facilities.

Outcome The result has been reassurance and physical security for witness. This has led to a

> reduction in the anxiety about the prospect of appearing in court or accidentally meeting a defendant. Witnesses are better able to focus on the case. The case manager is also able to keep witnesses informed of progress and to manage the case more effectively.
>
> **Contact** Bill Pitt, Nuisance Strategy Group, b.pitt@notes.manchester.gov.uk, 0161 234 4611

Witness support is an area where the benefits of partnership working can be clearly seen: local authorities and the police have different skills and resources and can combine them to give well-rounded support.

Methods of supporting witnesses currently being used by agencies also include:

- enclosing a letter with the summons advising the respondent to stay away from witnesses
- a higher police presence in the vicinity
- giving witnesses the personal mobile telephone number of a named police officer who can be called if they are threatened
- visits from neighbourhood wardens at pre-arranged times (sometimes daily)
- phone calls from the local authority at pre-arranged times.

The interim order enables witnesses to be protected from the outset of the court process.

Sections 48 and 49 of the Criminal Justice and Police Act 2001 make it an offence to intimidate witnesses in civil proceedings such as those for ASBOs.

Information sharing

Section 115 of the Crime and Disorder Act 1998 empowers any person to disclose information, where necessary or expedient for the purposes of the Act, to a chief officer of police, a police force, local authorities, probation service or health authority, or to a person acting on their behalf. Where the agency requesting the information clearly needs it for the purposes of reducing anti-social behaviour, the presumption should normally be that it will be supplied.

Information sharing and registered social landlords

A 'relevant authority' (as defined by section 115 of the Crime and Disorder Act 1998) may disclose information to a registered social landlord where the RSL is acting on behalf of the relevant authority for the purposes of the provisions of the Act.

In order to be 'acting on behalf of' the relevant authority the person or body so acting must have authority and must have consented to do so. Such authority may be derived in writing or orally. Authority may also be implied from the conduct of the parties or from the nature of employment. Authority may be confined to a particular act or be general in its character. If authority is general then it will still be confined to acts which the relevant authority itself has power to do.

It may be useful for partners to negotiate information-sharing protocols, examples of which can be obtained from the Home Office Information Sharing Team at:

Email: informationsharing@homeoffice.gsi.gov.uk

Website: www.crimereduction.gov.uk/informationsharing

The model protocol can be accessed at:

www.crimereduction.co.uk/infosharing21.htm

Information sharing issues can also be discussed with the Office of the Data Protection Registrar. If possible the protocol should be published, so that the public can see that information is being shared in an appropriate way.

The terms of the order (the prohibitions)

Although it is for the court to decide what prohibitions are to be imposed by the order, the applicant agency should propose conditions (including duration) to the court. A full order should be drawn up using the form in the court rules.

In the county court the proposed order should accompany the application. The process for the county court will be set out in the relevant Practice Direction.

Where the order is made on conviction in criminal proceedings an agency concerned in the case such as the police may propose prohibitions or the court may draw them up of its own volition. It should be noted that the order may not impose positive requirements, only prohibitions.

Careful thought needs to be given to the formulation of the conditions so they cannot be easily circumvented.

The prohibitions:

- Should cover the range of anti-social acts committed by the defendant
- Should be necessary for protecting person(s) within a defined area from the antisocial acts of the defendant (but as a result of the recent changes that defined area may be as wide as necessary and could in appropriate cases include the whole of England and Wales)
- Should be reasonable and proportionate
- Should be realistic and practical
- Should be clear, concise and easy to understand
- Should be specific when referring to matters of time if, for example, prohibiting the offender from being outside or in particular areas at certain times
- Should be specific when refering to exclusion from an area, include street names and clear boundaries such as the side of the street included in the order (a map with identifiable street names should also be provided)
- Should be in terms which make it easy to determine and prosecute a breach
- Should contain a prohibition on inciting/encouraging others to engage in antisocial behaviour
- Should protect all people who are in the area covered by the order from the behaviour (as well as specific individuals)
- May cover acts that are anti-social in themselves and those that are precursors to a criminal act, for example a prohibition on entering a shopping centre rather than on shoplifting
- May include a general condition prohibiting behaviour which is likely to cause harassment, alarm and distress
- May include a prohibition from approaching or harassing any witnesses named in the court proceedings.

Examples of ASBO prohibitions can be found on the Crime Reduction website at www.crimereduction.gov.uk

Duration of an order

The minimum duration for an order is two years. There is no maximum period and an order may be made for an indefinite period. It is for the court to decide the duration of an order, but the applying agency should propose a time period as part of its application.

The duration applied for should take into account the age of the recipient, the severity of his or her anti-social behaviour, the length of time it has gone on and the recipient's response to any previous measures to deal with the behaviour. A longer order will generally be appropriate in the case of more serious or persistent anti-social behaviour.

Summons procedure

Magistrates' court (acting in its civil capacity)

The lead individual in charge of the case should arrange for a summons form to be completed, with a copy retained on the application file, and for the defendant to be served with the following:

- The summons
- A copy of the completed ASBO application
- Documentary evidence of statutory consultation
- Guidance on how the defendant may obtain legal advice and representation
- Any notice of hearsay evidence
- Details of evidence in support of the application as agreed with the applicant agency's solicitor
- A warning to the defendant that it is an offence to pervert the course of justice, and that witness intimidation is liable to lead to prosecution.

Wherever possible the lead officer in charge will ensure that service of the summons is made on the defendant in person. If personal service is not possible, the summons should be served by post as soon as possible to the last known address.

Where a child or a young person is concerned, a person with parental responsibility must also receive a copy of the summons. This could be a local authority social worker in the case of a looked-after child as well as, or instead of, the parent. ('Parent' has the same meaning as under section 1 of the Family Law Reform Act 1987 and 'guardian' is defined in section 107 of the Children and Young Persons Act 1933.)

The summons forms will be set out within the Magistrates' Courts (Anti-Social Behaviour Orders) Rules 2002.

County court

The process for the county court will be set out in the Practice Direction of the updated Civil Procedure Rules published in January 2003.

Disclosure

Before evidence is disclosed the applicant should consult the police and other agencies to ensure that all reasonable stages have been taken to support witnesses and minimise any potential for witness intimidation. Evidence should not be disclosed without the express permission of the witness. However, evidence that is not disclosed cannot be relied on.

The applicant should seek to maintain witness anonymity and ensure that it does not identify them by default (for example through details of location, race, personal characteristics or age).

Court procedures

It is important that those hearing the case are fully briefed on the purpose of an ASBO. There should be no confusion as to the purpose of the order, which is to protect the community. The welfare of a child is of course to be considered and indeed the making of the order should contribute to this by setting standards of expected behaviour. But the welfare of the child is not the principal purpose of the order hearing.

Whether or not the subject of the application is present the court should be asked to make the order. Adjournments should be avoided unless absolutely necessary.

Magistrates' court (acting in its civil capacity)

An application for an ASBO in the magistrates' court is made by complaint. This means that the court will act in its civil capacity. The provisions governing applications for orders in the magistrates' courts are set out in the Magistrates' Courts Act 1980.

Under section 1(3) of the Crime and Disorder Act 1998 the application should be made to the magistrates' court whose area includes the local government area or police area where persons need to be protected from the anti-social behaviour.

The lead officer in charge of the case should ensure that all the evidence and witnesses are available at the hearing, including any evidence in support of the need for the court to make an immediate order.

Under section 98 of the Magistrates' Courts Act 1980 evidence will be given on oath. Any magistrate or judge may hear the case.

A power of arrest is attached to non-attendance at court in civil procedures under section 55 of the Magistrates' Court Act 1980. Various provisions for adjournment, non-attendance at court and the issue of a warrant for arrest are contained in sections 54 to 57 of the Magistrates' Courts Act 1980.

How to prepare a court file for an ASBO application – Lancashire Constabulary

A file to support the application for an ASBO should be prepared by the lead agency or the solicitor acting on their behalf.

A minimum of eight identical court bundles will be required as follows:

   3 Magistrates

   1 Clerk to the Court

   1 Applicant Solicitor

   1 Defence Solicitor

   1 Defendant

   1 Witness Box

The files are in loose leaf format (A4 ring binder).

The files should be indexed and paginated.

The index and contents to include as appropriate:

- Summons for anti-social behaviour order together with proof of service

- Application for anti-social behaviour order (in format provided by the Magistrates' Court (Anti-Social Behaviour Orders) Rules 2002)
- Defendant's details
- Defendant's previous convictions
- Defendant's ABC agreements
- Summary of incidents being relied upon by applicant
- Map and description of exclusion area
- Association chart (showing relationships and connections where the alleged anti-social behaviour is by a group of people)
- Documentation of statutory consultations
- Supporting statements from multi-agency consultation
- Statement from the officer in the case
- Any other statements obtained
- Hearsay notices
- Draft order for endorsement by court
- Home circumstances report where the subject of the order is a juvenile (if necessary and completed).

The bundle should be prepared and served on the solicitor for the defendant as soon as the summons is served.

The applicant's solicitor should attempt to have the contents of the bundle agreed prior to any pre-trial review.

Disclosure should be transparent and complete.

Contact Niamh Noone, Lancashire Constabulary niamh.noone@lancashire.police.uk 01772 412919

County court

An application for an order in the county court must be made in accordance with the procedure set out in the appropriate Practice Direction of the Civil Procedure Rules. Where the relevant authority is the claimant in the principal proceedings, the application for the order should be included in the claim form. Where the relevant authority is the defendant in the principal proceedings, the application for an ASBO should be made by way of an application notice which should accompany the defence. If the relevant authority is not a party to the principal proceedings, an application to be made a party and for the order must be made to the court in the same application notice.

Orders made on conviction in criminal proceedings

After a defendant has been convicted of a criminal offence any agency which is concerned in the case, and would be entitled to apply for an ASBO, may make a request to the court that an order be imposed in addition to the sentence. Alternatively, the court may make an order of its own volition.

Court procedures for juveniles

Applications to the magistrates' court acting in its civil capacity

Since the youth court has no civil jurisdiction, applications for orders against under 18s will be heard by the magistrates' court (except where the youth court is asked to impose an order on conviction).

The officer in charge of the application should contact the justices' clerk in advance of the hearing to ensure that it will be conducted in a way that is suitable for the child or young person.

- Unlike a youth court, which is closed to the general public, the magistrates' court is open to the general public and has no automatic restrictions to prevent public and press access or to prevent reporting of the proceedings or to protect the identity of a juvenile (or adult) who is the subject of an application.
- The court should have to have a good reason, aside from age alone, to impose a discretionary order under section 39 of the Children and Young Persons Act 1933 to prevent the identification of a child or young person concerned in the proceedings.
- The applicant may resist a call from the defendant's representatives for such restrictions if the effectiveness of the ASBO will largely depend on the wider community knowing the details.
- The applying agency should note that:
  - Under Section 98 of the Magistrates' Courts Act 1980 evidence will be given on oath, except the evidence of a child under 14 years which is given unsworn;
  - Section 34 of the Children and Young Persons Act 1933 requires the attendance of a parent or legal guardian at court for any person under 16 years of age. Every effort should be made before a hearing to ensure that this takes place to avoid unnecessary adjournments;
  - The court will require information about his or her background, home surroundings and family circumstances. Such information should be available to avoid the need for an adjournment.

Assessment of needs

When applying for an order against a young person aged between 10 and 17, an assessment should be made of their circumstances and needs. This will enable the local authority to ensure that the appropriate services are provided for the young person concerned and for the court to have the necessary information about him or her.

It is vital that any assessment made does not cause delay to the application for an order. The lead agency should therefore liaise closely with the local social services department or youth offending team from the start of the process so that where a new assessment is required it can be begun quickly. In some cases an up-to-date assessment may already be available.

Councils with social services responsibilities have a duty, arising from section 17 of the Children Act 1989, to safeguard and promote the welfare of children within their areas who may be in need. The assessment of the needs of such children is expected to be carried out in accordance with the Framework for the Assessment of Children in Need and Their Families. The guidance sets out the content and timescales of the initial assessment (seven working days) and the core assessment (35 working days). A core assessment is required when an initial assessment has determined that the child is in need. The assessment will cover the child's needs, the capacities of his/her parents and wider family, and environmental factors. This enables councils to determine whether the child is a 'child in need' and what services may be necessary in order to address the assessed needs.

The assessment of the child's needs should run in parallel with evidence gathering and the application process.

Statutory agencies, such as social services, the local education authority or the health authority, have a statutory obligation to provide services to under 18s. They should do so irrespective of whether an ASBO application is to be made and the timing of that application.

The ASBO application does not prevent such support and can proceed in parallel, or indeed prior to, that support.

Parenting orders

It is essential that parents and guardians take responsibility for the behaviour of their children. If an ASBO or an order on conviction is made against a juvenile the court should also consider making a parenting order in respect of the parents or guardians of the child or young person.[1]

Parenting orders are civil orders that help to engage parents[2] to address their child's offending or anti-social behaviour, and to establish discipline and a relationship with their child. This may help the conditions of the ASBO to be met and thereby reduce the chances of the young person breaching the order.

The parenting order consists of two elements:

- A requirement on the parent or guardian to attend counselling or guidance sessions for up to three months. This element is compulsory and must be imposed in all cases when an order is made (except where the parent or guardian has previously received a parenting order – section 8(5)). Sessions can cover setting and enforcing consistent standards of behaviour and responding more effectively to unreasonable adolescent demands.
- The second element, which is discretionary, requires the parent or guardian to exercise control over the child and can last for up to 12 months. It could include ensuring that the child attends school regularly, avoids certain places or is home by a certain time at night.

The court needs to consider an oral or written report before making a parenting order, unless the child or young person has reached the age of 16. To avoid unnecessary adjournments such a report should be available early in the court process.

A 'responsible officer', who will generally be an officer from the local youth offending team, social services, probation service or the local education authority, supervises delivery of the parenting order. The officer will have responsibility for, among other things, arranging the provision of counselling or guidance sessions and ensuring that the parent complies with any other requirements which the court may impose.

If the parent does not comply with the order, the responsible officer can refer the matter to the police for investigation. Such action is generally expected only where non-compliance is sufficiently serious to warrant possible prosecution – the responsible officer is expected to work with the parent to improve compliance. But if prosecuted and convicted for non-compliance, the parent can be fined up to £1,000 (level 3 on the standard scale).

---

[1] Provision for parenting orders is set out in sections 8, 9 and 10 of the Crime and Disorder Act 1998. The orders can be made in proceedings where a child safety order, an anti-social behaviour order or sex offender order has been made; a child or young person is convicted of an offence; or a person is convicted of an offence under Sections 443 or 444 of the Education Act 1996.

[2] For the purposes of the 1998 Act the term 'parent' has the same meaning as that contained within section 1 of the Family Law Reform Act 1987, that is either of the child or young person's natural parents whether or not married to each other at the time of their birth. 'Guardian' is defined in section 117 of the 1998 Act with reference to section 107 of the Children and Young Persons Act 1933, and includes any person who, in the opinion of the court, has for the time being the care of the child or young person. This may include people who may not have parental responsibility for the child or young person as defined in the Children Act 1989, such as step parents.

> **Good practice – managing procedures and timescales**
>
> Practitioners using ASBOs have taken a range of measures to minimise paperwork and delays, including:[1]
>
> - Breaking down the process into clear, manageable stages that are easy to follow for those unfamiliar with the process.
> - Setting timeframes for each stage of the application to keep the process focused, including a commitment to arrange problem-solving meetings within a short time.
> - Releasing key staff so that they can concentrate on the ASBO application process – this should result in evidence gathering being conducted quickly and efficiently.
> - Using other agencies, such as neighbourhood wardens and station staff, to collect evidence where additional evidence collection is required. (Evidence gathering and attending incidents are tasks that local authorities, RSLs and the police are already involved in and therefore not an additional cost.)
> - Adopting strategies to overcome challenges to witness evidence such as ensuring that witness statements corroborate.
> - Minimising court delays by forewarning the courts of the application and using pre-trial reviews.
> - Sharing costs between partner agencies and utilising the expertise from each agency.
> - Not engaging in non-essential problem solving meetings in more serious cases in order to get to court more quickly.

Immediate post-order procedure

Where an ASBO is granted it is preferable for a copy of the order to be served on the defendant in person prior to his or her departure from court.

Where an individual has not been personally served with the order at the court, the court should be asked to arrange for personal service as soon as possible thereafter. Proof of service of an ASBO is important, since any criminal proceedings for breach may fail if service is challenged by the defence, and cannot be proved by the prosecution. In the case of a child or young person the order should also be served and recorded as such on the parent, guardian or an appropriate adult.

An order comes into effect on the day it is made. But the two-year period during which no order shall be discharged except with the consent of both parties, starts from the date of service.[2]

The lead agency, if not the police, should ensure that a copy of the ASBO is forwarded immediately to the police. The agency should also give copies of the order to the ASB co-ordinator of the local crime and disorder reduction partnership, the other partner agencies, and to the main targets and witnesses of the anti-social behaviour, so that breaches can be reported and acted upon.

The police should notify the appropriate police area command on the same working day so that details of the defendant and the conditions of the order can be recorded.

---

[1] Taken from Home Office Findings 160, 'Implementing Anti-social Behaviour Orders: messages for practitioners', Dr Siobhan Campbell, 2002.
[2] Sections 1(9), 1B(6) and 1C(8) of the Crime and Disorder Act 1998, as amended.

A copy of the order should be provided to the lead agency's legal representative on the same day as the court hearing, and in the case of a juvenile the court will provide a further copy for the youth offending team (YOT).

The YOT should arrange for action to be taken by an appropriate agency (for example, social services) to ensure that the young person understands the seriousness of the ASBO. It should also consider the provision of appropriate support programmes to help avoid a breach of the ASBO by diverting the offender from the behaviour that led to it, although such programmes cannot as the law currently stands (November 2002) be a condition of the order.

3. After the order is made

The obtaining of the order is not the end of the process. The order must be monitored and enforced.

Partnership-working after the order is made should include information exchange to ensure early warning of problems and clarification of who should do what to safeguard witnesses and what other action should be taken to challenge the perpetrator in such cases.

It is essential that breaches of an order, appeals against the sentence and any other actions relating to the management of the case are reported to the agency which is responsible for the management of the case.

Police National Computer (PNC)

Recording of orders on the PNC will enable police forces to effectively enforce breaches. Arrangements are being made for orders to be placed on the PNC so that police officers are able to identify those with an order and are aware of the conditions of the order so that the necessary action can be taken in case of a breach (which is an arrestable offence).

Appeals

Magistrates' court (acting in its civil capacity) and orders on conviction in criminal proceedings

Section 4 of the Crime and Disorder Act 1998 provides the offender with the right of appeal against the making of an order. Appeal is to the Crown Court. Rules 74 and 75 of the Magistrates' Courts' Rules 1981 and 6 to 11 of the Crown Court Rules 1982 apply to appeals against orders. Both parties may provide additional evidence.

By virtue of section 79(3) of the Supreme Court Act 1981, an appeal is by way of a re-hearing of the case. In determining an appeal, the Crown Court should have before it a copy of the original application for an order (if applicable), the full order and the notice of appeal. The lead agency should ensure that copies are sent to the court.

Notice of appeal must be given in writing to the clerk of the court and the applicant body within 21 days of the order (Crown Court Rules, rule 7). But the Crown Court has the discretion to give leave to appeal out of time (rule 7(5)).

The agency which brought the initial application should take charge of defending any appeal against the order. It should also lead in action to guard against witness intimidation.

The Crown Court may vary the order or make a new order. Any order made by the Crown Court on appeal shall be treated for the purpose of any later application for variation or discharge as if it were the original magistrates' court order, unless it is an order directing that the application be re-heard by the magistrates' court.

Although on hearing an appeal it is open to the Crown Court to make any incidental order, for example, to suspend the operation of a prohibition pending the outcome of the appeal where this appears to the Crown Court to be just, there is no provision for automatic stay of an order pending appeal. The order remains in force pending the outcome of the appeal and breach is a criminal offence even if the appeal subsequently succeeds.

An appeal against the ruling of the Crown Court is to the High Court by way of case stated under section 28 of the Supreme Court Act 1981, or by application for judicial review by virtue of section 29(3) of that Act.

It is also open to the applying authority to seek to challenge a magistrates' decision to refuse to grant an order by way of case stated (judicial review of the decision to the Divisional Court) by virtue of Section 111 of the Magistrates' Courts Act 1980.

County Court

Any appeal against an ASBO made in the county court must be made in accordance with Part 52 of the Civil Procedure Rules. Appeals against orders made by district judges will be to a circuit judge and against orders made by circuit judges to the High Court.

Breaches

Breach of an order is a criminal offence, which is arrestable and recordable. Responsibility for prosecuting a breach of an ASBO lies with the Crown Prosecution Service (CPS). Such prosecutions must therefore pass both the evidential and public interest test.[1]

The lead officer managing the case should keep the other partner agencies informed of the progress and outcome of the breach investigation. A particular consideration will be the need to protect witnesses.

The standard of proof for prosecution of a breach of an order is the criminal standard 'beyond reasonable doubt'. Provision is made in section 1(10) of the Crime and Disorder Act 1998 for a defence of reasonable excuse.

In the case of an adult (see below for juveniles), the maximum penalty on conviction in the magistrates' court is six months in prison or a fine not exceeding £5,000 or both; at the Crown Court the maximum penalty is five years in prison or a fine or both. Community penalties are available but a conditional discharge is not.

Agencies and courts should not treat the breach of an anti-social behaviour order as just another minor offence. (It should be remembered that the order itself would normally have been the culmination of a course of persistent anti-social behaviour.) An anti-social behaviour order will only be seen to be effective if breaches of it are taken seriously.

---

[1] See www.cps.gov.uk.

Persistent anti-social behaviour train stations – British Transport Police
Issue Ticket touting is a serious problem at London Underground stations. A particular case involved an individual causing a severe nuisance by touting for tickets and abusing and threatening staff. This happened on an almost daily basis over a period of many years. The individual was the subject of continuous calls for police assistance. He was reported and arrested on numerous occasions but received only fines for individual minor offences, which had no deterrent effect.
Approach The British Transport Police (BTP) worked with the local authority to apply for an ASBO. Staff and the community were used to gather evidence of behaviour for the application. An ASBO was considered to be effective because proceedings for breach are criminal and previous convictions for breach of the ASBO can be cited prior to sentencing. This allows sentences for breach to reflect the impact of the behaviour on the community.
Outcome The individual has been sentenced twice for breach (custodial sentences were given both times). The ASBO has without doubt improved the quality of life for the community by protecting customers and staff from abuse.
Contact Chief Inspector David Dickason, British Transport Police, 020 7222 5600, daviddickason@gtnet.gov.uk

Information on breaches can be received from any source including the local authority housing department and other local authority officers, neighbours and other members of the public. Any information received by a partner agency should be passed immediately to the police and lead officer, who should inform the other agencies involved.

Breach penalties are the same for all orders, including the interim order. Court proceedings should be swift and not fractured by unnecessary adjournments either during the proceedings or before sentencing.

Where the offender is found guilty of the breach, the court may take reports from the local authority or police and any applicant agency before sentencing. The court should also consider the original reasons for the making of the order. The sentence given should be proportionate and reflect the *impact* of the behaviour complained of.

Breaches by juveniles

Breach proceedings for children and young people will be dealt with in the youth court. Breach proceedings in the youth court are subject to automatic reporting prohibitions (Section 49 Children and Young Persons Act 1933) unless lifted. The court has a wide discretion to lift the reporting restrictions. Section 49(5)–(8) sets out the circumstances in which it may do so, prior to and irrespective of, any conviction. Section 49(4) sets out the circumstances after conviction.

Under Section 98 of the Magistrates' Courts Act 1980 evidence will be given on oath, except the evidence of a child under 14 which is given unsworn.

Section 34 of the Children and Young Persons Act 1933 requires the attendance of a parent or legal guardian at court for any person under 16 years of age.

The court will require information about the young person's background, home surroundings and family circumstances prior to sentence. This should be provided by the youth offending team or social services.

The maximum sentence for breach by a juvenile is a detention and training order (DTO), which has a maximum term of 24 months – 12 months of which is custodial and 12 months is in the community. The DTO is available for 12 to 17 year olds (although a juvenile aged between 12 and 14 years must be a persistent (criminal) offender to be given a DTO). Those aged 10 and 11 years old can be given a community order for breach of ASBO. As with adults, community penalties are available but a conditional discharge is not.

In addition the youth court should consider whether to make a parenting order.

Variation and discharge of an order

Variation or discharge of an order, including an interim order, may be made on application to the court that originally made it.

An application to vary or discharge an order made on conviction in criminal proceedings may be made to any magistrates' court within the same petty sessions areas as the court that made the order.

The application can be made either by the original applicant in the case or the defendant. An order cannot be discharged within two years of its service without the agreement of both parties. An order made on conviction cannot be discharged before the end of two years.

The procedure for variation or discharge will be set out in The Magistrates' Courts (Anti-Social Behaviour Orders) Rules 2002, The Crown Court (Amendment) Rules 2002 and the Civil Procedure Rules. These are published separately to this guidance and available on introduction on the Crime Reduction Website at www.crimereduction.gov.uk

If the individual asks for a variation or discharge of an order, the agency that obtained the order needs to ensure that a considered response is given to the court.

If it is decided that the lead agency should contest the application for variation or discharge, it should give the court its reasons, supported as appropriate by evidence gathered in the course of monitoring the effectiveness of the order.

The magistrates' court clerk will send details of the variation or discharge of any ASBO to the local police force and local authority. The police should record any discharge or variation of the ASBO on their computer system and arrange for any changes to be reflected in the Police National Computer record.

Monitoring and recording

Local agencies should agree common procedures for recording and monitoring both their successful and unsuccessful applications. Details of orders granted should be sent to the local crime and disorder reduction partnership ASB co-ordinator and the local authority or police as appropriate as well as other agencies involved with the offender (including the local youth offending team if the offender is under 18 years old).

As a minimum there should be a record of:

- The original application (or details of the prosecution and hearing for the order in the case of an order on conviction) including the name, address, date of birth, gender and ethnicity of defendant
- The order itself including, where applicable, the map showing the exclusion area
- Date and details of any variation or discharge of the order
- Action taken for any breach.

The following information could also be recorded:

- Name, address, age, gender and ethnicity of the victim – or a statement that the case involved no identified victim
- Details of the person or persons who complained of the behaviour
- Details of any contributory issues, for example, drugs, alcohol and substance misuse and/or mental health problems
- Details of any aggravating factors, for example, racial motivation
- Assessment of outcome in terms of whether or not the anti-social behaviour ceased.

Consistency of information will help to assess the effectiveness of orders and inform future local audits and crime reduction strategies.

Promoting awareness of orders

The purpose of ASBOs is to protect local communities from the harassment, alarm or distress that can be caused by anti-social behaviour. An effective media strategy by the crime and disorder reduction partnership (CDRP) is therefore essential if local residents and businesses are to be aware of orders and their implications. Using the local press to ensure the community knows the subject and conditions of the order is often a cost-effective strategy.

At the same time, the staff of the partner agencies need to understand how and when ASBOs can be used, and how they relate to the other tools to combat anti-social behaviour available to the partnership.

Local agencies and CDRPs should, within the context of their overall strategies for combating anti-social behaviour, devise a strategy for promoting awareness of orders. A designated officer should have responsibility for its delivery. This might most naturally be the CDRP ASB co-ordinator. Disclosure of information should be necessary and proportionate to the aim it seeks to achieve.

Suggested aims of the strategy:

- To increase community confidence in reporting anti-social behaviour and expectations that it can be reduced
- To deter potential offenders from anti-social behaviour
- To ensure that the *local population is aware* of ASBOs, the powers of the local authority, registered social landlords and the police (including the British Transport Police) to apply for them and who to approach if they believe that an ASBO may be appropriate
- To ensure that agency staff have confidence in using ASBOs
- To ensure that potential witnesses are aware of the support available to them.

Acceptable behaviour contracts

What are acceptable behaviour contracts?

An ABC is a written agreement between a person who has been involved in anti-social behaviour and one or more local agencies whose role it is to prevent such behaviour. ABCs are most commonly used for young people but may also be used for adults.

The contract is agreed and signed at a meeting with the individual and the lead agencies. Where the person whose behaviour is at issue is a child or young person, parents or guardians should be encouraged to attend.

The contract specifies a list of anti-social acts in which the person has been involved and which they agree not to continue. Where possible the individual should be involved in drawing up the contract. This may encourage them to recognise the impact of their behaviour and take responsibility for their actions.

Support to address the underlying causes of the behaviour should be offered in parallel to the contract. This may include diversionary activities (such as attendance at a youth project), counselling or support for the family. It is vital to ascertain which agencies are already involved, especially where the individual is aged between 10 and 17 years.

Legal action in the form of an anti-social behaviour order or possession order (if the young person is in social housing) should be stated on the contract where this is the potential consequence of breach. The threat of legal action provides an incentive to ensure that the contract is adhered to.

Types of behaviour ABCs have been used for

ABCs have been used to address a wide range of anti-social behaviour including:

- Harassment of residents or passers by
- Verbal abuse
- Criminal damage
- Vandalism
- Noise nuisance
- Writing graffitti
- Engaging in threatening behaviour in large groups
- Racial abuse
- Smoking or drinking alcohol while under age
- Substance misuse
- Joy riding
- Begging
- Prostitution
- Kerb-crawling.

Acceptable behaviour contracts for kerb crawlers – Lancashire Constabulary

Approach In February 2002 Preston police launched 'Operation Kerb' to tackle the problem of street prostitution in an area of the city. This involved targeting kerb crawlers, as well as prostitutes, all of whom were asked to sign a generic ABC on arrest. All of the 15 kerb crawlers arrested at the time signed contracts.

Outcome The ABCs were extremely successful with the kerb crawlers – none of these contracts were breached. The scheme was less successful with the prostitutes and applications for ASBOs have been made against them.

Lessons learned In future the contracts used will be tailored to the individual concerned rather than generic.

Contact Steve Little, Lancashire Constabulary, 01772 614444

Multi-agency working

The flexible nature of ABCs allows for various agencies to take the lead according to the circumstances in each case, local practice and which agencies can have greatest impact on reducing unacceptable behaviour.

In Islington, for example, the Anti-Social Behaviour Team running the ABC scheme is led by representatives from the local authority housing department and the local police. In other areas the lead agency is the youth offending team working closely with the local police.

Other agencies involved with ABCs – either as signatories on the contract or in providing support to the individual and family – are registered social landlords, social services, schools, environmental health and health services. This is not a prescriptive list.

Providing training for staff in partner agencies involved in ABCs will enable schemes to work more effectively. In particular, training should cover the practical implications of contracts (such as the paperwork required) and how to deal with breaches.

Multi-agency working has a number of benefits. It can:

- Increase the speed of evidence gathering
- Improve background information on the individual's circumstances
- Help to ensure that interventions are tailored to the individual
- Improve monitoring of contracts
- Reduce breaches by the provision of other support
- Enhance the effectiveness of the scheme through joint training and planning
- Utilise a variety of expertise to intervene early in anti-social behaviour.

Tackling youth anti-social behviour – Stockport Youth ASB Action Team

Approach The team make good use of acceptable behaviour contracts as an intervention with persistent young offenders, usually as a precursor to an ASBO. ABCs have been useful in preparing ASBO applications as they indicate to the court that an offender is unwilling to change their pattern of behaviour voluntarily and this negates any attempt by defence counsel to argue that the ASBO is unnecessary. The team has also had success in using records of previous criminal convictions together with a statement from the area police officer and the local anti-social behaviour officer as the main evidence in an ASBO application.

With younger offenders or those who are on the cusp of offending behaviour, the team offers intervention work tailored to the individual's needs and often use ABCs as a part of this intervention work to set boundaries and enable parents to regain some authority. On such occasions the team tend to work closely with specialist education staff and sports development officers.

The team has surveillance staff who use surveillance equipment to gather evidence for the team and other agencies such as the local authority housing department. Community beat officers also draw on this information to extend their operational capabilities.

Outcome By November 2002 over 30 ABCs have been issued with only five being breached; four ASBOs have been granted and a further five are at an advanced stage of preparation. Three breached ASBOs have resulted in detention and training orders. The team found that the use of the record of previous criminal convictions speeded up the process of getting the ASBO granted as it showed a pattern of anti-social behaviour.

> **Contact** Keith Swindell, Youth Anti-Social Behaviour Action Team, Stockport YOT, 0161 476 2876, keith.swindell@stockport.gov.uk

Publicity

It is important that agencies and the community are aware of the full range of services available to tackle anti-social behaviour. This will encourage reporting of complaints and let those involved in anti-social behaviour see that effective action can be taken against them.

The ABC scheme should be well publicised amongst young people. In particular it could be publicised within local schools and amongst other agencies working with young people.

Identifying individuals for ABCs

People for whom a contract may be beneficial can be identified using a wide variety of evidence sources:

- Complaints to housing staff or police officers
- Housing staff observations
- Police stops or arrests
- Other police intelligence
- Photographic evidence
- Self admission
- Video evidence
- Discussions with residents
- Information from the education service, especially relating to truancy and exclusions
- Information from and about the victims of anti-social behaviour
- Social services data
- Referrals from other schemes and agencies, for example youth services.

Once agencies identify a suitable candidate for a contract, checks should be made into whether the individual or family is subject to any other investigations or support. In the case of a young person the local youth offending team should be informed and if appropriate the social services or education welfare.

It is vital that consideration is given to whether an individual is really suitable for the scheme. Where there is offending behaviour which is serious and persistent an ASBO or other legal action is likely to be more effective.

> **Targeting individuals for ABCs – Islington Anti-Social Behaviour Team**
>
> An area or housing estate with increased disorder levels is identified.
>
> A letter is sent to all residents on the estate outlining the aims and objectives of the ABC scheme. The letter discusses the problems caused by anti-social youths on the estate, and includes a general description of the unacceptable behaviour occurring. It invites residents to record the details of all problem behaviour experienced or witnessed and to complete incident record books that can be used for evidential purposes. The local authority housing department, police and other agencies are also encouraged to monitor activity and gather evidence to identify the people involved.
>
> A second letter is sent specifically to the parents or legal guardian of any young person who has come to the attention of the police or the local authority housing department informing them of their child's unacceptable behaviour. This second letter invites both the young person and their legal guardian to attend an interview with police and housing officers at

> their local housing office to discuss the behaviour of the young person. The letter informs the family that on completion of this interview the child will be expected to sign an acceptable behaviour contract and adhere to its terms and conditions for a period of 6 months.
>
> Contact Paul Dunn or Alison Blackburn, Islington Anti-Social Behaviour Team, 020 7421 0111, paul.e.dunn@met.police.uk, alison.blackburn@islington.gov.uk

The ABC meeting

Once the appropriate agencies have been consulted the individual involved should be formally invited to take part in a meeting with the all the relevant parties.

The ABC meeting should be used as an opportunity for the individual involved in the anti-social behaviour and his or her family, where appropriate, to discuss the meaning of the term 'anti-social behaviour' and the impact it has on others.

The meeting can be used as an early intervention process to stop the inappropriate behaviour becoming worse and to outline possible repercussions should the behaviour be repeated. It can also be used as an opportunity to provide support to address underlying causes such as family problems. Further action may then be taken by the lead agencies after the meeting to ensure that other agencies become involved as necessary.

It is worth thinking about where the meeting should take place. While the use of police premises may reinforce the importance attached to an ABC it is important that care is taken to ensure that the interview is not misinterpreted as being part of a criminal investigation.

Parents or guardians, housing or local police officers and any other interested party such as a social worker or family friend may be present if it is considered appropriate.

If the individual who is to become subject to an ABC does not attend without notification or good reason further attempts, by letter or a visit, should be made to contact them. If this fails their non-appearance can be documented and used at any future proceedings if the inappropriate behaviour is repeated. Written warning of this should be sent to the person concerned.

The meeting where the contract is signed does not constitute legal proceedings.

Key points when arranging and conducting the ABC meeting:

- Publicise the scheme prior to holding the meeting so that those concerned are aware of the scheme and its aims
- Make the interview less formal to avoid intimidating the family
- Choose a spacious room and only invite key stakeholders
- Involve other agencies prior to this meeting, for example youth services and schools
- Hold a pre-meeting with key stakeholders to share relevant information. This will help to keep attendance at the actual interview to a minimum
- Allow adequate preparation time.

Also see Appendix G for suggested Do's and Don'ts of the ABC meeting.

> **Addressing the underlying causes of ASB – Islington ASB Team**
>
> **Issue** A young person was entering a housing association estate and continually damaging property, smoking and drinking until the early hours and abusing a number of the vulnerable residents.
>
> **Approach** Police and housing staff held an ABC meeting with the young person and his mother. It became apparent that he was not aware of the effect of his behaviour on others and his mother was unaware of his actions. Through discussions at the meeting the underlying cause of the problem was identified: due to the lack of space in their accommodation the mother was asking her son to leave the property at night. An ABC was signed by the young person and the lead agencies. In addition, the housing officer placed the family on the priority housing list for more suitable accommodation on the condition that the son kept to the terms of the contract.
>
> **Outcome** The family were moved during the six month period of the ABC. Since signing the contract the young man has not come to the attention of police or housing staff.
>
> **Contact** Paul Dunn or Alison Blackburn, Islington Anti-Social Behaviour Team, 020 7421 0111, paul.e.dunn@met.police.uk, alison.blackburn@islington.gov.uk

Drawing up the contract

An ABC normally lasts for six months, though since it is not a statutory document any reasonable period may be specified.

While the terms of the contract should reflect the behaviour to be addressed they should not be so numerous that the individual is overwhelmed. About half a dozen might be the norm. In addition there needs to be a balance between general and specific conditions. If they are too general it may be unclear precisely what acts are covered, but if they are too specific it may be possible to evade them too easily.

The contract should be written in language that the individual can easily understand.

Examples of terms agreed in ABCs:

I will not:

- damage property
- verbally abuse passersby
- write graffiti
- throw stones or other objects
- congregate in groups
- climb on public or private property
- spit
- smoke in public
- set fire to things
- physically harass people
- damage the environment
- smash glass
- damage cars

Some schemes define all criminal offences committed by the individual as breaches irrespective of whether the behaviour is prohibited by the contract.

The contract can be renewed after further discussions have been held if breaches have occurred or other forms of anti-social behaviour are continuing. Second contracts should be considered if the behaviour does not improve during the first contract or resumes soon after. However, where an ABC is not likely to tackle the problem behaviour other measures, such as an anti-social behaviour order, should be pursued quickly.

A copy of the original contract should be made available to all those involved in monitoring the behaviour of the individual. Other interested parties should be informed of the agreed conditions of the contract where appropriate, which may include the youth offending team and other agencies.

Monitoring

Continued monitoring is vital for the contract to be effective. Information on breaches can be collected from the same sources as those from which the original anti-social behaviour was identified (see above). Accurate and systematic data collection techniques – such as standard forms and reporting systems – will assist with the monitoring and evaluation of contracts.

If the contract is breached there must always be a response. Agencies and organisations involved will need to consider the circumstances and decide upon the best course of action.

Key points for ensuring effective monitoring:

- Ensure enough staff and resources are available for monitoring.
- Keep the number of contracts in each geographical area of responsibility relatively low.
- Ensure that there is good communication between the agencies involved, especially in relation to sharing information. If one agency is primarily responsible they need to inform others of their findings and also make sure evidence is collected from other agencies. Breaches can be overlooked if data is not shared.
- Make sure that there are an adequate number of home visits (at least two) during the contract.
- Ensure that there are regular meetings of those involved in monitoring and implementing the scheme.
- Ensure that there is good information for residents who may act as witnesses to anti-social behaviour.
- Ensure parents of children who have entered into contracts receive regular feedback about their behaviour.

Dealing with breaches

The action taken should be determined by the nature of the breach. A structured approach can be taken to breaches, leading to legal action if the behaviour does not cease. Such a structured approach may involve:

- Verbal warnings
- Written warnings (however this assumes a good level of literacy and visits may be more appropriate)
- An interview to discuss and reiterate the contract terms. This will also help to identify why the breach has occurred and enable agencies to provide additional support that may be required to prevent further breaches
- Proceedings for an anti-social behaviour order
- Proceedings for a possession order.

Agencies such as the youth offending team (in the case of a young person) should be involved to identify appropriate measures to address the continued unacceptable behaviour. However, where the community is facing on-going anti-social behaviour, legal action should be considered.

ABCs are not a substitute for anti-social behaviour orders (ASBOs) and should not be seen as a necessary precursor to an application for an order.

Evidence collected for an ABC and breach of the contract may be cited in court for an application in support of a possession order or an anti-social behaviour order.

Appendices

A. Summary of legislation governing ASBOs

Adapted from material produced by the Judicial Studies Board.[1]

When were they introduced

The power to impose anti-social behaviour orders came into force in April 1999 under the terms of the Crime and Disorder Act 1998. The legislation was amended by the Police Reform Act 2002.

The Police Reform Act:

- Introduced an interim order
- Extended the geographical area over which an order can be made to any defined area of England and Wales, or the whole of England and Wales
- Introduced orders on conviction in criminal proceedings
- Enabled the British Transport Police and registered social landlords to apply for orders
- Introduced orders in county court proceedings (alongside related proceedings).

Purpose of the order

To prevent anti-social behaviour by named individuals.

Who can apply for an order

The police or local authority in consultation with each other can apply for the order.

Under the Police Reform Act 2002 the British Transport Police and registered social landlords (RSLs) are also able to apply after consultation with both the local police and local authority.

Consultation is required, agreement of the other agency is not.

Grounds for an order

The individual's behaviour is anti-social i.e. it causes alarm, distress or harassment to one or more persons not in the same household as him/herself

and

the order is necessary to protect persons from further anti-social acts.

---

[1] Judicial Studies Board 'Anti-Social Behaviour Orders: Revised Training Material for Section 1 & 4 of the Crime and Disorder Act 1998', November 2002.

Appendix 3 – Guide to Anti-social Behaviour Orders and Acceptable Behaviour Orders 223

When an order can be made

- When an application has been specifically made for an order
- In addition to the sentence for an offence of which the person has been convicted

Interim orders

The court can make an interim order pending the determination of the case.

Geographical validity of an order

Under the Police Reform Act 2002 an order can now extend across any defined area within, or the whole of, England and Wales.

Civil proceedings

Applications are made to the magistrates' court acting in its civil capacity. This will affect how the courts deal with applications in the following way:

- The civil rules of evidence apply which permit the use of hearsay evidence provided certain procedural points relating to notice requirements have been complied with
- In the case of applications for ASBOs, the criminal standard of proof applies to past acts of anti-social behaviour alleged against the defendant.

Adjournments should only be allowed in exceptional circumstances.

Vulnerable and intimidated witnesses

If those subject to the anti-social behaviour feel unable to come forward, for example, for fear of reprisals or intimidation, provision has been made for the use of professional witnesses.

In addition special measures directions can be made by the court before a trial to protect distressed witnesses by the use of screens in court and video link evidence.

Duration of the order

The minimum duration for an order is two years. There is no specified maximum but the court should make the order only for so long as it considers that it is necessary for the protection of the community from the individual in question.

What should the order contain?

The prohibitions in the order must be such as are necessary to protect person(s) from further anti-social acts by the defendant in the locality. The prohibitions must be specific in time and place so it is readily apparent both to the defendant and to those enforcing the order what does or does not constitute a breach.

The terms of the order must be negative i.e. not to take particular actions. There is no power to compel an individual to do anything.

Juveniles

Children aged 10 and upwards can be made the subject of an order and their cases will similarly be dealt with in the magistrates' court acting in its civil capacity. Because these are civil proceedings, they are not dealt with in the youth court. Courts may need to consider special arrangements in the conduct of these proceedings in view of the European Court of Human Rights decision in the Thompson and Venables case and the subsequent Practice Direction issued by the Lord Chief Justice.

Reports of proceedings

Since the magistrates' court is acting in its civil capacity, there is no presumption in favour of reporting restrictions, including a prohibition on publishing photographs, in cases involving juveniles. There will be no such restrictions unless the court decides to impose them under Section 39 of the Children and Young Persons Act 1933 to protect the identity of the person under 18.

Against the need to protect a young person, and a consideration of his or her rights under the Human Rights Act, the court will need to bear the following points in mind:

- Unless the nuisance is extremely localised, enforcement of the order will normally depend on the general public being aware of the order and of the identity of the person against whom it is made.
- Effective enforcement may require the publication of photographs of the offenders as well as their names and addresses.
- The need to keep the local community informed and make the subject of the order face up to the fact that he or she will be expected by the community to abide by its terms.

Breach of an order

A breach of an order is a serious criminal offence and should be tackled quickly and effectively. The Crown Prosecution Service will conduct prosecutions.

The standard of proof is the criminal standard 'beyond reasonable doubt'.

- The maximum penalty on conviction in the magistrate's court is six months in prison or a fine not exceeding £5,000 or both
- At the Crown Court the maximum penalty is five years in prison or a fine or both. A conditional discharge is not available to the court.

B. Anti-social behaviour orders and orders on conviction – step by step

Identification of anti-social behaviour
There is behaviour that is causing, or likely to cause, harassment, alarm or distress to one or more person(s) not of the same household as the perpetrator.

Identification of the need to protect the community
An order is necessary to protect person(s) from further anti-social acts by the perpetrator.

Partnership working
Liaison between lead agencies and other agencies which can add value to the application. Involve youth offending team and social services at the start of the process if the subject of the application is a juvenile in order to ensure that any assessment required is carried out in parallel with the application process.

Identify the most effective route to seek an order		
Anti-social behaviour orders	*Orders in county court proceedings*	*Orders on conviction in criminal proceedings*
under section 1 of the Crime and Disorder Act 1998	under section 1B of the Crime and Disorder Act 1998	under section 1C of the Crime and Disorder Act 1998
if individual not subject to relevant court action	if the individual is party to civil action in the county court	if the individual is subject to a criminal prosecution
		The matter can be raised for the first time post-conviction
See below	The stages for orders in county court proceedings will be available on publication of the Practice Direction in the updated Civil Procedure Rules	See page [228]

Process for anti-social behaviour orders

Undertake statutory consultation
Documentary evidence of consultation, not agreement, is required.

Collect evidence
Agencies applying for orders should strike a balance and focus on what is most relevant and necessary to provide sufficient evidence for the court to arrive at a clear understanding of the matter.

Draw up prohibitions
The order should be drafted in full including its duration and a court file prepared.

Make an application to the magistrates' court
An application for an ASBO is by complaint to the magistrates' court using the appropriate form in the Magistrates' Courts (Anti-Social Behaviour Orders) Rules 2002. The complaint must be made within six months from the time when the matter of the complaint (the behaviour) arose. A complaint may be made on the basis of one incident if sufficiently serious. Earlier incidents may be used as background information to support the case and show a pattern of behaviour. The application is made to the magistrate's court whose area includes the local government or police area in which the 'relevant persons' (i.e. those subjected to the ASB) reside A summons together with the application, as set out in the Rules, should be either given to the defendant in person or sent by post to the last known address.

Applying for an interim order
Where there is an urgent need to protect the community an application for an interim order may be made with the application for the main order. The appropriate form in the Magistrates' Courts (Anti-Social Behaviour Orders) Rules 2002 should be used. An application for an ex parte interim order (i.e. without notice being given to the defendant) may be made subject to agreement of the justices' clerk or other court clerk with delegated authority. The clerk shall grant leave for an application for an interim order to be made where he or she is satisfied that it is necessary. The hearing for an ex parte interim order will take place without the presence of defendant. Where the hearing is made on notice the defendant should be summoned to attend the hearing. If an interim order is granted the application for the main order (together with a summons giving a date for the defendant to attend court) should be served on the defendant in person as soon as practicable after the making of the interim order. The interim order will not take effect until it has been served on the defendant. If the interim order is not served on the defendant within seven days of being made then it shall be set aside. The interim order shall cease to have effect if the application for an anti-social behaviour order is withdrawn or refused.

The hearing

The lead officer in charge of the case should ensure that all the evidence and witnesses are available at the hearing, including any evidence in support of the need for the court to make an immediate order

The defendant(s) should attend but an order can be made in his or her absence.

Immediate post order procedure

Where an ASBO is granted it is preferable for a copy of the order to be served on the defendant in person prior to his or her departure from Court. If this is not possible, personal service should be arranged as soon as possible thereafter. In the case of a juvenile the order should also be served on the parent, guardian or an appropriate adult. In all cases service should be recorded.

The lead agency, if not the police, should ensure that a copy of the order is forwarded immediately to the police. Copies should also be given to the ASB co-ordinator of the local crime and disorder reduction partnership, the other partner agencies, and to the main targets and witnesses of the anti-social behaviour.

An order comes into effect on the day it is made. But the two-year period during which no order shall be discharged[1] starts from the date of service.

Other matters

Application for variation or discharge by either the applicant or the defendant is to the same magistrates' court that made the order. Appeal is to the Crown Court. Breach of the order will go to the magistrates' court, which may refer it to the Crown Court in the more serious cases.

---

[1] Except with the consent of both parties (this does not apply to the order on conviction which cannot be discharged during the two-year period)

Process for an order made on conviction in criminal proceedings (in the magistrates' court or the Crown Court)

Collect evidence

Evidence may be collected for presentation to the court post-conviction. This is not a requirement as the court may make an order on conviction on its own initiative.

Draw up prohibitions

The police or other agency involved in the case may draw up the prohibitions necessary to protect the community from the subject's anti-social behaviour for consideration by the court post conviction. This is *not* a requirement.

Signal intention to seek an order

Prior to, or at the start of, the criminal stage or hearing the police, CPS or local authority involved in the case may advise the subject and court that an order will be sought on conviction.

This is not a requirement, the issue can be raised for the first time post-conviction.

Criminal hearing

This is to establish guilt of criminal charge only.

Verdict

If found guilty the offender is convicted or given a conditional discharge.

Post verdict – hearing for order on conviction

The hearing for the order post-conviction is civil.

The issue of an order may be raised by the magistrates or judge without any request from the prosecution or the police or local authority; the Crown Prosecution Service (CPS) may remind the court of the general powers available to it as appropriate.

The police and/or other agencies may be asked to or may offer to submit additional evidence relating to the request for the order and need for the prohibitions.

Immediate post order procedure

If the offender is given a custodial sentence the court may make provision for the requirements of the order to come into effect when he or she is released from custody.

See details for immediate post-order procedure for ASBOs.

Other matters

Application for variation or discharge by either the applicant or the defendant may be made to any magistrates' court within the same petty sessions area as the court that made the order. Appeal is to the Crown Court. Breach of the order will go to the magistrates' court, which may refer it to the Crown Court in the more serious cases.

C. Relevant court judgements

1. House of Lords – *Clingham (formerly C (a minor)) v Royal Borough of Kensington and Chelsea* (on Appeal from a Divisional Court of the Queen's Bench Division); *Regina v Crown Court at Manchester Ex p McCann (FC) and Others (FC)*, October 2002
2. *R on application of the Chief Constable of West Midlands Police v Birmingham Justices*; citation number: [2002] EWHC 1087 (Admin)

This judgement determined a chief constable's right to delegate authority to apply for ASBOs to any suitable officer notwithstanding their rank.

D. Public funding for defendants

Criminal public funding is available for any proceedings under sections 1 and 4 of the Crime and Disorder Act 1998 relating to anti-social behaviour orders, including interim orders, where they are made in the magistrates' court or where an appeal is made in the Crown Court.

Advocacy Assistance is available for an anti-social behaviour order (ASBO), an interim order under Section 1D of the CDA, variation or discharge of an ASBO, or an appeal against the making of an ASBO under Section 4 of the CDA, in accordance with the Criminal Defence Service General Criminal Contract. Solicitors can self grant advocacy assistance for these matters. There are no financial criteria for the grant of Advocacy Assistance. Advocacy Assistance may not be provided where it appears unreasonable that approval should be granted in the particular circumstances of the case, or where the interests of justice test, set out in Schedule 3 of the Access to Justice Act 1999, is not met. In applying this test, there is an additional factor of whether there is a real risk of imprisonment if an anti-social behaviour order is made and subsequently breached.

A representation order may be sought on application to the Legal Services Commission in respect of these proceedings. Provision for representation is made under Regulation 3(2)(criminal proceedings for the purposes of Section 12(2)(g) of the Access to Justice Act 1999) of the Criminal Defence Service (General)(No.2) Regulations 2001, and Regulation 6(3) of the same regulations. An application to the Commission must be made on form CDS3. An application will be determined in accordance with the Interests of Justice Criteria. The availability of Advocacy Assistance will be a relevant factor which the Legal Services Commission will take into account when considering the grant of representation.

Where an application for a representation order is refused, the Legal Services Commission shall provide written reasons for the refusal and details of the appeal process. The applicant may make a renewed application in writing to the Funding Review Committee, which may grant or refuse the application.

Advocacy Assistance is available for proceedings in the Crown Court, where an appeal is made under section 4 of the Crime and Disorder Act 1988. The merits test is slightly different from that on application for an interim or a full ASBO. It is based only on the general reasonableness test. Advocacy Assistance may not be granted if it appears unreasonable that approval should be granted in the particular circumstances of the case. The prospects and merits of an appeal should be taken into account as well as whether the individual has reasonable grounds for taking the proceedings. Representation is also available for an appeal against an order under section 4 of the CDA. An application should be made to the Legal Services Commission who will consider grant against the availability of advocacy assistance.

Any challenge against the ruling of the Crown Court to the High Court by way of case stated or by application for judicial review, falls outside the scope of criminal funding. Legal representation would have to be applied for in accordance with the Funding Code procedures to the Legal Services Commission. This work is funded through the Community Legal Service although it falls within the scope of the General Criminal Contract.

Advocacy Assistance is available for a breach of an interim or full anti-social behaviour order. Representation is also available for breach proceedings on application to the Commission as above.

Guidance on public funding for proceedings in the county court will be available on introduction.

E. The process of obtaining and monitoring an ABC – Islington Anti-Social Behaviour Team

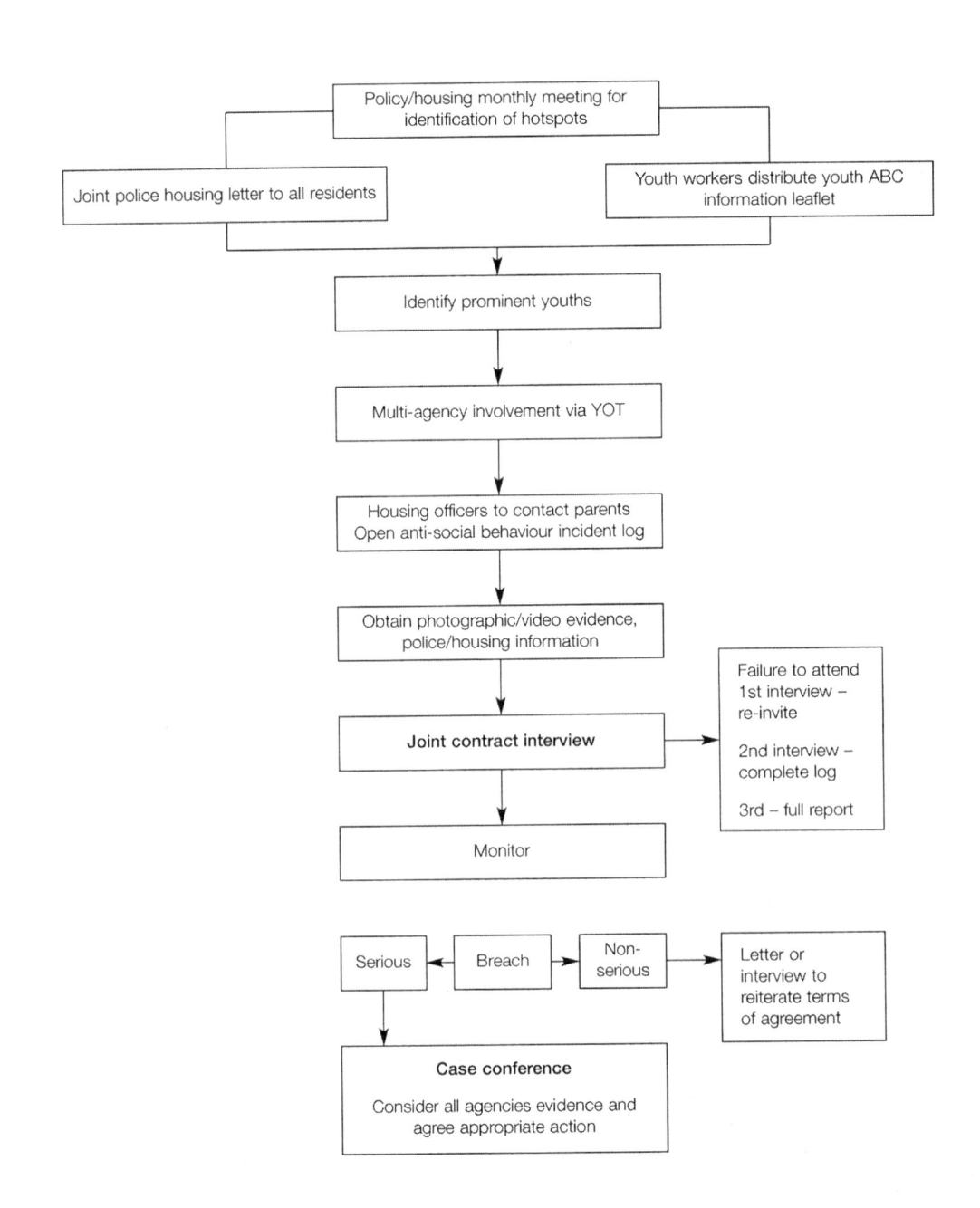

```
Policy/housing monthly meeting for
identification of hotspots
         │
    ┌────┴────┐
    ▼         ▼
Joint police housing    Youth workers distribute youth ABC
letter to all residents      information leaflet
         │
         ▼
   Identify prominent youths
         │
         ▼
   Multi-agency involvement via YOT
         │
         ▼
   Housing officers to contact parents
   Open anti-social behaviour incident log
         │
         ▼
   Obtain photographic/video evidence,
   police/housing information
         │
         ▼
   Joint contract interview  ───▶  Failure to attend
         │                         1st interview –
         ▼                         re-invite
      Monitor                      2nd interview –
                                   complete log
                                   3rd – full report

Serious ◀── Breach ──▶ Non-serious ──▶ Letter or interview to
   │                                    reiterate terms of agreement
   ▼
Case conference
Consider all agencies evidence and
agree appropriate action
```

F. An example of an acceptable behaviour contract

ACCEPTABLE BEHAVIOUR CONTRACT

THIS CONTRACT is made on the [date]

BETWEEN [name and address of lead agency/agencies]

AND [name of individual]

[name of individual] AGREES the following in respect of future conduct –

> 1. I will not write graffiti or damage any property in and around the [specify area].
> 2. I will not congregate in groups in communal areas of [specify the area], i.e. stairways and walkways.
> 3. I will not climb on any rooftops, lift shafts or any other prohibited areas.
> 4. I will not throw anything at residents or passersby in or around the estate.
> 5. I will not threaten or abuse residents or passersby. This includes swearing.

FURTHER [name of individual] enters into a commitment with the [name of agency/agencies] not to act in a manner that causes or is likely to cause harassment, alarm or distress to one or more persons not in the same household.

Breach

If [name of individual] does anything which he/she has agreed not to do under this contract which the [agency/agencies] considers to amount to anti-social behaviour, an application may be made to the magistrates' court for an ANTI-SOCIAL BEHAVIOUR ORDER to prohibit [name of individual] from acting in a manner likely to cause harassment, alarm or distress to one or more persons not of the same household.

> DECLARATION
>
> I confirm that I understand the meaning of this contract and that the consequences of breach of the contract have been explained to me.
>
> SIGNED   Youth
>
> [signature of individual]
>
> DATE   ....
>
>
> SIGNED   Parent
>
> [signature of parent or guardian]
>
> DATE   ....

WITNESSED	
SIGNED	Police Officer
[name of police officer, for example]	
DATE	
SIGNED	Housing Manager
[name of housing officer, for example]	
DATE	

G. Conducting an ABC meeting – Islington Anti-Social Behaviour Team

This draws on the experience of housing and police officers but can adapted for other agencies, such as youth offending teams.

Before the meeting

Do

- Consider other measures for tackling anti-social behaviour alongside this action. A notice seeking possession may still be appropriate.
- Identify individuals likely to benefit from the ABC scheme at regular meetings involving police and housing officers. Once a person is being considered, start an Incident Record Book.
- Give reasonable notice of the meeting and hand-deliver the letter where possible.
- Seek to involve both parents or guardians if there is a joint parenting role, even if they do not live at the same address.
- Where the family are known to social services, advise them of the interview, the purpose, and if appropriate ask if they would like to be present. Where the local authority is looking after a young person (i.e. 'in care'), a representative from social services must be invited to attend.
- If the young person is known to attend a local school, encourage their involvement. The young person could be on a school sponsored scheme that could assist with tackling the unacceptable behaviour.
- Try to find out if the young person is involved in activities organised by the play and youth service. They may be able to assist with diversion activities.
- Contact the youth offending team (YOT) to establish whether they know the young person and to ensure that the action proposed does not conflict with action being pursued by them.
- Contact the police to check whether there are currently any related criminal charges being considered by the Crown Prosecution Service in relation to the young person. If there are, an interview can still go ahead but without the police and without the use of an ABC. The interview would be used simply to clarify to the young person and his parents the terms and conditions of their tenancy agreement. If the CPS find insufficient evidence to make a criminal charge then the ABC interview may be considered again.
- Pre-meet with professionals, such as social services, to clarify the procedure and purpose

of the meeting/ABC. Ideally this meeting should *not* take place immediately before the interview in case there are concerns that need to be resolved. Ensure that if officers from other departments are to be present at the meeting they are clear on who is taking the lead.

- Pre-meet to agree who will take the lead and clarify the latest position on reported incidents and action against the youth or the tenancy.
- Try to establish in advance which other agencies/individuals may attend, if any.
- Consider involving other siblings within the same family in the same meeting if you think they could be vulnerable to becoming involved in anti-social behaviour, even if an ABC is not thought to be appropriate at this stage.
- Be clear in your own mind what the purpose of the meeting is. Remember the aim is not simply to come away with a signed contract, but *to stop the anti-social behaviour*. The idea of the interview is to talk with the young person and his/her parents so that they both have an understanding of what we mean by anti-social behaviour and what the implications are should further incidents take place.
- Be prepared for the fact that both young people and parents may deny all involvement and that feelings could run high.
- Give consideration to a suitable venue and seating plan so that the meeting can take place in relative comfort with enough chairs and space for everyone. Avoid setting up barriers or creating an 'us-and-them' situation.
- Give consideration to the type of activities the young person has been involved in *and* those that are particularly relevant on the estate, which you may wish to include in the contract. These should not be used to prepare the contract in advance but to include in the discussion about which activities should be included in the contract.
- Nominate a suitable officer to take notes during the interview. Although you should aim to keep the number of officers to a minimum it is recommended to have a note-taker that will not be involved in the discussion. Detailed notes are not required but the main points do need to be jotted down.
- Try to ensure that the same people are involved for the duration of the contract and monitoring period. The ABC creates an opportunity to establish rapport with young people on contracts.

DON'T

- Hold the meeting at the police station (unless necessary).
- Expect to be able to follow a script and for all interviews to be the same. They are all different. Of the interviews carried out so far a significant number of parents have been extremely positive about the meetings once they overcome their initial suspicion and concern. The attitude of the young people has ranged in extremes from total silence to hostility and abuse, but the latter is not usual and in most cases it has been possible to have a discussion about anti-social behaviour and what it means.
- Underestimate the importance of the preparation in advance of the meeting. You cannot expect to be able to turn up on the day and carry out an effective interview without being clear on the background to the case. Also, if you fail to involve other relevant departments or organisations you are potentially compromising the council's position in being able to pursue further action.
- Prepare the final version of the contract in advance of the meeting. This is defeating one of the key points of the meeting, which is to encourage the young person to list the activities he/she has been involved in or could become involved in future. A draft list of activities that you may wish to include is, however, a good idea.

During the meeting

Do

- Arrive promptly to allow for a pre-meeting, and allow enough time for the meeting so you are not rushed. Some meetings have been known to last two hours, others have been more straightforward. N.B. The attention span of a young person is about twenty minutes.
- If the young person and his or her parent/guardian fail to attend write once more with a further date for a meeting. If they fail to attend the second meeting, consider moving straight to legal action, write setting out the seriousness of the issue including details of action proposed. Monitor the case as you would had a contract been signed.
- Wear name badges.
- Use simple language that is free from council/police jargon.
- Aim to get the message across that anti-social behaviour and the signing of the contract is an extremely serious issue, however at the same time you should aim to keep the meeting informal and relaxed to encourage full participation of the young person and their parents.
- Make the young person and their parents aware of the consequences of breach.
- Support each other and be mindful of the issues relevant to both the police and the housing department e.g. possible criminal or civil action.
- Talk to the young person. Find out how they spend their time, what their understanding is of anti-social behaviour and how it may impact upon residents, the council, his/her parents, him or herself.
- Listen to what is being said about home circumstances and any other pressures or difficulties the family is experiencing. This will help to put together information for dealing with the case and involving any other relevant agencies.
- Explain the purpose of the contract, how it will be monitored and the implications of any further incidents, both in terms of civil action such as possession orders and anti-social behaviour orders or criminal action such as criminal damage, *before* the contract is signed.
- Take any concerns raised by the young person and his/her parents seriously and attempt to address them.
- Produce the final typed version of the contract as quickly as possible once those present have agreed the activities to be included. Ideally arrange for someone outside the meeting to do this for you so that you do not leave your colleague on his/her own. Remember that any delay could be a source of irritation to those present and may result in a contract not being signed.
- Remember to get everyone present to sign the contract and to provide a copy for the young person and their parents to take away with them.
- Allow 'time out' if the meeting becomes heated. Consider the provision of tea/coffee if appropriate but remember that a hot drink could be used as a missile.
- Take notes of the meeting and any issues that are raised.
- Sum up the main points at the end of the meeting.
- Provide contact details of lead officers to parents.
- End on a positive note. If there are no further incidents there'll be no further action.
- Thank everyone for his/her attendance.

Don't

- Behave in a confrontational manner but state any allegations calmly. Remember that the aim is not to accuse but to stop bad behaviour.
- Single out the families for all the problems in the area, if they are told that their children are one of a number of young people and others will also be interviewed, you will find that the parents more readily accept this and be prepared to work with you.

- Attempt to force the young person to sign the contract but *do* explain why it is important and persuade them as far as possible.
- Worry if you have been unable to get a signature. This does not mean that the meeting has been a waste of time. Try to establish why there is a reluctance to sign, attempt to address their concerns and keep a record of their responses. It may be that they need time to think it over and you can suggest meeting again in a few days time. You do need to advise that we would like a signed contract as this demonstrates a commitment on their part to taking the issue seriously, and that if they still refuse to sign we can still pursue further action should the bad behaviour continue. This must be followed up in writing.
- Disclose details of complainants.

After the meeting

Do

- Complete the *Incident Record Book* straight after the interview. This is a very important document which will be used as evidence should further action be pursued.
- Copy the contract to social services, children and families team, where they know the young person. The police are responsible for sending a copy to the youth offending team.
- Notify patrolling police officers.
- Notify the estate services officers, other housing officers, housing assistants, senior caretaker and relevant caretakers that a contract has been drawn up and request assistance in monitoring further activities.
- Write to thank those present for their attendance and to confirm the outcome, attaching a further copy of the agreement. Advise who has been given copies of the contract. This will help to serve as a reminder of what the implications are should the young person carry out further anti-social acts.
- Monitor the contract for 6 months. If there is a further incident, regardless of how minor it may seem, you must bring this to the attention of the lead officer so that consideration can be given to any further action. This could range from sending a letter to re-iterate the terms of the contract, to applying for a possession order or an anti-social behaviour order. *It is most important not to let a further incident pass by seemingly unnoticed.*
- Liaise with partner agencies if there is a report of a further incident or trouble on the estate. At very least monthly updates must be provided at meetings between police and housing officers. Officers should visit the young person with the contract, as part of the monitoring process, on at least two occasions within the six-month monitoring period. A written record of the outcome must be kept on file.
- Ensure that any further incidents are documented in the incident record book promptly.
- Write to the young person at the end of the 6 month period. In the letter acknowledge that the contract period has come to an end, thank them for keeping to the terms of the agreement and remind them of the implications should there be a repeat of the unacceptable behaviour in future.

Don't

- Generally provide complainants (or others) with details of the young people with a contract, but *do* publicise the fact that a number of young people within the area have signed a contract. This could act as a deterrent to others as well as encourage the reporting of incidents.

H. ABC Good Practice Tips – Circle 33 Housing Group

1. Provide support packs for targets of anti-social behaviour when this is thought appropriate.
2. Provide advice and support packages for the perpetrator and family members when specific concerns are identified, for example drug and alcohol misuse.
3. At the end of the contract where no breach has been identified look for ways of recognising this and reinforcing improved behaviour.
4. Recognise and encourage the contribution of family members to the successful outcome of the contract, particularly where there is a breakdown in the family home.
5. Encourage other agencies to contribute to addressing the underlying causes of a young person's anti-social behaviour.

Further copies of this publication can be obtained by telephoning 0870 241 4680.

APPENDIX 4

USEFUL CONTACTS

Home Office

www.homeoffice.gov.uk

The Together Actionline
tel: 0870 220 2000
www.together.gov.uk

Information Commissioner

www.dataprotection.gov.uk

Crime Reduction

www.crimereduction.gov.uk

The Social Landlords Crime and Nuisance Group

Tim Winter, SLCNG, c/o Whitefriars South, 42B New Union Street, Coventry CV1 2HN